Exploring
Southern
Maine

NATURAL WONDERS and HISTORIC SITES

RUSSELL DUNN

Down East Books
Camden, Maine

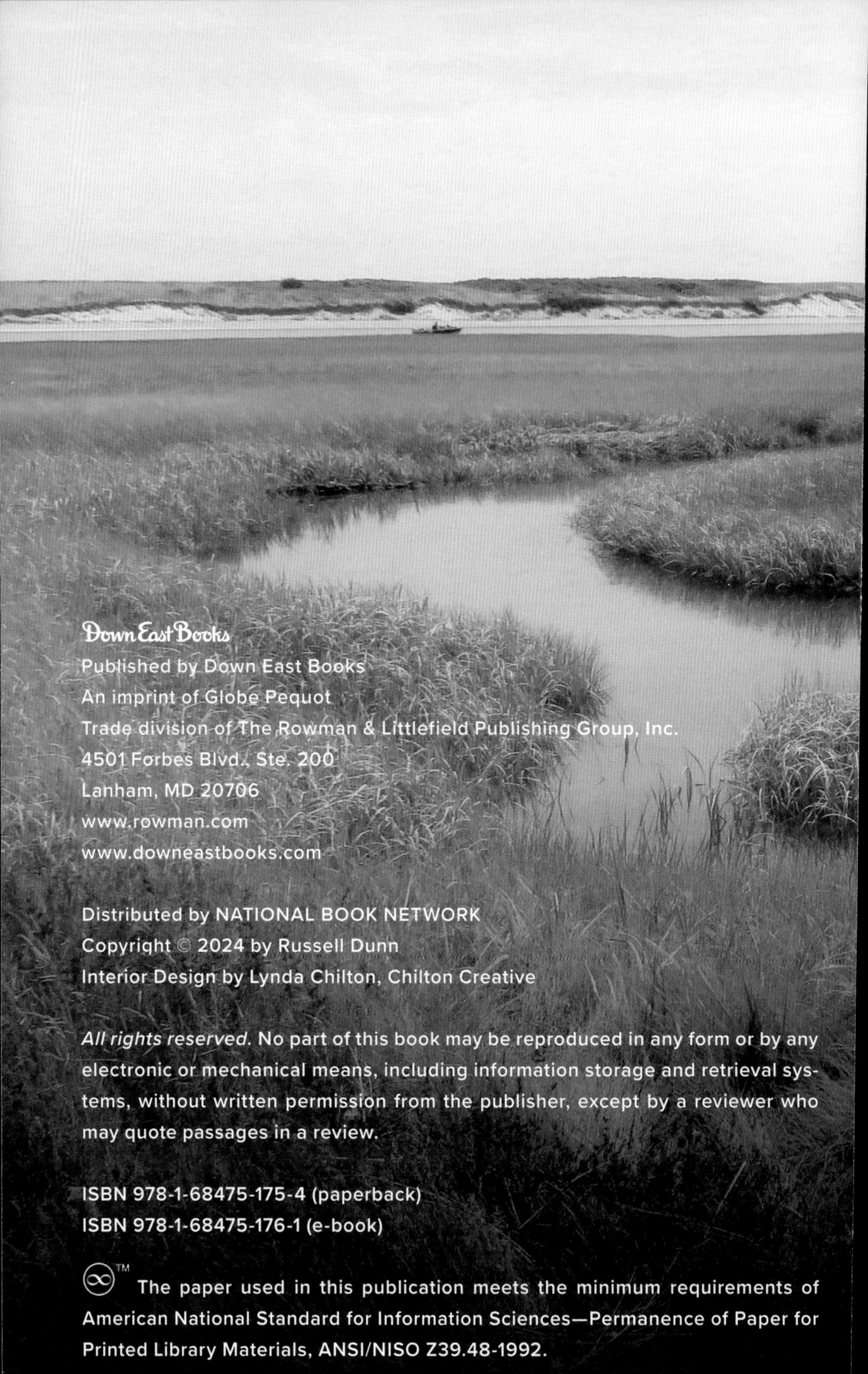

Down East Books

Published by Down East Books

An imprint of Globe Pequot

Trade division of The Rowman & Littlefield Publishing Group, Inc.

4501 Forbes Blvd., Ste. 200

Lanham, MD 20706

www.rowman.com

www.downeastbooks.com

Distributed by NATIONAL BOOK NETWORK

Copyright © 2024 by Russell Dunn

Interior Design by Lynda Chilton, Chilton Creative

ISBN 978-1-68475-175-4 (paperback)

ISBN 978-1-68475-176-1 (e-book)

∞™ The paper used in this publication meets the minimum requirements of American National Standard for Information Sciences—Permanence of Paper for Printed Library Materials, ANSI/NISO Z39.48-1992.

CAUTION: Outdoor recreational activities are by their very nature potentially hazardous and contain risk.

The publisher and author have done their best to ensure the accuracy of all the information contained in *Exploring Southern Maine: Natural Wonders and Historic Sites;* however, they can accept no responsibility for any loss, injury, or inconvenience sustained by any traveler as a result of information or advice contained in this guidebook.

Contents

Introduction

The south coastal part of Maine is a smorgasbord of villages and towns with historic sites, land trusts, conservation areas, and fabulous beaches. It literally has a little bit of something for everyone, be it for history buffs, hikers, explorers, or those who just want to get out and enjoy the sun and sand. Kittery, Kittery Point, Eliot, South Berwick, Berwick, North Berwick, York, Old York, Cape Neddick, Ogunquit, Wells, Kennebunkport, Kennebunk, Biddeford, and Seco offer much for those looking to enrich their understanding of Maine's five centuries of European history.

HUMAN HISTORY; The human history of Maine goes back thousands of years, long before Europeans set foot on the continent. The region was first settled around 13,000 years ago as Native Americans advanced northward following the retreating Laurentide Ice Sheet, which had covered most of Canada and a large portion of the Northern United States. Native Americans used the multitude of rivers and lakes left behind as their routes of travel, using dugout canoes (hollowed out trees) and birchbark canoes for transportation. They frequently lived in wigwams (semi-permanent domed dwellings) and were hunters-gatherers and fishers. The various tribes, consisting of the Penobscot, Mi'kmaq, Maliseet, Passamaquoddy, and Western Abenaki, were all part of the Wabanaki Confederacy, or "people of the dawn." Their glorious dominion over the land began to come to an end with the arrival of European settlers in the 1600s.

The first English settlement in Maine, which lasted for just over one year, was the Popham Colony, aka Sagadahoc Colony, near the mouth of the Kennebec River, that was sponsored by the Plymouth Company and established in 1607 by George Popham, who died that winter. The colonists had severely underestimated the severity of Maine's winter, believing it would be similar to what they experienced in England whose winters were moderated by the Gulf Stream.

It didn't take many centuries for European, possessing higher levels of technology and no longer ignorant of the severity of Maine's winters, to displace Native Americans, the indigenous people. Five centuries ago, the population of Maine consisted of ~17,000 strictly indigenous inhabitants. Today, the population of Maine numbers well over 1.3 million, primarily of European ancestry.

GEOLOGICAL HISTORY: Maine's geological history is the confluence of multiple tectonic forces. Through the eons, the bedrock has been subjected to sedimentation (with vast amounts of sediment being laid down), deformation (involving land being folded or displaced), metamorphism (with the bedrock undergoing compression without melting) and igneous activity (where rock has been turned into magma and then solidified again). Mountains have been raised only to be whittled down through weathering and erosion.

Geologists can trace the geological history of Maine as far back to at least 650 million years. Some contend that the record goes back even further in time to over 1 billion years.

To be sure, more recent geological events have had their effect on shaping the landscape. As the last glacier retreated north to its present position after planning the landscape, it left behind over 6,000 lakes and ponds, and 32,000 miles of rivers.

MAINE FUN FACTS: Maine is famous for its rocky coastline (a main tourist attraction) and for being the leading U.S. producer of lobsters and blueberries. The seaboard of Maine measures approximately 230 straight miles, but if you factor in the craggy coastline with its innumerable nooks and crannies, the shoreline turns out to be 3,478 miles long. Maine has over 4,000 islands, most of which are less than one acre in size.

Maine also has the distinction of being the largest of the six New England States, covering approximately the same surface area as the other five combined. It was the 23rd state to join the union. Maine achieved statehood through the Missouri Compromise, which allowed it to enter the union in 1820 as a slave-free state, along with Missouri as a slave state.

Maine is the only state in the union to border just one other state—New Hampshire.

Its nickname, the "Pine Tree State," came from the abundance of evergreens covering over 17 million acres of land. The white pine, the tallest tree in the eastern United States, is Maine's official tree.

The state has more than 60 lighthouses. Of these, three are mentioned in this book.

Exploring Southern Maine covers the part of Maine from Kittery to Saco, a somewhat arbitrary delineation, yet sufficient to offer an abundance of outings for those interested in exploring the hidden wonders of an area that has a high density of tourism.

Also included is a brief section on museums and libraries not covered in the main text, golf courses for golfers, family-fun attractions, and places where dog-owners can take their dog to get exercise.

How was Maine named? No one knows for sure. Possibly, to honor the ancient Province of Maine, France. Possibly, from sailors who used the word "main" for mainland to distinguish it from the thousands of offshore islands. What we do know is that Maine is the only state in the union that contains just one syllable.

HOW THE BOOK IS PUT TOGETHER: To create a consistent, fixed point of reference for destinations, the directions for each chapter begin from Ogunquit Square in Ogunquit at the intersection of U.S. 1/Main Street, Beach Street, and Shore Road. From this starting point, eight somewhat arbitrary subcategories have been created to group chapters, starting with Ogunquit and then proceeding south through Perkins Cove and York to Kittery Point; followed west to South Berwick and North Berwick; then north through Wells, and Kennebunkport, ending at Biddeford and Saco.

As such, this is an eclectic book, guiding you to geological points of interest such as waterfalls, glacial boulders, rock profiles, and towering cliffs; to historic houses, garrisons, and mansions; to hiking trails and scenic walkways; to museums, historic churches, and nineteenth-century libraries; to beaches, rivers, parks, and launch sites for cartop watercraft; and to golf courses. We make no pretense of being comprehensive. New attractions and land trusts are always coming into existence.

For those who are familiar with GPS coordinates and Google Earth, you can reconnoiter the desired area in advance by inserting the GPS coordinates for the parking area and destinations into Google Earth. By doing so, you will be able to visualize exactly where you are going and what you will see. These coordinates can also be used once you have arrived at your destination.

The GPS coordinates listed were mostly determined by using Google Earth as opposed to taking onsite readings. As a result, slight discrepancies may occur between computer generated coordinates and coordinates taken onsite. The reason for this is that Google Earth had to stitch together thousands of individual maps to create its world-wide map, necessitating minor compromises here and there to make everything fit together seamlessly.

Mileages, too, may very slightly due to small differences between automobile odometers. Hopefully, such discrepancies will be minor.

Driving time is always a critical factor when it comes to planning excursions. During tourist season, U.S. 1 and Route 9 become heavily trafficked, with bottlenecks frequently developing in Ogunquit, Wells, Kennebunk and Kennebunkport. Allow extra time to get to your destination even though the distance involved may seem at first inconsequential.

Most of the directions given follow either U.S. Route 1 or Route 9. U.S. 1

was numbered as a highway in 1925 and follows parts of one of Maine's oldest roads—the King's Highway. The road was established in the late 1600s to connect Boston and Machias and follows along the east coastline.

Route 9 is more inland than U.S. 1 and passes through the cities of Biddeford and Saco and, beyond that, South Portland, Portland, Augusta, and Bangor.

The Kittery to Portland section of the Maine Turnpike/I 95, which opened in the fall of 1947, may be useful for reaching farther-away sites like Biddeford and Saco. In general, the exits from the Maine Turnpike pertaining to the area covered in this book proceed as follows: Exit 1 for Kittery and South Eliot; Exit 7 for York; Exit 19 for Wells and North Berwick; Exit 25 for the Kennebunks; Exit 32 for Biddeford and Saco; and Exit 36 for Old Orchard Beach.

Each chapter has been designed so that parts of the text can be skipped over as needed. For example, if your interest is strictly on walking the Marginal Way, you can pass over the history part, and vice versa. This applies to virtually all the chapters.

It is our hope that the outings listed in this book will take you to new and interesting destinations—places, perhaps, that you had never been to before or even knew existed.

CAUTION: Safety Tips for Hikers and Paddlers

Nature is inherently wild, unpredictable, and uncompromising. Outdoor recreational activities are by their very nature potentially hazardous and contain risk. All participants in such activities must assume responsibility for their own actions and safety. No book can replace good judgment. The outdoors is forever changing. The author and the publisher cannot be held responsible for inaccuracies, errors, or omissions, or for any changes in the details of this publication, or for the consequences of any reliance on the information contained herein, or for the safety of people in the outdoors.

TIPS FOR HIKERS:

1. Always hike with two or more companions so that should one member become incapacitated, a second member can stay with the person needing help while the others go for assistance.

2. Make it a practice of bringing along a day pack complete with emergency supplies, compass, whistle, flashlight, dry matches, raingear, power bars, extra layers, gorp, duct tape, lots of water (at least twenty-four ounces per person), mosquito repellent, emergency medical kit, sunblock, and a device for removing ticks.

3. Wear sunblock when exposed to sunlight for extended periods of time. Apply repellents when you know that you are going into an area brimming with mosquitoes, black flies, and other insects that view you as mealtime.

4. Hike with ankle-high boots for additional support and gripping power.

5. Be cognizant of the risk of hypothermia and stay dry. The air temperature doesn't have to be near freezing for you to become over-chilled. Equally of concern is the danger of hypothermia (overheating). Be sure to drink plenty of water when the weather is hot and muggy.

6. Stay out of the woods during hunting season. If you do enter wooded areas when hunters are about, wear an orange-colored vest and make noise periodically.

7. Unless you are proficient in orienteering, stay on trails whenever possible to avoid becoming disoriented and lost.

8. Be flexible and adaptive to a wilderness environment that can change abruptly. Trails described in this book can become altered by blowdown, beaver dams, and other natural elements.

9. Always let someone know where you are going, when you will return, and what to do if you have not shown up by the designated time.

10. Avoid any creature acting erratically. If an advancing animal cannot be frightened off, assume that it is either rabid or operating in a predatory mode.

11. Allow for extra time if hiking in the winter when darkness arrives early.

12. Be mindful of ticks, which have become increasingly prevalent and virulent as their range expands. Check yourself thoroughly after every hike and remove any tick immediately. The longer the tick remains in contact with your skin, the greater the risk that you will contract Lyme disease or worse.

TIPS FOR PADDLERS: The following tips are for intermediate paddlers who are comfortable being on the water and (hopefully) well versed in self-rescue procedures:

1. If you don't know how to swim, learn now!

2. Wear a brightly colored personal flotation device (PFD) with reflective tape.

3. Be cognizant of tides if you are on a river affected by tidal impulses from the ocean. You don't want to end up stuck on a mudflat during low tide.

4. Pack a waterproof dry bag with all the small items that may be needed during the trip, e.g. sunblock, SPF-rated lip balm, whistle, bug repellent, compass, sunglasses, gloves (in case blisters developed on your hands), car keys, money, first-aid kit, cell phone, extra clothing layers to keep warm, a Swiss army knife or "Leatherman," and duct tape.

5. Alcohol and paddling is one cocktail that doesn't mix well.

6. Return to your launch site immediately if you become unexpectedly immersed and feel chilled. Maine water is punishingly cold, even on the hottest days of summer. Avoid hypothermia.

7. Tell someone where you are going and when you expect to return.

8. Take along three to four liters of water to ward off dehydration and hypothermia (over-heating).

9. Pack food and snacks to maintain proper energy levels. Keep them stored in a waterproof container when you're not munching.

10. Pay attention to the wind. Surprisingly, wind speed over water can be as much as 50 percent greater than over land.

11. Be sure to familiarize yourself with how the launch site looks from the water as you paddle away so that you can return without confusion.

12. Remember that not all power-boaters think to slow down when they pass by a paddler. If you are on a river shared with motorized craft, be prepared to turn bow-first into waves in order to avoid being swamped.

13. Apply liberal portions of sunscreen to your face, arms, and legs, and wear sunglasses if you are paddling under a hot, glaring sun. Wear a wide-brimmed hat as well. Remember that water reflects light and heat, intensifying both.

14. Stash an extra paddle (if you are in a canoe) in case the one you're using becomes lost or broken. A paddle leash will prevent you from losing your paddle. For long distance paddles, wear paddling gloves to minimize blisters.

15. Check your body over thoroughly after each trip for ticks. The likelihood of picking up a tick increases if you have been near brushes or have had to push your way through areas of overhanging trees and weeds—so pay attention.

16. Always take along personal identification, including emergency contacts and relevant medical information should you become unconscious and require emergency treatment.

{1}

Ogunquit Area

Ogunquit—the Algonquin word for "beautiful place by the sea"—is a natural starting point for all of the ventures in this book due to its high density of tourism.

Originally, Ogunquit was a shipbuilding center in the seventeenth and eighteenth century; then an arts center in the twentieth century, becoming a vacation mecca beginning the last century into the present.

Ogunquit was part of Wells until 1980, when it seceded and became incorporated as a town.

All the hikes in this section begin from the center of Ogunquit (junction of U.S. 1/Main Street, Shore Road & Beach Street).

For answers to general questions about Ogunquit, contact the Chamber of Commerce, 102 Main Street/U.S. 1, P.O. Box 2289, Ogunquit, ME 03907; (207) 646-2939. or consult their website at https://www.ogunquit.org/faqs.

MARGINAL WAY

LOCATION: Ogunquit (York County)

MAINE ATLAS & GAZETTEER: Map 1, A5

GPS PARKING (GENERAL AREAS): *North end*—43.250381, -70.598224 & 43.248987, -70.598503 & 43.245608, -70.598745; *South end*—43.237270, -70.590608

GPS MAIN ENTRANCES TO THE MARGINAL WAY: *Shore Road*—43.246010, -70.597089; *Perkins Cove*—43.237715, -70.590919

GPS POINTS OF INTEREST ALONG THE MARGINAL WAY: *Ontio Beach*—43.244721, -70.591373; *Little Beach*—43.244533, -70.590279; *Lobster Point Lighthouse*—43.243738, -70.589983; *Israel's Head*—43.244069, -70.588654; *Marginal Way Plaque*—43.242533, -70.589250; *Informational plaque & tablets listing Friends of the Marginal Way* --- 43.240147, -70.588526; *Footbridge*—43.239500, -70.589123; *Oarweed Cove*—43.237845, -70.587294; *Oarweed Restaurant*—43.237734, -70.590944

HOURS: Generally, dawn to dusk

FEE: None

RESTRICTIONS: Regular Park rules & regulations apply

ACCESSIBILITY: *Marginal Way*—1.2-mile walk

SPECIFIC DISTANCES STARTING FROM SHORE ROAD BY THE SPARHAWK OCEANFRONT RESORT: *Ontio Beach, Little Beach, Lobster Point Lighthouse & Israel's head*—~0.5-mile walk; *Informational plaques*—0.8-mile walk; *Footbridge*—0.9-mile walk; *End of walk at Oarweed Restaurant*—1.2-mile walk

DEGREE OF DIFFICULTY: Moderately easy

ADDITIONAL INFORMATION: *Marginal Way Map — www.marginalwayfund.org/wp-content/uploads/2017/04/marginal-way-map.pd*

Dogs are not allowed from April until October

DIRECTIONS: From the center of Ogunquit (junction of U.S. 1/Main Street, Shore Road & Beach Street), walk southeast on Shore Road for 0.2 mile. The Marginal Way begins to your left by the Sparhawk Oceanfront Resort marked by a sign indicating "Marginal Way Walkway Entrance."

Marginal Way, from Perkins Cove: From the northeast end of Perkins Cove, start from the east side of the Oarweed Restaurant & Lobster Pound, a famous Perkins Cove restaurant that opened in 1963.

DESCRIPTION: Marginal Way is a 1.25-mile-long, undulating, paved walkway above the rocky coastline of Ogunquit. On the east side of the walkway are sandy beaches and cliffs, barriers of rock, and the Atlantic Ocean; on the west side are private homes, resorts, and natural areas. The Lobster Point Lighthouse is encountered midway along the walk.

The next area of significance is where the path divides momentarily. The cobblestone path straight ahead takes you past tablets listing Friends of the Marginal Way and a plaque describing the origin of the rocks and structure of the Marginal Way. This short cobblestone path immediately reunites with the paved path.

Near the south end is the walkway's only footbridge, spanning a tiny chasm. At each end of the footbridge are 5-foot-high cement pillars.

WALK: The walk can be done from one end to the other with return either on foot or by using the trolley system when it's operating. The north entrance, in the village of Ogunquit, is next to the Sparhawk Oceanfront Resort. The south entrance, in the tiny hamlet of Perkins Cove, is next to the Oarweed Restaurant & Lobster Pound.

There are also paved paths and roads leading down to or coming up from sections of the Marginal Way: Locust Grove Lane (starting by the 1826 Locust Grove Cemetery), Israel's Head Road (named for Israel's Head, a rocky prominence), Stearns Road (named for George Stearns who constructed the Rockmere Bed & Breakfast in 1899), Frazier Pasture Road (probably named for where sheep or cattle were once pastured), and Ontio Way (named for a hotel).

Note: If you follow the Locust Grove Lane Path southwest from the Marginal Way for >250 feet, you will be treated with an unexpected surprise.

To your left is a tiny path with wooden steps that lead in 10 feet to a babbling brook making its way through a tiny Japanese garden on a hill, complete with a Buddha and a miniature footbridge (GPS: ~43.244753, -70.592823). Pay attention to the sign that states "Private. Please enjoy without entering" and go no further.

HISTORY: In 1925, Josiah Chase, Jr., a veteran of the Civil War, a former State legislator and conservationist, donated a strip of oceanside property extending from Perkins Cove to Israel's Head that became the nucleus of the Marginal Way. This was at the behest of Frederick Raymond Brewster, an architect and childhood friend of Chase, who grew increasingly alarmed at the prospect of the rocky oceanfront being lost forever to the public by private landowner acquisitions.

Chase's gift to Ogunquit encouraged other landowners to make similar donations, including land easements at the north and south entrances, and within a short span of time, the walkway extended north from Israel's Head for another 0.25 mile. It now encompasses 12 acres of land.

The walkway is called the Marginal Way according to Kathryn M. Severson, Susan Day Meffert and Marie D. Natoli's in *Then & Now: Ogunquit* (2009), "... because it was defined originally by the easterly margins of multiple properties." It is said to be the longest paved, coastal walkway in New England.

In 1991, 2007, and 2018 the Marginal Way was severely damaged by storms. The damage incurred in 2018 is still being undone thanks to the Marginal Way Committee and the nonprofit Marginal Way Preservation Fund, a 501.c.3 organization.

Sparhawk Oceanfront Resort (85 Shore Road) at the north end of the Marginal Way—The original Sparhawk Oceanfront Resort, called Sparhawk Hall, was built in 1897 by Nehemiah P. M. Jacobs (Dorothea Jacobs Grant's uncle). It burned down two years later and was rebuilt. The second Inn was later razed, and the current Sparhawk Oceanfront Resort complex took its place. The Barbara Dean Restaurant (named for Barbara Dean Knapp) opened in 1934 in front of the resort. At some point, it closed as a restaurant, was assimilated into the Sparhawk Resort and converted into seven suites and three apartments.

In the 1960s and 1970s, two additional buildings were added to the Sparhawk complex.

It is believed that the resort was named Sparhawk in honor of Nathaniel Sparhawk, an eighteenth-century Kittery Point merchant who later married into the Pepperrell family.

Ontio Beach is one of three tiny beaches between the Beachmere Inn and Israel Head Road, the other two being Little Beach and Mother's Beach. It is named for its proximity to Ontio Hill, the Ontio (hotel), and Ontio Way (a road and walkway coming down from Israel Head Road to the Marginal Way). The original Ontio Hotel was built in 1899 by Oliver Merrill and Frank Knight.

Lobster Point Lighthouse is a tiny, 23-foot-high, faux "lighthouse" that was built in 1947 and named for its proximity to Lobster Point, a section of land between the Ogunquit River's outflow and Israel's Head. The lighthouse was designed by Grover S. Perkins and constructed by Winfield Charles Little-field. It was renovated in 1993, with the top section repaired and replaced with fiberglass, and recon-structed in 2009 when the entire structure was upgraded. Despite appearances, the lighthouse was strictly built to serve as a pumping station for the Ogunquit Sewer District. Until its installation, untreated water issuing from sewer pipes was polluting the ocean and endangering the beaches.

In *On the Rocks of Ogunquit* (1957), George Towar, a metallurgist and engineer, writes, "At low tide, Lobster Point . . . seems to have the most tide pools and these teem with animals and vegetable life."

The Marginal Way, Ogunquit, Maine

Israel's Head is a prominent, rocky mound extending out into the ocean at the end of Israel's Head Road. As you look northward, it offers superb views of Ogunquit Beach. According to Esselyn Gilman Perkins, in *History of Ogunquit Village* (1951), the rocky promontory was named for Israel Littlefield, a local resident who is buried in the 1826 Locust Grove Cemetery (GPS: 43.243343, -70.595782) along Shore Road.

Wharf's Lane—Many folks think of Wharf Lane as an extension of the Marginal Way because it does continue north along the shoreline for another 0.1 mile from where the Marginal Way is interrupted by the Sparhawk Oceanfront Resort, Sea Chambers (occupying the site of the former Littlefield Inn), Revelations Gift Shop (a former Methodist church) and several other businesses. Originally named Sawyer's Lane after Christopher Sawyer, a trader who lived nearby on Shore Road, the street later came to be called Wharf's Lane for the five wharves—Sullivan Wharf, Sawyer's Wharf, Town Dock, Captain Sam's Wharf, and Joe-Not-Littlefield Wharf—and fishermen shacks and storehouses located at its east end that turned Ogunquit into a hub of coastal shipping

activity during the early years. Products like dried salt fish, blueberries, lumber, and firewood were transported on schooners to Boston and other port cities. Larger vessels made the trip to as far away as the West Indies to trade for rum and molasses.

Invasive species—The Marginal Way is under constant assault from such invasive species as Asian Bittersweet, Japanese Knotweed, Black Swallowwort, phragmites, nightshade and a host of other invaders. These species threaten biodiversity, out-compete native species, and do not support local insects, birds, and animals.

The Marginal Way Committee (https://www.ogunquit.gov/283/Marginal-Way-Committee) and a bevy of volunteers have fought back tirelessly, pulling out by hand the roots of unwanted species and replanting flora native to the coast. It is a fight that is ongoing and never-ending.

In 2022, the Marginal May was put on the Register of Historic Places by the United State Department of the Interior, an extraordinary honor considering that very few trails in the United States have received such an honor.

OGUNQUIT BEACH

MAINE ATLAS & GAZETTEER: Map 1, A5-Map 3, E1

GPS PARKING: OGUNQUIT BEACH: *East end of Beach Street*—43.249795, -70.594459; *Southwest end of Beach Street*—43.248997, -70.598522; *Off River Road*—43.250375, -70.598143; *Off Cottage Street*—43.246343, -70.598462; *Jacobs Lot*—43.247802, -70.599679 (2-hour limit)
FOOTBRIDGE BEACH: *Footbridge Beach*—43.263394, -70.591548; *South end of Ocean Avenue*—43.267560, -70.587976

GPS POINTS OF INTEREST: *Beach Street Bridge*—43.250237, -70.595802; *Norseman Resort area at beach entrance*—43.250418, -70.593204; *Mouth of Ogunquit River*—43.246407, -70.591675

GPS OGUNQUIT DUNES: *South entrance*—43.253849, -70.592436; *North entrance*—43.258270, -70.590950

HOURS: Generally, from dawn to dusk

FEE: *Parking*—fee charged. *Beach*—no charge.

RESTRICTIONS: *Beach*—Regular beach rules & regulations apply. *Ogunquit Dunes*—Walkers must stay on paths; walking on the dunes is not permitted.

ACCESSIBILITY: *Ogunquit Beach*—10-foot walk down ramp to beach; *Footbridge Beach*—0.1-mile walk from parking area to beach; *Ocean Avenue*—150-foot walk to beach The public bathhouse is in the parking area near the main beach entrance.

Dogs are not permitted on Ogunquit Beach from April 1st to September 7th. Dogs are permitted on the beach from September 8th to March 31, but must be on a leash. Dogs are not permitted at any time in the Ogunquit River Estuary—the area behind Ogunquit Beach where the Ogunquit River flows into the area. Lifeguards are on duty during the summer daily from 10:00 a.m. to 5:00 p.m. For further details, contact https://www.ogunquit.org/our-beaches.

Website for parking lots in Ogunquit—https://ogunquit.gov/289/Ogunquit-Parking-Lots

DIRECTIONS: *Ogunquit Beach*—From the center of Ogunquit (junction of U.S. 1/Main Street, Shore Road & Beach Street), drive northeast on Beach Street (in the early days known as Ocean Avenue) for >0.3 mile to its end. Turn right into a large parking area and park.

ALTERNATE PARKING: *River Road parking*—Drive northeast on Beach Street for <0.2 mile, turn left onto River Road and, after >200 feet, left into a large parking area.

Worster parking lot—Drive northeast on Beach Street for 0.1 mile and turn right into a medium-sized parking area.

Cottage Street lot—Drive southeast on Shore Road for <0.2 mile and bear right onto Cottage Street. After >200 feet, turn left into the large parking area opposite the rear of the S. Judson Dunaway Community Center.

Footbridge Beach—From the center of Ogunquit, drive north on U.S. 1/Main Street for ~1.1 miles. Turn right onto Ocean Street, head southeast for >0.3 mile, and park in the large area to your left.

Ocean Avenue Access—From the center of Ogunquit, drive north on U.S. 1/Main Street for ~1.8 miles. Turn right onto Bourne Avenue and head southeast for <0.7 mile, passing through marshlands on both sides along the way. When you come to Ocean Avenue, turn right and proceed southwest for 0.4 mile to the parking area at the end of the road for North Beach.

DESCRIPTION: *Ogunquit Beach, aka Main Beach; Footbridge Beach;* and *North Beach, aka Moody Beach (which may be slightly farther north)*—Although Ogunquit Beach is a continuous 3.0-mile-long stretch of white sand and surf, it can be thought of as three separate beaches—Ogunquit Beach, starting at the mouth of the Ogunquit River; Footbridge Beach, where a pedestrian bridge crosses the Ogunquit River; and 1.0-mile-long Moody Beach, which is fronted by private homes. Walkers are allowed to walk along Moody Beach but are not permitted to set up beach chairs, umbrellas, or beach towels except in the intertidal zone (the area between high tide and low tide), and even that is open to dispute. In [Edward B.] *Bell v. Town of Wells* (the Moody Beach case), litigated in 1984, Maine's Supreme judicial court found that a 1640s Puritan ordinance still held, limiting public access to the intertidal zone to just fishing, fowling

(hunting birds), and navigation. This ruling was upheld in 1986. Readers should conclude that their ability to stroll along Moody Beach remains tentative, and mainly at the acquiescence of private landowners.

Ogunquit Dunes—The Ogunquit Dunes, averaging 25 feet in height, form an impressive 3.0-mile barrier between the ocean and the Ogunquit River and its salt marshes. Except for designated areas, however, the dunes are off limit to beach walkers. Regrettably, no restrictions were in place during Ogunquit's early years and the heavily grassed dunes were partially ruined by dune walkers who found the soft sand to their liking—even for sledding. Damage was also done by blustery storms and high winds, particularly during a storm in 1978 when the ocean broke through the dunes in several places. Replacement sand had to be brought in by the U.S. Army Corps of Engineers from nearby glacial deposits, and stalks of grass had to be replanted.

It's interesting to note that rivers are constantly changing, and the Ogunquit River is no exception. In his 1880 book *History of York County, Maine with Illustrations and Biographical Sketches of Its Prominent Men and Pioneers*, W. Woodford Clayton quotes Jeremiah Hubbard and Jonathan Greenleaf, who write, "*Within the memory of man now living the outlet of the [Ogunquit] river into the sea has shifted nearly a mile. It formerly ran out where it now does; but in a great storm the outlet became somewhat obstructed, and the main river broke through the beach nearly a mile to the eastward. The river having thus found vent, its former channel was wholly filled up. However, the river gradually wore away the beach, and with it a small island, which lay very near to it, and in a few years regained its former channel, where it has ever since remained.*"

Looked at with a yardstick measuring centuries, the rivers, rocky shorelines, and beaches of Ogunquit are constantly undergoing transformation.

In his 1957 book *On the Rocks of Ogunquit*, based upon a lecture given in 1945 to the Ogunquit Art Association, George Towar puts forward an interesting observation, the accuracy of which I leave for the reader to judge: "*There is one feature of sand beaches in general that I would like to call to your attention:*

every good, long sands beach which I have ever seen has low marsh land or a river or a bay behind it. This seems to be a geological requisite of beaches." This certainly applies to Ogunquit Beach.

HIKE: *Ogunquit Beach*—This is a highly desirable area for beach goers, most of whom choose to congregate on the part of the beach between the north end of the Norseman Resort and the mouth of the Ogunquit River.

It is great fun to walk the entire length of the beach from the mouth of the Ogunquit River to the rocks at the end of Moody Beach, some >3.0 miles distant. From the north end of Moody Beach, looking east, you may be able to make out Bibb Rock (GPS: 43.278217, -70.555629), 1.0 mile distant, located at the south end of a mostly underwater, 0.5-mile-long rocky bar.

Ogunquit Dunes—From the Norseman Resort beach entrance to Ogunquit Beach, walk north along the shoreline for >0.2 mile and then bear left onto a path that takes you up and over the dunes to the Ogunquit River side of the sandbanks. From here, turn right and walk north for 0.3 mile; then cross back over the dunes to the beach area again, returning south to your starting point in 0.6 mile.

A second option for exploring the dunes is to walk north for 0.6 mile along the shoreline from the Norseman Resort beach entrance and turn left onto the northernmost path up over the dunes. Once on the Ogunquit River side, turn left and walk south for 0.3 mile, and then back over the dunes to the beach.

Take note that you must stay on the pathways. Walking on the dunes, which are fenced in for good reason, is not permitted.

There is also a short pathway between the north side of the Norseman Resort and the south end of the dune that extends from the beach to the Resort's parking area.

HISTORY: Ogunquit Beach began to really take off as a tourist attraction when the Beach Street Bridge was constructed in 1888, connecting the mainland with an isthmus-like strip of land between the ocean and the Ogunquit River. Quickly, a pavilion, dancehall and bowling alley were established, and the beach became a popular, festive public destination.

Hotels began to spring up in Ogunquit and Wells in the 1880s, spurred on by the development of the Boston & Maine Railroad bringing guests from New York City and Philadelphia, and the Atlantic Shore Line Trolley, completed in 1907, bringing in guests from more immediate areas.

Meanwhile, at the same time, Charles Tibbetts, a Dover, New Hampshire developer, purchased Wells Beach from the State of Maine on a quitclaim deed for $100,000. From 1903 to 1919, summer cottages began sprouting up at the north end of the beach (now known as Moody Beach) as Tibbets divided the property into 10-building lots, and then leased those lots for subdivision.

Residents of Ogunquit began to take notice and realized that their beach, long taken for granted as public and free for all to enjoy, was in danger of becoming privatized through development. Because Ogunquit was still a part of Wells, citizens of Ogunquit felt that their concerns regarding this issue as well several others were being ignored and pushed for more representation.

A group of prominent residents, including Roby Perkins Littlefield of Wells [see chapter on Beach Plum Farm], appealed to the State Legislature, and the Town of Ogunquit was given the right of eminent domain over the land between the Ogunquit River and the Atlantic Ocean.

The Ogunquit Beach District was formed in 1923 to purchase the beach through a supplemental tax added onto Ogunquit's regular property tax and to make it a public park. Since then, Ogunquit Beach has remained open for public recreation and, starting in 1938, has become one of only two municipally owned beaches in the State of Maine.

In 2020, *TripAdvisor's* Travelers Choice (citing the "Best of the Best"), designated Ogunquit Beach as one of the top twenty-five beaches in the United States, and the #1 beach in New England.

What makes Ogunquit Beach so special? Unlike many coastal public beaches that extend, at best, for only several hundred yards, Ogunquit Beach is over three miles long. Secondly, the beach is sandy and rock-free throughout its entire length. Many of Maine's other beaches are riddled with rocks, stones, pebbles, and rocky outcrops. Thirdly, it possesses high sand dunes, backed by the Ogunquit River behind it, which only breaks through to the ocean at the south end of Ogunquit Beach.

The Norseman Resort, at the entrance to Ogunquit Beach, occupies the site of the former Perkins Bathing Pavilion, which was owned by a sea captain named Walter Perkins.

The present 200-foot-long Beach Street Bridge was built in 2008, replacing an older one.

OGUNQUIT RIVER PADDLES

LOCATION: Ogunquit (York County)

MAINE ATLAS & GAZETTEER: Map 1, A5—Map 3, E1

GPS PARKING: *Ogunquit Beach*—43.249795, -70.594459; *Footbridge Beach*—43.263448, -70.591528

GPS LAUNCH SITES: *Ogunquit Beach Area*—43.250127, -70.595187; *Footbridge Area*—43.262800, -70.591354; *World Within Kayaking Rentals*—43.272114, -70.596195

HOURS: *Beach areas*—continuously, but generally from dawn to dusk; *World Within Kayaking Rentals*—Consult website, https://www.world-within.com, for specific hours

FEE: *Ogunquit Beach/Ogunquit River*—parking fee charged; *Ogunquit River Inn/World Within Kayaking Rentals*—fee charged; *Footbridge launch*—parking fee charged

RESTRICTIONS: Regular beach and watercraft guidelines apply

ACCESSIBILITY: *Ogunquit Beach parking*—100-foot carry; *Footbridge Beach parking*—100-foot carry; *World Within Kayaking Rentals*—Immediate put-in

DEGREE OF DIFFICULTY: Easy

ADDITIONAL INFORMATION: World Within Kayaking Rentals, 17 Post Road, Wells, ME 04090, (207) 646-0455

DIRECTIONS: *Ogunquit Beach Area*—From the center of Ogunquit (junction of U.S. 1/Main Street, Shore Road & Beach Street), drive northeast on Beach Street for >0.3 mile to its end. Turn right into a large parking area. From the Ogunquit Beach parking area, carry your watercraft north for >100 feet to the Ogunquit River.

See chapter on Ogunquit Beach for additional parking areas.

Ogunquit River Inn Launch Site (private) for rentals—From the center of Ogunquit (junction of U.S. 1/Main Street, Shore Road & Beach Street), drive north on U.S. 1/Main Street for ~1.6 miles. Turn right at the Ogunquit River Inn and park to your left, where the World Within Kayaking Rentals operates at the north end of the Inn next to the private launch site. Walk downhill past the side of the hotel on your right and swimming pool on your left to the lower level, where multi-colored kayaks stashed at the launch site can be rented. There is an observation deck on the shore overlooking the Ogunquit River and from where, if you look to your right, you can readily see Moody falls if the foliage is sparse.

Footbridge Beach area—From the center of Ogunquit (junction of U.S. 1/Main Street, Shore Road & Beach Street), drive north on U.S. 1/Main Street for ~1.1 miles. Turn right onto Ocean Street and head southeast for >0.3 mile and park in the large area to your left.

DESCRIPTION: The Ogunquit River is a 10-mile-long river that rises in South Berwick, flowing into the Atlantic Ocean at the south end of Ogunquit Beach—an area that, according to W. Woodford Clayton, in *History of York County, Maine: with illustrations and biographical sketches of its prominent men and pioneers* (1880), forms a small harbor *"which can be entered by small vessels only, the depth of water there being about eight feet."* The river has a watershed of ~21 square miles.

PADDLE: The Ogunquit River is a delightful river to paddle on between U.S. 1 and the Atlantic Ocean. It runs through a marshland and is a fairly shallow stream as you might expect due to it being tidal. For this reason, it is best to paddle within the span of two hours before high tide and two hours after high tide. At low tide, you could very well end up stuck on a mud flat if you are too far upriver.

To add to the paddle's enjoyment, time your outing so that you are going with the direction of the tide, not against it.

Ogunquit River Launch—Although you can paddle downstream to the Atlantic Ocean in 0.4 mile, it makes for a more interesting trek to paddle upriver, passing under the footbridge leading to Footbridge Beach in >0.9 mile and then coming to the junction of the Ogunquit River and Stevens Brook in >1.3 miles. If you turn left and head west on the Ogunquit River, the trek will end in 0.4 mile near the base of Moody Falls, close to the launch site at the Ogunquit River Inn.

The second option, and by far the longer trek, is to continue north from the junction of the Ogunquit River and Stevens Brook, now paddling on Stevens Brook and the backed-up waters of the Ogunquit River. In another 0.5 mile, you will pass under the Bourne Avenue Bridge, and, after another ~1.0 mile, come to the Furbish Road Bridge. From here, the paddle continues into the Wells National Estuarine Research Reserve.

Body surfing option on the Ogunquit River up to the Beach Street Bridge—If you wish, you can join other swimmers who wait until an hour or two before high tide and then body surf the inrushing Ogunquit River from near the mouth of the river to the Beach Street Bridge. It's exhilarating to watch the shoreline race by you at an astonishing pace while you are swept along by the current.

Take note that beach users are not allowed to use flotation devices when the tidal waters are flowing out of the Ogunquit River into the Atlantic Ocean.

Interestingly, the ocean by the mouth of the Ogunquit River is one of the best-known breaking spots for surfboarding in Maine, where big waves break off Lobster Point, becoming quite sizeable at times.

Ogunquit River Inn launch site—From the launch site at the north end of the

inn, paddle east for 0.4 mile until you come to the junction of the Ogunquit River and Stevens Brook. If you turn right, you will head south down the Ogunquit River, eventually reaching the Atlantic Ocean. Along the way, a footbridge is passed under at 0.4 mile; then, the Beach Street Bridge at 1.3 miles.

At 1.7 miles, the mouth of the Ogunquit River is reached where it is best to turn around and return upriver unless you wish to do some sea kayaking. Hopefully, the tide is coming in as you head back upriver.

If you choose to turn left at the junction of the Ogunquit River and Stevens Brook, follow Stevens Brook and the backed-up waters of the Ogunquit River north. In 0.5 mile, you will pass under the Bourne Avenue Bridge. In another 1.0 mile, the Furbish Road Bridge is reached. If you continue further, you will enter into the Wells National Estuarine Research Reserve.

Footbridge Beach area launch—From the parking area, put in via the launch site at the northwest end of the footbridge. There are two directions you can go from here: Heading south takes you down the Ogunquit River. Along the way, at >0.9 mile, you will pass under the Beach Street bridge and, at 1.3 miles, approach the mouth of the Ogunquit River at the Atlantic Ocean. Unless you're into sea kayaking, it is best to stop here and turn around, hopefully timing your trip so that the tide is coming in.

Heading north takes you up the Ogunquit River to the junction of the Ogunquit River and Stevens Brook. If you turn left here and paddle west, you will dead-end in 0.4 mile at a large pool below Moody Falls, close to the Ogunquit River Inn launch site. If you instead continue straight north, now on Stevens Brook and the backwaters of Ogunquit Creek, you will pass under the Bourne Avenue Bridge in another 0.5 mile and then, in another 1.0 mile, reach the Furbish Road Bridge. Should you continue further north, you will end up paddling into the Wells National Estuarine Research Reserve.

If you are curious about the blockhouse structure in the Footbridge Beach parking lot, it is analogous to the Lobster Point Lighthouse on the Marginal Way in that both serve as disguised pumping stations for the Ogunquit Sewer District.

HISTORY: Stevens Brook is a small-to-medium-sized stream that rises in the uplands west of U.S. 1 and flows into the Ogunquit River behind private houses and dunes that front Moody Beach. It benefits greatly from the backed-up Ogunquit River at high tide.

THE LEAVITT THEATER

LOCATION: Ogunquit (York County)

MAINE ATLAS & GAZETTEER: Map 1, A5

GPS PARKING: Parking is free in the evenings in the upper parking area (43.250413, -70.599484) and lower parking area (43.250285, -70.598448) directly across the street from the theater

GPS LEAVITT THEATER: 43.250459, -70.600262

HOURS: Open seasonally from May through October; Consult website, https://www.leavittheatre.com, for more details

ADDITIONAL INFORMATION: Leavitt Theater, 259 Main Street, Ogunquit, ME 03907; (207) 646-3123; https://www.leavittheatre.com

DIRECTIONS: From the center of Ogunquit (junction of U.S. 1/Main Street, Shore Road & Beach Street), head north on U.S. 1/Main Street for 0.1 mile. The Leavitt Theater is on the west (left) side of the road.

DESCRIPTION: The Leavitt Theater is a seasonal theater that provides *"a place of community, entertainment and support for the performing arts."* It has expanded to include a bustling lounge with nightly entertainment, as well as an outdoor seating area with cocktail and food options.

HISTORY: The original Leavitt Theater was built in Sanford, Maine, northwest of Ogunquit, by Frank and Annie Leavitt in 1910. After a fire destroyed the building, the Leavitts moved to Ogunquit in 1923 and opened the 500-seat Leavitt Fine Arts Theater in 1924. The first cinema shown at the theater was *Dante's Inferno*, a 1924 silent era movie that contained nudity as well as disturbing images. It created a firestorm of controversy, but the theater did well, probably due to all the free advertising that the uproar created.

When Frank died, Annie continued running the theater. Later, Dan Levenson took over, but only briefly.

In 1976, Peter Clayton bought the theater and turned it into a family-run business. In 2013, the theater's obsolete projectors were replaced by state-of-the-art digital equipment following a fundraising campaign that raised nearly $71,000.

In 2017, Peter's son, Max Clayton, became the new owner, along with his partner, Emily Knight. They have kept The Leavitt moving ahead despite the digital age onslaught of in-home theater.

Today, the theater is *predominantly* a restaurant and bar, although its auditorium is still used for live comedy, local music, free films, and much more.

Ogunquit Square Theater—The Leavitt Theater wasn't the only cinema in town. There was also the Ogunquit Square Theater, which was located on 15 Shore Road (GPS: 43.248598, -70.599390) and has its own fascinating history. It began as a commercial garage near the center of Ogunquit. In 1933, Walter and Maud Hartwig converted the garage into a playhouse for their Manhattan Theater Colony troupe. After the Hartwigs relocated in 1937 to a new playhouse that they built on 10 Main Street [see chapter on Ogunquit Playhouse], the building was remade into the 465-seat Ogunquit Square Theater, which opened in 1939. Visitors best remember the walls being hung with buoys in the local color of individual lobstermen. The theater no longer exists, having been closed since the 1990s and replaced by the Front Porch General Store and Sea Bags.

OGUNQUIT MEMORIAL LIBRARY

LOCATION: Ogunquit (York County)

MAINE ATLAS & GAZETTEER: Map 1, A5

GPS PARKING: There is no library parking other than on the street or in designated parking areas [see chapter on "Ogunquit Beach"].

GPS OGUNQUIT MEMORIAL LIBRARY: 43.243944, -70.596621

HOURS: Consult website, https://ogunquitlibrary.com, for specific hours

FEE: None

ADDITIONAL INFORMATION: Ogunquit Memorial Library, 166 Shore Road, Ogunquit, ME 03907; (207) 646-9024

DIRECTIONS: From the center of Ogunquit (junction of U.S. 1/Main Street, Shore Road & Beach Street), head southeast on Shore Road for <0.4 mile. The library is to your right, on the west side of Shore Road. There is space for a couple of cars in front of the library.

DESCRIPTION: The Romanesque Revival-style Ogunquit Memorial Library was a gift to the Town by Nannie D. Conarroe in memory of her deceased husband, George Conarroe, a Philadelphia attorney who summered with his wife in Ogunquit [See chapter on St. Peters-by-the-Sea Episcopal Chapel for additional information].

HISTORY: The Ogunquit Memorial Library was designed by Philadelphia architect Charles M. Burns and built in 1897 by York contractor Edward B. Blaisdel. It opened to the public in 1898.

The interior of the library is made of stained, dark oak.

In 1914, the library was enlarged by Luther Weare who also constructed the magnificent grandfather clock now on display in the library. Weare fashioned the grandfather clock out of a black walnut piano case.

Additional work was done on the library in 2007 when the majestic entrance doors had to be replaced. The new doors were handcrafted by Matthew Browne and the Rovnack Group, a family-owned cabinet shop.

The 2-foot miniature replica of the library facing the clock was crafted by Winaloe U. Stonehill in the 1930s. It, along with a number of other miniatures town buildings, were originally displayed in a garden in front of Stonehill's home. He called his collection of small-scale buildings "Tiny Town."

The Ogunquit Memorial Library was listed on the National Register of Historic Places in 1983.

LOCATION: Ogunquit (York County)
MAINE ATLAS & GAZETTEER: Map 1, A5
GPS OGUNQUIT BAPTIST CHURCH: 43.244306, -70.596350
GPS OGUNQUIT PARKING (CHURCH ONLY): 43.244447, -70.596478
ADDITIONAL INFORMATION: Ogunquit Baptist Church, 157 Shore Road, Ogunquit, ME 03907; (207) 646-2160
The church is open seasonally.

DIRECTIONS: From the center of Ogunquit (junction of U.S. 1/Main Street, Shore Road & Beach Street), head southeast on Shore Road for <0.4 mile. The church is on your left, along the east side of the road.

HISTORY: A congregation of like-minded believers began meeting in 1830 and soon had erected a small church. In 1859, a new church (the one that you presently see) was built, expanding over the years and even surviving a fire.

The historic church is of a classic Greek Revival design with cornices, and a pedimented roof surmounting four unfluted columns that are more in the Tuscan column style.

The church stands in the L-shaped crook of the historic Colonial Inn, c. 1890 (GPS: 43.244698, -70. 596386). The Inn has the distinction of being the only surviving nineteenth-century hotel in Ogunquit that has retained its original appearance and that still operates as a hotel.

OGUNQUIT HERITAGE MUSEUM & DOROTHEA JACOBS GRANT COMMON

LOCATION: Ogunquit (York County)

MAINE ATLAS & GAZETTEER: Map 1, A5

GPS PARKING: 43.244606, -70.600137

GPS DESTINATIONS: *Ogunquit Heritage Museum*—43.244681, -70.600382; *Dorothea Jacobs Grant Commons*—43.244774, -70.599976

MUSEUM HOURS: Consult website, ogunquitheritagemuseum.com or https://chamber.ogunquit.org/list/memberogunquit-heritage-museum-405, for specific details (presently June-October, Tuesday-Saturday, 1:00 p.m.—5:00 p.m.)

FEE: Donations appreciated

ADDITIONAL INFORMATION: Ogunquit Heritage Museum, 86 Obeds Lane, Ogunquit, ME 03907; (207) 646-0296

DIRECTIONS: From the center of Ogunquit (junction of U.S. 1/Main Street, Shore Road & Beach Street), head southeast on Shore Road for >0.2 mile. Turn right onto Obeds Lane and head southwest for <0.2 mile, turning right into the small parking area for the museum.

DESCRIPTION: The Ogunquit Heritage Museum, located on the Dorothea Jacobs Grant Commons land, occupies the former Cape-style house of Captain James Winn Sr., constructed in ~1780.

Adjacent to the Museum is the Dorothea Jacobs Grant Commons, a small park that has a short, winding path that takes you along the edge of the woods.

HISTORY: *Ogunquit Heritage Museum*—The integrity of the Winn Home, originally located on U.S. 1, north of Ogunquit, has not changed significantly over the years despite numerous owners and tenants. We do know that during the early nineteenth century, a central staircase and front door were added.

The building was placed on the National Register of Historic Places in 1979 for its historic value.

After the house was donated to the town by Phyllis Perkins and moved to its present location by the Rotary Club of Ogunquit in 2001, further restoration work was done. In addition to repainting the house, workers replaced its L-shaped section ("the ell") in 2005. The original ell was sold for $1 by Ms. Perkins to another party.

The Heritage Museum offers exhibits and artifacts featuring Ogunquit's history of fishing, lobstering, and shipbuilding; its social and cultural heritage; the rise of the art colony and summer theater; and its architectural heritage, including the Winn Home itself, which still possesses most of its original paneling, flooring, and hardware. In addition, the museum houses the extensive Charles Littlefield Seaman Library. Seaman, along with his second wife, Dorothy, founded the Littlefield Family Newsletter, a quarterly genealogical journal, in 1991.

Ogunquit Dory—In front of the museum (or, off season, moored in Perkins Cove) is a replica of the Ogunquit Dory that William Henry Perkins built at his boathouse on Sawyer's Lane (now known as Wharf Lane). The boats were typically 16 to 21 feet in length.

Dorothea Jacobs Grant Commons—The property was previously part of the Sparhawk owned by Dorthea Jacobs Grant's family. In Grant's will, the land, starting from behind what would eventually become the Seacastles Resort, southwest to U.S. 1, was donated to the Town of Ogunquit.

The Park contains two entrances. One is by the Heritage Museum; the other is from a large parking area off Cottage Street. A brick sidewalk leads around the perimeter of the park under shady trees and well-placed benches. At the southwest corner of the garden is a birdhouse perched on a pole that is a replica of the old Riverside Hotel [see chapter on Perkins Cove].

As a point of interest, Grant's former home is located on the south side of the Marginal Way entrance (GPS: 43.246026, -70.596836), directly in front of the Sparhawk Oceanfront Resort, into which it has been assimilated.

At the time of her death in 1983, Dorothea established an endowment fund for the Ogunquit Memorial Library and a perpetual care fund for three local cemeteries. She also donated a significant parcel of land along the Marginal Way by Israel's Head to the Town of Ogunquit.

Obeds Lane was named for Dorothea Jacobs Grant's uncle, Obediah. The road was originally a continuation of Agamenticus Road.

BARN GALLERY

LOCATION: Ogunquit (York County)
MAINE ATLAS & GAZETTEER: Map 1, A5
GPS PARKING: 43.241197, -70.597426
GPS BARN GALLERY: 43.241291, -70.597160
HOURS: Consult website, https://barngallery.org, for specific details
ADDITIONAL INFORMATION: Barn Gallery, 3 Hartwig Lane, Ogunquit, ME 03907; (207) 646-8400

DIRECTIONS: From the center of Ogunquit (junction of U.S. 1/Main Street, Shore Road & Beach Street), head southeast on Shore Road for >0.5 mile and turn right onto Bourne Lane and then immediately left into a small parking area for the Barn Gallery next to the side of the building.

DESCRIPTION: The Barn Gallery was constructed in 1958 by the Barn Gallery Associates (BGA) in collaboration with the Ogunquit Art Association (OAA) to be a permanent site for the Ogunquit Art Association to exhibit their works, present gallery talks, provide lively panel discussions, and offer workshops and demonstrations. The gallery opened in 1959.

The Art Association was founded in 1928 at the Perkins Cove Studio by Charles H. Woodbury and a group of local artists and friends. Their first exhibition took place at the Ogunquit Beach Pavilion (now the site of the Norseman Resort).

The name "Barn Gallery" dates from the time when the Art Association conducted their annual art show, starting in 1936, at Edwin C. Perkin's large, yellow barn on Shore Road.

HISTORY: The Ogunquit Art Association was founded in 1928 in the Perkin Cove studio of painter and art instructor Charles Herbert Woodbury, who became the organization's first president. Woodbury was well known long before then, becoming the youngest honoree of the Boston Art Club at age 17.

It is owned and administered by the Ogunquit Arts Collaborative, a not-for-profit corporation.

JOSIAS RIVER PUBLIC PARK

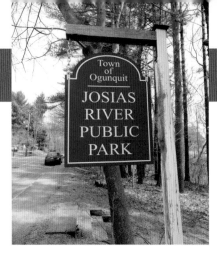

LOCATION: Ogunquit (York County)

MAINE ATLAS & GAZETTEER: Map 1, A5

GPS PARKING: Pull-off-road in front of the Park

GPS JOSIAS RIVER PUBLIC PARK: 43.241521, -70.600784

HOURS: Dawn to dusk

FEE: None

RESTRICTIONS: Regular Park rules & regulations apply

ACCESSIBILITY: <0.1-mile walk

DEGREE OF DIFFICULTY: Easy

ADDITIONAL INFORMATION: The Park lies across the road from Jonathan's Ogunquit

DIRECTIONS: From the center of Ogunquit (junction of U.S. 1/Main Street, Shore Road & Beach Street), proceed southeast on Shore Road for >0.5 mile. Turn right onto Bourne Lane and head west for 0.2 mile. The Park is on your left, nearly opposite Jonathan's Ogunquit (a restaurant that includes live jazz and concerts) on 92 Bourne Lane.

DESCRIPTION: Josias River Public Park is a 1-acre parcel of land that was donated to the Town of Ogunquit by Phil Cavaretta (proprietor of the Meadowmere Resort) and Joseph Gallo (owner of Josephs Farms) and was officially dedicated in 2006 to the memory of Eve Cavaretta.

HIKE: This very short hike leads you through the woods and down to the Josias River within 100 feet.

HISTORY: The river and the Park were named for Josiah Littlefield, a property owner who erected a sawmill at Josias River Falls (slightly farther downstream) in 1643. The Park abuts a tiny segment of the ~5.8-mile-long Josias River that rises principally from marshes east of 2.3-mile-long Chases Pond (formerly called Cape Neddick Pond) and Mt. Agamenticus and drops 220 feet before reaching the ocean. It encompasses a watershed of <7.5 square miles.

According to *New England Miniature: A History of York, Maine* (1961) by George Ernst, *"There were at least five mills on the Josias River and its tributaries, the oldest was last operated by descendants of Ebenezer Moulton.*"

The two benches in the Park near the river are dedicated to the mothers of Phil Cavaretta and Joseph Gallo.

OGUNQUIT PLAYHOUSE

LOCATION: Ogunquit (York County)

MAINE ATLAS & GAZETTEER: Map 1, A5

GPS PARKING: 43.239589, -70.601088

GPS OGUNQUIT PLAYHOUSE: 43.238988, -70.600307

HOURS: Consult website, https://www.ogunquitplayhouse.org, for specific details

FEE: Admission charged

ADDITIONAL INFORMATION: Ogunquit Playhouse, 10 Main Street/U.S. 1, Ogunquit, ME 03907; (207) 646-5511; www.ogunquitplayhouse.org

For more detailed information, consult the book *The Ogunquit Playhouse: 75 Years* (2007) by Carole Lee Carroll, Bunny Hart and Susan Day Meffert.

DIRECTIONS: From the center of Ogunquit (junction of U.S. 1/Main Street, Shore Road & Beach Street), head south on U.S. 1/Main Street for 0.7 mile and turn left into the parking area for the playhouse.

DESCRIPTION: The 654-seat Ogunquit Playhouse is Maine's largest performing arts organization, producing up to six Broadway-caliber productions each year from May through October, with an additional two co-productions in the spring and for the holidays with The Music Hall in Portsmouth, NH.

HISTORY: Ogunquit Playhouse was the brainchild of Broadway showman Walter Hartwig and his wife, Maude, who brought their band of performers and artisans from New York, Connecticut, and New Hampshire to Ogunquit in 1933, establishing summer theatre and theater education as part of the industry's Little Theater Movement. Their first performance was held in a renovated garage in Ogunquit's Town Square [see chapter on Levitt Theater for additional information], and they quickly established a Theatre Colony for developing new works and new performers.

Four years later, the Hartwigs purchased a 27-acre parcel of land along U.S. 1/Main Street and built the present Ogunquit Playhouse, opening its doors for the first time on July 17, 1937, with a production of *Boy Meets Girl* written by Bella and Samuel Spewack. Upon Walter's untimely death in 1941, Maude continued to run the theater until 1950 when she sold the organization to actor/producer John Lane. Lane ushered in the Playhouse's second golden age drawing to the stage big name stars from film and television.

Upon Lane's retirement in 1994, Ogunquit Playhouse became a 501c3 nonprofit organization and continued to thrive. During the last 17 years under Executive Artistic Director Bradford T. Kenney, the Playhouse has grown into a major player in the industry, producing at least one world premiere or new work each season while nurturing multiple productions at other regional theaters throughout the country.

The theater was listed on the National Register of Historic Places in 1995.

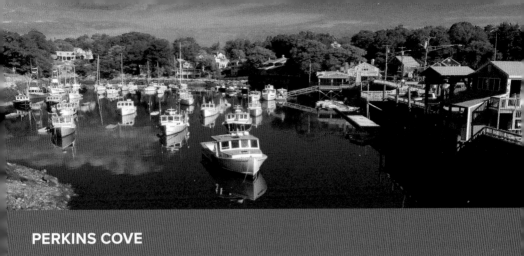

PERKINS COVE

LOCATION: Ogunquit (York County)

MAINE ATLAS & GAZETTEER: Map 1, A5

GPS PARKING: *Near drawbridge*—43.237345, -70.590613; *Adjacent to the Oarweed Restaurant*—43.237968, -70.591794; *Junction of Shore Road & Perkins Cove Road*—43.238714, -70.594462

GPS DESTINATIONS: *Perkins Cove*—43.236708, -70.589769; *Drawbridge*—43.236398, -70.590265; *Perkins Cove (Basin)*—43.236983, -70.591640; *Josias River Falls*—43.237207, -70.593687

ADDITIONAL INFORMATION: Historic Walking Tour of Perkins Cove is presently conducted June-October on Monday & Wednesdays at 10:00 a.m. Reservations are mandatory. Modest fee charged.

DIRECTIONS: From the center of Ogunquit (junction of U.S. 1/Main Street, Shore Road & Beach Street), proceed southeast on Shore Road for >0.8 mile. At a fork marked by a colorful blue and white sign stating "Perkins Cove," bear left and head southeast on Perkins Cove Road for 0.2 mile to reach Perkins Cove.

For those wishing to drive, three parking areas in Perkins Cove are available, but fill up quickly.

DESCRIPTION: Perkins Cove is a quaint fishing community, resplendent with boutique shops and retail outlets on both sides of Perkins Cove Road. It is also still an active working waterfront for lobstermen, fishermen and tuna men. The Oarweed Restaurant is located at the south end of the Marginal Way.

A looped, one-way road, starting at Rotary Park (43.236763, -70.590209), leads around through the tiny community and back out.

Near the south end of the hamlet, Perkins Cove Road changes to Harbor Lane and enters a small community of homes (off-limits to the public), including

the historic Island House that was renovated and enlarged prior to 1910 by Hamilton Easter Field (a New York artist who opened an art school in 1911), on what at one time was Adams Island until it was joined to the mainland. When Field arrived in Ogunquit in 1902, he wanted the island in order to specifically create a summer home for himself, his mother, and Robert Laurent, whom he had mentored.

Adams Island was named for George Adams, who built a house on the island in 1850.

HISTORY: *Perkins Cove Harbor*—The picturesque harbor is usually occupied by dozens or more moored pleasure craft and a few lobster boats. There are 68 moorings in total (47 which are commercial and 21 which are recreational).

Originally, there was no harbor, just the unnavigable Josias River that dropped over Josias Falls into Flat Pond and then ran through a marshland and out into the Atlantic Ocean. What's interesting is that the course of the river was different in those early days. It emptied into Oarweed Cove (GPS: 43.236628, -70.588595), forming a crescent-shaped beach north of Adams Island, and not into Fish Cove (GPS: 43.234635, -70.587332) as it does today.

Old dory fishermen called the cove simply "The Cove" or "Fish Cove." The name may have changed to Perkins Cove when Daniel Perkins and his wife started taking borders into their home, which they later called the Perkins Cove House.

In those days before the marshlands were turned into a harbor, Joel Perkins used to harvest the salty hay that grew in the marshes around the Josias

River. The salt marshes were mostly owned by Lyman Staples, who also owned the nearby Riverside Farm (which became the Riverside Hotel after he started renting rooms on his farm).

Salty hay had many uses, including bedding for stables, protecting docks and bulkheads, and preventing erosion at construction sites. Salty hay, aka salt hay and Saltmeadow Cordgrass, typically grows above mean high tide, forming the cowlicked meadows that are associated with a high tide marsh.

Because there was no headland or breakwater to protect boats from stormy weather, fishermen had to drag their dories onto the riverbank in the winter and during bad weather or take their chances leaving the boats in Fish Cove. This proved to be an onerous task year in and out. To resolve the problem, the Fish Cove Harbor Association was formed in 1857 and a channel was dug to connect Fish Cove, to the south, with the Josias River, to the north. In time, this trench was further enlarged through natural erosive processes, resulting in the creation of a small tidewater basin.

In order to permit larger boats to moor in a safe harbor, two-thirds of the marshland was dredged by the U.S. Army Corps of Engineers in 1941-1942. At the same time, the old river channel was filled in with dredge removed from the marshlands and Adams Island became joined to the mainland.

The basin has been dredged five times since—in 1951 to increase the depth of the harbor; in 1959-1960 to expand the harbor's size by removing the remaining marshland; in 1966-1967; in 1976; and finally in 1991-1992, the latter three dredgings being for routine maintenance or increasing the depth of the basin or channel. More dredging is due to be done by the Army Corps of Engineers in the near future.

Josias River Falls—This small, 10-15-foot-high waterfall is formed on the Josias River, a 3.0-mile-long stream that drains an area of 7.4 square miles. In the past, the stream was also known as Josiah's River and Four Mile Brook. The waterfall is located at the north end of the Perkins Cove basin. It can be seen from the west side of the Auberge on the Cove behind Apartment #15, as well as from boats mooring in the harbor.

Drawbridge—The Perkins Cove Drawbridge at the entrance to the harbor basin is an iconic landmark. The original footbridge—a small, rickety structure—was erected by Lyman Staples in 1896 to enable guests at his Riverside Hotel, today known as "Auberge on the Cove" (GPS: 43.236148, -70.591830), to readily access the hamlet without having to go around the harbor. Every winter, the bridge would have to be repaired or replaced due to surging tides or winter ice floes. Lyman dutifully maintained the bridge until Hamilton Easter Field purchased half of the cove and took over the task.

The bridges that followed were fairly insubstantial until 1944 when the prototype of today's dual span bridge was built, with one side capable of being raised or lowered by a hand crank to allow vessels with masts to make their way under. William Tower, Jr. was appointed the first harbor master at this time.

Later, the hand crank was replaced by an electro-mechanical device, and then, still later, that was replaced by a hydraulic device. Major work on the footbridge occurred in 1964, 1977, and 2000. Recently, the Town received funding for a major upgrade of the bridge in 2024.

The Perkins Cove bridge that you see today is the only remaining, wooden, double leaf draw footbridge in the United States.

Near the northwest end of the drawbridge is a monument honoring "Fisherman Christopher L. Linney age 18 [who] lost his life at sea June 28, 1984. Dedicated to all fishermen who have sailed away forever."

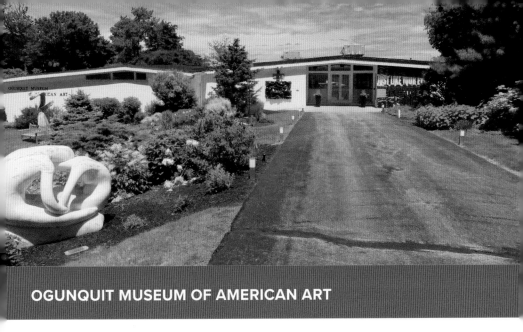

OGUNQUIT MUSEUM OF AMERICAN ART

LOCATION: Ogunquit (York County)

MAINE ATLAS & GAZETTEER: Map 1, A5

GPS PARKING: 43.233239, -70.589572

GPS DESTINATIONS: *Ogunquit Museum of American Art*—43.233767, -70.589108; *Pond with footbridge*—43.233602, -70.589600; *Narrow Cove Overlook*—43.234177, -70.588419

HOURS: Consult website, https://ogunquitmuseum.org, for specific details

FEE: Admission charged

ADDITIONAL INFORMATION: Ogunquit Museum of American Art, 543 Shore Road, Ogunquit, ME 03907; (207) 646-4909

DIRECTIONS: From the center of Ogunquit (junction of U.S. 1/Main Street, Shore Road & Beach Street), drive southeast along Shore Road for ~1.3 miles and turn left onto the entrance for the Ogunquit Museum of American Art where parking is available.

DESCRIPTION: The Ogunquit Museum of American Art is an art museum with over 3,000 works in its permanent collection. The museum organizes ongoing exhibitions of modern and contemporary art, and offers regular educational programs and events.

The museum sits within three acres of gardens overlooking the Atlantic Ocean with stunning panoramic views of Maine's iconic coves and outcroppings. Outdoor sculptures are integrated throughout the grounds.

WALK: Short walking paths behind the museum provide views from rocky bluffs of Narrow Cove, the Atlantic Ocean, and Perkins Cove.

Walks can also be taken on the grounds in front of and to the side of the museum, including crossing over a footbridge that spans a small pond.

HISTORY: The Ogunquit Museum of American Art was founded by the artist Henry Strater, who purchased an oceanfront property known as Narrow Cove from Charles H. Woodbury in 1951. Charles S. Worley, Jr. designed the building that opened in 1953 as the Museum of Art of Ogunquit. The modernist building, with its signature sloping roofline, was constructed from local stone and wood. In 1992, the museum changed its name to the Ogunquit Museum of American Art.

The museum shares close historic and geographic ties to the art schools of Charles Woodbury, who opened the Ogunquit Summer School of Drawing & Painting in Perkins Cove in 1898, and Hamilton Easter Field, who founded the Summer School of Graphic Arts in Perkins Cove in 1911. The core of the museum's collections features works by artists associated with the modern arts community that grew from these schools, including Marsden Hartley, Walt Kuhn, Marguerite Zorach, and Yasuo Kuniyoshi.

The museum continues its tradition of celebrating the arts community in Maine and beyond by collecting and showing works by contemporary artists.

CAPE NEDDICK AREA

I n Charles Edward Banks' *History of York Maine. Vol. 1* (1931), the author writes, *"The shore line from Bald Head Cliff to Braveboat Harbor forms an almost straight line, broken in the middle by the curious projection extending into the ocean for a mile and terminating in a small cliff-like rock, separated from it by a narrow and deep channel through which the tide flows with great velocity. The detached portion on which stands the lighthouse is called The Nubble..."* This is the Cape Neddick area, a truly magical place!

CLIFF HOUSE & BALD HEAD CLIFF

LOCATION: Bald Head (York County)

MAINE ATLAS & GAZETTEER: Map 1, A5

GPS PARKING: 43.220974, -70.579662

GPS DESTINATIONS: *Cliff House*—43.220093, -70.577905; *Bald Head Cliff*—43.221537, -70.575837; *Stairway leading partway down to base of cliff*—43.219819, -70.577401

ADDITIONAL INFORMATION: Cliff House, 591 Shore Road, Cape Neddick, ME 03902; (207) 361-1000

Resort map—https://www.cliffhousemaine.com/pdf/resort-map.pdf

DIRECTIONS: From the center of Ogunquit (junction of U.S. 1/Main Street, Shore Road & Beach Street), drive southeast along Shore Road for ~1.7 miles. Turn left onto the entrance for the Cliff House and go northeast for 0.2 mile to the parking area.

DESCRIPTION: Cliff House is a massive hotel with 226 guest rooms, a luxury spa, the Tiller (a restaurant with ocean views), and several ancillary buildings, situated on 70 acres of land atop Bald Head Cliff.

The name Cliff House really doesn't do justice to this establishment. This hotel is not just on a cliff. It is massive and over 0.2-mile long,

WALK: An 0.4-mile-long, dirt/paved walkway goes around the back of the hotel, interrupted by a swimming pool. The walk provides superb views of the ocean and bluffs.

Near the southeast end of the hotel by The Tiller, a stairway descends to an observation deck positioned near the bottom of the cliff.

Along the Bald Head walk, take note of the brownish-colored seams in the rock, extending from a few inches up to 10 feet across, that are dikes filled in by basalt (a volcanic rock) 175 million years ago.

Across from the parking area is the Cliff House Woods Trail, which provides an alternative to the open views of the Cliff Walk.

A second swimming pool is located near the north end of the hotel. It offers a unique experience for swimmers where a vanishing edge creates the illusion of bobbing right out in the ocean.

HISTORY: The Cliff House was founded in 1872 by Elsie Jane Weare, wife of Captain Theodore Weare (a local merchant and ship owner). The hotel was built by Elsie Jane's brother, Captain Charles Perkins, using wood that was milled in his sawmill on Beach Street in Ogunquit. The hotel has since gone through many additions and renovations. During World War II, it was commandeered and used as a radar station to detect offshore Nazi submarines. Major renovations were undertaken in 1948 to undo damage inflicted by the military occupation, and in 2000 a new lobby, conference room, retail space, and fitness center and spa were added on. In 2016, a complete renovation was done.

ST. PETERS BY THE SEA EPISCOPAL CHAPEL

LOCATION: Bald Head (York County)

MAINE ATLAS & GAZETTEER: Map 1, A5

GPS PARKING: 43.217950, -70.583479

GPS DESTINATION: *St. Peters by the Sea Episcopal Chapel*—43.218280, -70.583293; *Memorial Garden*—43.217969, -70.583349

ADDITIONAL INFORMATION: St. Peters by the Sea Episcopal Chapel, 535 Shore Road, Cape Neddick, ME 03902; (207) 361-2030; www.st-peters-by-the-sea.org (St. Peter's Bald Head newsletter)

Services are held at the chapel on Sundays, 8:00 am and 10:00 am, from June to October. Consult website, https://st-peters-by-the-sea.org, for special events.

DIRECTIONS: From the center of Ogunquit (junction of U.S. 1/Main Street, Shore Road & Beach Street), drive southeast along Shore Road for ~1.7 miles. Just past the Cliff House entrance, turn left onto a paved driveway that leads up to the church. Follow the driveway past the St. Peters Memorial Garden and park in a large field to the south of the chapel.

DESCRIPTION: St. Peters by the Sea Episcopal Chapel is an historic chapel dating back to the end of the nineteenth century.

The St. Peters Memorial Garden, opened in 2008 for cremated remains, is near the south side of the chapel. The first interment—that of Royce Morgan—occurred that same year.

HISTORY: The Episcopal stone chapel was designed by George C. Burns and constructed by Edward B. Blaisdell of York in 1897 from monies donated by Nannie Conarroe in memory of her late husband, George M. Conarroe [see chapter on Ogunquit Memorial Library]. In the *History of York Maine. Vol. 2* (1935) by Charles Edward Banks, the author writes, "*A beautiful stone church, St. Peters-by-the-sea, built in 1898 next to the Canarroe estate where services, according to the rites of the Episcopal Church, are held during the summer for the convenience of visitors temporarily domiciled in that section, gives a sober touch to his landscape. George M. Conarroe and family from Philadelphia were for many years patrons of this church and sponsor of the Cliff [House], as a resort.*" Of note are the spectacular stained-glass windows that were designed and built by Connick Studios of Boston.

Major restoration work was done on the chapel's rectory, the Marmion House, in 2021 and 2022. The rectory, which was built in 1900 next to the chapel, was originally named Bonnie Brae, Gaelic for "pleasant hill." The named changed in 1992 to honor the Marmion family for their long and devoted service to the church.

Fittingly, the chapel resides on 92-foot-high Christian Hill, a promontory high enough to allow the church's cross to be visible to sailors far out to sea.

MOUNT AGAMENTICUS

LOCATION: Agamenticus Village (York County)

MAINE ATLAS & GAZETTEER: Map 1, A4

GPS SUMMIT PARKING: 43.222962, -70.692283

GPS PARKING FOR POINTS OF ACCESS TO THE RING TRAIL: *#1: By entrance road*—43.216786, -70.692125; *#2: Part way up Agamenticus Road, to left*—43.218507, -70.692231; *#3: Part way up Agamenticus Road, to right*—43.219621, -70.691889

GPS SUMMIT DESTINATIONS: *Mt. Agamenticus Learning Lodge*—43.223575, -70.691694; *Old fire tower*—43.223740, -70.692689; *Observation deck*—43.224380, -70.692120

HOURS: *Summit drive*—April—September, 6:00 a.m.—Sunset; October—March, 7 a.m.—Sunset; *Hiking*—Daily, dawn to dusk
Consult website, https://agamenticus.org, for specific details

FEE: None

RESTRICTIONS: Regular Park rules & regulations apply

ACCESSIBILITY: Variable depending upon trails hiked

DEGREE OF DIFFICULTY: Easy-Moderate

ADDITIONAL INFORMATION: Mount Agamenticus, 21 Mount Agamenticus Road, York, ME 03902; (207) 361-1102

Trail map—https://agamenticus.org/wpcontent/uploads/ 2018/01/ MT.A-MAP.pdf

DIRECTIONS: From the center of Ogunquit (junction of U.S. 1/Main Street, Shore Road & Beach Street), drive south on U.S. 1/Main Street for 0.4 mile. Turn right onto Agamenticus Road/Clay Hill Road, and head southwest for ~4.0 miles. When you reach Mountain Road, turn right and proceed west for ~1.5 miles until you come to Agamenticus Road.

Summit—Turn right onto Agamenticus Road and head north, going steadily uphill, for 0.6 mile to reach the summit parking area.

Hiking Trailheads—#1—At the beginning of Agamenticus Road is a large parking area for hikers; #2—Drive up Agamenticus Road for >0.1 mile and pull into a small parking area on your left; #3—Drive up Agamenticus Road for 0.2 mile and turn into a small parking area on your right.

DESCRIPTION: Mt. Agamenticus is a 682-foot-high mountain that was used by early sailors as a navigational point of reference. It is said to be the highest point on the Atlantic seaboard between Mount Desert Island and Florida taking into account that it is not right on the seaboard but rather five miles inland. The mountain is part of a 10,000-acre conservation region.

HIKE: All the trailheads described eventually take you to the white-blazed Ring Trail which, as the name suggests, circles around the mountain. Several secondary trails spin off from this central trail to a variety of locations.

It is best to have a trail map in hand when undertaking the hike.

On a clear day on the summit, you can see as far as the skyscrapers of Boston and the Presidential Range of New Hampshire. Looking out to sea, 7.5 miles east of York Harbor, the *Isles of Shoals* (GPS: 42.987991, 70.613862), which lie below the horizon, can sometimes be seen with binoculars if conditions are right. The shoals consist of nine islands: *Duck Island* (named for being a resting stop for migrating birds. At one time, the U.S. government used it as a bombing target); *Appledore Island* (housing the Shoals Marine Laboratory); *Smuttynose Island* (containing the graves of Spanish sailors); *Lunging Island* (formerly known as Londoner's Island); *Cedar Island* (named for the cedar trees that grow on the island); *Star Island* (containing the historic 1873 Oceanic Hotel); *Malaga Island* (connected to Smuttynose Island by a breakwater built in the late 1700s by Captain Samuel Haley); *Seavey Island* (used for studying nesting Tern populations); and *White Island* (with its White Island Lighthouse, aka Isles of Shoals Lighthouse). In addition, there is *Boon Island* (GPS: 43.121314, -70.475733) and its lighthouse, 7.0 miles southeast of Kittery.

HISTORY: In *The Rocks of Ogunquit* (1957), George Towar writes, "*Mt. Agamenticus is an excellent example of the rounding off of the rock into a dome by the glacier.*" Towar points out that at one time, Mt. Agamenticus was considerably higher and more irregular in shape.

According to Sandy Nastor in *Indian Placenames in America. Volume 2* (2005), *Agamenticus* may be Abenaki for "other side of the river." Another source states that Agamenticus is Native American for "the little river which lies behind an island in its mouth" referring to an earlier time when the York River was called the Agamenticus River.

Native Americans called the mountain *Sasanoa* after an Abenaki chieftain. Sophie Sweet, in *Stories of Maine* (1899), adds that "*the name is applied to a beautiful elevation, or rather three elevations joined together, well wooded, and rising up*

gentle slopes, not rocky or steep like the Mount Desert mountains, but with a large crowning rock upon its summit."

It is alleged that a Mi'kmaq leader named Aspinquid, who was the chief sachem of all Native American tribes in the northern section of North America, was murdered in 1696, declared a martyr and a saint, and then buried on top of Mt. Agamenticus. A stone cairn atop the mountain that was initially thought to mark St. Aspinquid's grave site was later found to have been erected by the United States Coast Geodetic Survey in 1847. St. Aspinquid's real burial site remains unknown.

It is from Chief Aspinquid that the "Aspinquid at Norseman Resort" on Beach Street in Ogunquit takes its name.

During the time that the "Big A" Ski Resort operated on the mountain, Mt. Agamenticus was affectionately known as the "Big A." A summit lodge, ski shop, and parking area for 400 cars were located at the top of the mountain, along with nine ski trails. Rusted remnants of the ski resort's chair lift, which operated from 1960 to 1974, can be seen near the summit, northeast of the Mount Agamenticus Learning Lodge. In order to produce artificial snow when needed, the ski resort created an artificial pond (now called Kilgore Swamp) in 1970.

Earlier, in 1918, a wooden fire tower was erected on the summit and the mountain used for fire detection. It was replaced several times.

In 1941, the mountain summit was taken over by the U.S. Army and used as an anti-aircraft spotting station and as an SCR-271 early-warning radar base. It was manned by twenty-five soldiers. The base was destroyed by fire in the winter of 1944. Due to severe wintery conditions, fire-fighting equipment simply could not get up the summit road to save the buildings. In the 1980s, any military structures that had survived were demolished.

There are a fair number of things to see on top of Mount Agamenticus: The Mount Agamenticus Leaning Lodge (formerly the Big A Ski Area lodge); a variety of informational plaques; a two-level wooden viewing deck; the abandoned and cordoned-off Mount Hope Fire Tower that was helicoptered over from Sabattus, Maine; the "Big A" 1.0-mile-long, summit trail, designed for universal access; and many additional features. Birders find the summit particularly advantageous for viewing migrating hawks.

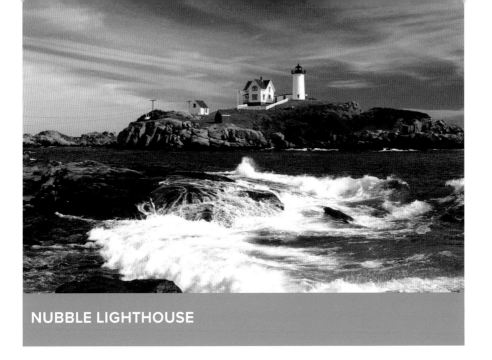

NUBBLE LIGHTHOUSE

LOCATION: Cape Neddick (York County)

MAINE ATLAS & GAZETTEER: Map 1, B5

GPS PARKING: 43.165596, -70.593064

GPS DESTINATIONS: *Sohier Park*—43.165688, -70.593156; *Nubble Lighthouse*—43.165349, -70.5911

HOURS: *Visitor Center/Gift Shop in Sohier Park*—Consult website, nubble-light.org, for specific details

FEE: *Parking*—free

RESTRICTIONS: Regular Park rules & regulations apply

ACCESSIBILITY: There is no direct access to the lighthouse

DEGREE OF DIFFICULTY: Easy

ADDITIONAL INFORMATION: Sohier Park, 11 Sohier Park Road, York, ME 03909; (207) 363-1040

DIRECTIONS: From the center of Ogunquit (junction of U.S. 1/Main Street, Shore Road & Beach Street), drive south on U.S. 1 for >5.0 miles.

When you come to the junction of U.S. 1 & Short Sands Road, turn right onto Short Sands Road and head southeast for 0.9 mile. At Ridge Road, turn left and proceed northeast for 0.2 mile. Continue right onto Church Street and follow it southeast for another 0.2 mile.

When you reach Long Beach Avenue/U.S. 1A, turn right, and drive southwest for 0.2 mile. Bear left onto Nubble Road and proceed east for ~1.0 mile, following along the shoreline, to your right. Finally, turn right onto Sohier Park

Road, and continue east for another 0.1 mile to park in a large parking area that can become easily congested with cars during the busy season.

DESCRIPTION & HISTORY: *Nubble Lighthouse*—The 41-foot-high Nubble Lighthouse, aka Cape Neddick Lighthouse, was built in 1879 on a 2.5-acre "nubble" of rock (Cape Neddick Nubble) next to the mainland. Originally, it was painted dark red, but in 1902 was repainted bright white, and has remained so ever since. The building standing 50 feet from the conical lighthouse is the Victorian light-keeper's house, enhanced by its gingerbread trim, including a lantern with miniature cast-iron lighthouses on its railing.

The nubble is separated from the mainland by a shallow, 300-foot-wide channel.

In 1602, the English explorer Bartholomew Gosnold was sufficiently impressed by the Nubble to name it "Savage Rock," perhaps reflecting his first impression of Native Americans he encountered in the area. His first impression may not have been warranted, however. In *Old York: Proud Symbol of Colonial Maine. 1652-1952* (1950), Edward W. Marshall writes, *"To the surprise of the English sailors the Indians wore articles of clothing made by 'Christians...They spoke divers Christian words* [meaning "more than one"] *and seemed to understand much more than we, for want of language, to comprehend."*

Samuel Adams Drake, in his 1891 book, *The Pine Tree Coast*, writes that *"Cape Neddick is a long tongue of land on which no thing grows but coarse wiry grass—a succession of rocky knobs and deep spongy hollows—thrust off from the main shore into the sea, which the heated rocks lap with avidity."*

In 1614, a member of Captain John Smith's crew, while on an exploratory mission for the Plymouth Company, called it "the knubble," a name which stuck and has been dutifully recorded on maps and records ever since.

The construction of the Nubble Lighthouse was overseen by General James Chatham Duane, Chief Engineer of the Army of the Potomac. Nathaniel H. Otterson was appointed as acting lightkeeper in 1879 by the Secretary of the Treasury. Otteron resigned in 1885. A succession of lightkeepers followed, terminating with Russell Ahlgren, a coast guard petty officer.

Over the years, many changes have been made, including electricity being brought to the island in 1938 and the lighthouse becoming automated in 1987. The current lighthouse beacon is illuminated by a 1,000-watt blub enclosed in red plexiglass.

Today, the lighthouse is managed by York's Parks and Recreation Department. The lighthouse is so popular that a photograph of it was sent into space aboard Voyager II in 1977 in hopes that extraterrestrials encountering the spaceship might have a better understanding of our planet and its historic and natural beauty.

As to what the word Neddick means, Charles Edward Banks in *History of York Maine. Vol. 1* (1931) suggests that "*Neddick is a word derived from the dialect of the eastern Indians, the root of which is Nāoo, meaning solitary like a single tree, to which the terminal 'dik' conforms to the Micmac word Nāedich, the place name of a like nubble on the coast of Nova Scotia.*"

In *Roadside Geology of Maine* (1998), D. W. Caldwell writes, "*The nearly circular mass of dark grabbo [an intrusive rock] in the Cape Neddick pluton [a body of intrusive rock] is perhaps the youngest rock in Maine; it is dated at 118 million years old...*"

Sohier Park—Sohier Park, featuring park benches and rock formations, is the gateway to viewing the Nubble Lighthouse. The property was named for William D. Sohier, from whom the property was acquired in 1929.

Sohier Park contains a gift shop and restrooms which are open seasonally from mid-April through mid-October, weather dependent.

The 137-foot-high Boon Island Light, built in 1811, can be seen off the coast from Sohier Park. It remains the tallest lighthouse in Maine.

HISTORIC ROCK FORMATIONS

The following rock formations were of sufficient interest to the public that antique postcard reproductions were made of many of them. Over a century has passed since the postcards were printed, and whether any of these natural rock formations still exist in a recognizable manner is something that readers will have to decide for themselves.

OLD MAN OF THE SEA

LOCATION: Cape Neddick/York Beach (York County)
MAINE ATLAS & GAZETTEER: Map 1, AB5

DESCRIPTION: Charles Edward Banks, in the *History of Maine. Vol. II* (1935), writes that the Old Man of the Sea is "*a curious rock formation on the Nubble, resembling the human face.*" A circa 1906 postcard places the historic rock at "York Beach, ME." Still another just says "York, ME" and doesn't specifically mention the beach. Where-ever the rock formation is located, it probably has been worn down and blunted by the ocean.

DEVIL'S PULPIT & SPOUTING ROCK

LOCATION: Bald Head (York County)
MAINE ATLAS & GAZETTEER: Map 1. A5

DESCRIPTION: *Devil's Pulpit*—Esselyn Gilman Perkins, in *History of Ogunquit Village* (1951), writes that the Devil's Pulpit "*is found near the residence of Norman Braser. At low tide one is able to walk in this cave of brown granite origin, when the sea runs high again, each wave closes the mouth of the cave, and air compressed. This results in a stream of water which is forced out of the top of the cavern.*"

If you can figure out where Norman Braser once lived over 70 years ago, then you are half-way there to finding this rock formation. There are tantalizing clues to its possible location, however, as you drive along Shore Road. For instance, 0.1 mile south of the Cliff House entrance is Pulpit Rock Lane (unfortunately, a private road) that leads to a rocky area between Jack's Cove to the east, and Perkins Cove to the west.

A circa 1901 postcard is captioned, "Devil's Pulpit, Bald Head Cliff, York Maine," which suggests that the rock formation is at the end of Bald Head Cliff. After over a century, what are the odds of a rock formation surviving that is so perilously close to the ocean and its erosive power?

Spouting Rock—Perkins mentions that Spouting Rock (a name also used to describe a natural phenomenon at Cape Arundel) is "*...located about halfway between Perkins Cove and Bald Head Cliff (York).*" This would place it somewhere near a GPS reading of 43.228807, -70.581389 where there are 60-foot-high cliffs fronted by large, modern homes. "*The best time to observe this interesting feature is at half-tide and when the surf is running well. The water fills and leaves this cave at intervals, and the display is well-worth observing.*"

In *The Rocks of Ogunquit* (1957), George Towar writes that Spouting Rock "*... can be located by the fact that it is near a dike which has a unique feature. The dike is about five feet wide and the molten rock brought up many solid pieces of rock of much lighter color. These light spots are about as big as your fist and show all over the surface of this dark gray dike...Follow this dike down to the water's edge and at half tide with a fair surf running, a nearby cave in the rocks under water will spout a very pleasant display.*"

ROARING ROCK

LOCATION: York Beach (York County)
MAINE ATLAS & GAZETTEER: Map 1, B5
GPS ROARING ROCK POINT:
43.142594, -70.623679
GPS ROARING ROCK: Unknown
ACCESSIBILITY: Unknown. Private homes at Roaring Rock Point make access dubious at best.

DESCRIPTION: In the *History of York Maine. Vol. II* (1935), Charles Edward Banks describes Roaring Rock as "*a narrow chasm in the rocky cliff on the northeast shore of Alcock's Neck [*named for farmer John Alcock who bought the rocky point in 1643*]. This was first described in 1709 as 'a hollow rock known by the name of the Roaring Rock.' The opening at the top is a yard wide for a distance of seventy-five feet inland at right angles with the sea; at the bottom the mouth is six feet wide and the crevice twenty feet deep at low tide. In a storm the inrushing tide rises like a fountain many feet above the top of the cliff. [E. P.] Tenney in his novel entitled 'Agamenticus' thus describes the natural sound effects: its music is its power; it is a roaring rock. Besides the common thunder of the waves there is a sound that stirs the blood like a sea trumpet, caused by the sudden expulsion of a great volume of air from below through the narrow opening on the surface; and there is also a wild roar with a rhythm, by the displacement of innumerable pebbles that run up and down with the wash of the waves. This is by far the most musical rock upon the coast of New England.*"

In *Ancient City of Georgeana and Modern Town of York Maine: from its earliest settlement to the present time* (1873), George Alex Amery states that "*Roaring Rock [is] one of the strange formations that the coast of Maine alone presents. The musical reverberations from this rock fall at all times with a pleasant rhythm of the air, while in storms the 'roaring' is terrific.*"

A line drawing of the rock can be seen in Charles Edward Banks' book.

Antique postcards identify the rock formation as being at York Beach.

Whether the rock phenomenon still exists is questionable. In *New England Miniature: A History of York, Maine* (1961), George Ernst writes, "*This peculiarity was lost when the hollow was at least partially blocked by falling boulders.*"

Possible clues to the rock's location are given away by the name of three roads clustered together off U.S. 1A—Roaring Rock Road, Roaring Rock Point Road, and Sea Trumpet Drive.

WATCH DOG

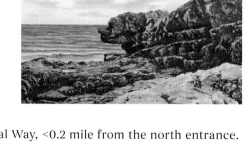

The Watch Dog, Ogunquit, Maine

LOCATION: Ogunquit (York County)
MAINE ATLAS & GAZETTEER: Map 1, A5
GPS WATCH DOG: 43.246066, -70.591948
ACCESSIBILITY: The rock formation is visible along the Marginal Way, <0.2 mile from the north entrance.

DESCRIPTION: A century-old postcard image of the Watch Dog reveals the projecting head of a dog or a similar creature. Although it would seem unlikely at first that the Watch Dog's distinctive profile could have outlasted years of crashing waves and the cycles of freezing and thawing during Maine winters, enough of it remains to be identifiable. The best vantage point is from the Marginal Way behind Anchorage-by-the-Sea.

As a point of interest, there is also a Bull Dog Rock in Narrow Cove (close to Perkins Cove) in George Towar's *The Rocks of Ogunquit* (1957) that was sketched by Louis H. Ruyl, an American etcher and illustrator, but that was over 65 years ago—an eternity for rocks exposed to the sea.

BALANCED ROCK

LOCATION: West of Chases Pond (York County)
MAINE ATLAS & GAZETTEER: Map 1, A4
GPS FOLLY POND: 43.203204, -70.694540
GPS FOLLY POND TRAILHEAD OFF MOUNTAIN ROAD: 43.215919, -70.686833
ACCESSIBILITY: Unknown

DESCRIPTION:

In the *History of York Maine. Vol. I (1931)*, Charles Edward Banks writes, "*There is a curious rock back of Folly Pond, resting on another, so well balanced that it can be easily tilted by the hand. It weighs many tons.*" Banks goes on to mention that Folley Pond is one of fourteen ponds, not all of them being natural.

A 5.4-mile-loop trail goes around Folly Pond starting opposite the Center or Wildlife at 385 Mountain Road. Finding the boulder without knowing its exact location, however, could prove exceedingly difficult. Furthermore, any balanced rock that was easily tilted a hundred years ago may already have been toppled by miscreants.

MORDANS CAVE

LOCATION: Mt. Agamenticus area (York County)
MAINE ATLAS & GAZETTEER: Map 1, A4 (guesstimate)
ACCESSIBILITY: Unknown

DESCRIPTION: Mordans Cave is a talus cave created by the tumbling together of rocks that formed tiny rooms and passageways. In *Settlement and Abandonment on Tatnic Hill: An Eclectic History of Wells. 1600-1900*, Joseph W. Hardy writes, "*They are a complex of large boulders which have been torn from the face of the cliff by the last glacier, resulting in some holes and passages that have the appearance of caves.*" Hardy also includes a photograph of the caves taken in 1908 with several children standing in front of it.

The cave is named for James Mordan who, along with his family, is said to have lived there during the eighteenth century.

According to Edward Emerson Bourne in *History of Wells and Kennebunk from the earliest settlement to the year 1820, at which time Kennebunk was set off, and incorporated* (1875), the cave was also inhabited later for a short time by Nathaniel Boston, and was located "*on the west side of the Tatnick Hills, not far from the road, near the house of Elisha Allen, deceased...*" If you can find out where Elisha Allen once lived, then you are halfway there to locating this historic talus cave, which, hopefully, is not on private property.

THE DEVIL'S INVENTION

LOCATION: Scituate (York County)
MAINE ATLAS & GAZETTEER: Map 1, AB4–5 (guesstimate)
ACCESSIBILITY: Unknown

DESCRIPTION: In Charles Edward Banks' book, *History of York, Maine. Vol. II* (1935), the author writes that the Devil's Invention was created when "*a stockade [was] built against a large boulder in 1679 by James Adams to imprison the children of Henry Simpson. It was in the region of Scituate, easterly from the main highway through that settlement. Nothing remains of it except the tradition of its location.*" A line drawing of the rock can be seen in Banks' book.

Edward C. Moody, in *Handbook History of the Town of York: from early times to the present* (1914), adds in further details: "*In a solitary place four or five miles from the dwelling houses of the inhabitants, he [Adams] built of logs, beside a ledge of perpendicular rocks, a pen or pound several feet in height with walls inclined from the bottom up.*" His intention was to leave the two children, ages 6 and 9 there to *"perish of famine"*—an act of revenge against Henry Simpson. Fortunately, the children were able to escape by digging under the logs.

James Adams was subsequently apprehended. In *Ancient City of Georgeana and modern Town of York Maine from its earliest settlement to the present time* (1873), George Alex Emery writes that "the depraved criminal was condemned to have thirty stripes well laid on; to pay the father of the children five pounds, the treasurer ten pounds besides fees and charges of the prison..."

MOUSAM RIVER POTHOLE

LOCATION: Kennebunk (York County)
MAINE ATLAS & GAZETTEER: Map 3, D1
ACCESSIBILITY: Unknown

HISTORY: According to Daniel Remich in *History of Kennebunk from its earliest settlement to 1890* (1911), *"If legend can be relied upon, the banks of the Mousam River were once visited by a personage whose fame has been known in all ages of man's existence and through all inhabited lands. There was a large boulder a few rods [~50 feet] below the village saw-mill which bore a mysterious imprint, said to be the impress of the cloven foot of his Satanic majesty. He must have bounded upon it with a heavy tread or placed the limb there while the one molten rock was yet stiff and pliable..."*

Although the story is fanciful, what it describes when you take away the hyperbole is a good-sized pothole worn into a boulder along the Mousam River. Whether the boulder and pothole still exist is anyone's guess, but unless it has been tampered with, the imprint should still remain.

{3}

YORK AREA

York has the distinction of being the second oldest town in Maine, incorporated in 1652. It went through a big hotel era starting in the 1870s, facilitated through mass transportation provided by steam railroads and electric trolleys, a phenomenon that lasted until the mid-1900s. Sea Cottage was the earliest hotel, which later became the Hotel Mitchell, and which today is the Anchorage Hotel, across from the Sun & Surf Restaurant at Long Sands Beach.

York is composed of four smaller communities—York Village, York Beach, York Harbor, and Cape Neddick. In the early days, York was noted for its lobstering, fishing, ship building, and farming.

The York Region Chamber of Commerce covers York, Cape Neddick, Kittery, Eliot, and South Berwick. They can be reached at 1 Stonewall Lane, York, ME 03909; (207) 363-4422 or at https://www.gatewaytomaine.org.

SHORT SANDS BEACH

LOCATION: York Beach (York County)

MAINE ATLAS & GAZETTEER: Map 1, A5

GPS PARKING: 43.174902, -70.609302

GPS DESTINATIONS: *Short Sands Beach*—43.174567, -70.607251; *Public bathrooms*—43.175183, -70.609571; *Ellis Park*—43.173728, -70.607681

HOURS: Check website, https://www.yorkparksandrec.org/ellispark, for specific details

FEE: *Parking*—fee charged by the hour using the kiosk; *Beach*—free

RESTRICTIONS: Regular beach rules & regulations apply; for further details, contact https://www.yorkparksandrec.org/ellispark

ACCESSIBILITY: The beach is in close proximity to the parking area

ADDITIONAL INFORMATION: Short Sands Beach, 13 Ocean Avenue Extension, York, ME 03909; (207) 363-1040

Seasonal lifeguards are present from the last week in June through Labor Day, 9:00 a.m. to 4:30 p.m. The public restrooms, which opened in 2014, are located by the parking area. The beach lies in close proximity to York's Wild Kingdom and Amusement Park.

For specific information on domestic animals and beach usage, consult https://www.yorkparksandrec.org/attractions/beaches. At present, domestic animals are not allowed on the beach between 8:00 a.m. and 6:00 p.m. from May 20th through September 20th. Pets must be leashed between 6:00 a.m. and sunrise from May 20th to September 20th.

DIRECTIONS: From the center of Ogunquit (junction of U.S. 1/Main Street, Shore Road & Beach Street), drive south on U.S. 1 for ~4.3 miles.

At the junction of U.S. 1 & U.S. 1A, turn left onto U.S. 1A /Cape Neddick Road and head southeast for ~0.8 mile. When you converge onto U.S. 1A/Main Street, bearing right, head southwest for 0.6 mile. Then turn left onto Main Street (a one-way street) and in <0.1 mile you will be at the parking area for Short Sands Beach.

If you drive too far on U.S. 1A/Main Street, you will come to Ocean Avenue, which is a one-way street facing towards you.

DESCRIPTION: Short Sands Beach is a 0.3-mile-long, coarse, gray sandy beach located on the north side of Cape Neddick, tucked between rocky cliffs. The rocky bluff to your northeast is Barn Point (GPS: 43.180447, -70.602041), a projection of land that extends northeast into Cape Neddick Harbor.

In *Ancient City of Georgeana and Modern Town of York Maine: from its earliest settlement to the present time* (1873), George Alex Amery describes "Short Sands" as *"...a firm, hard beach...so sheltered by projecting points that the heavy sea-swells never interfere with bathing or boating...Boulders and ledges are scattered upon the shore in inextricable confusion creating a picturesqueness delightful to the eye of the beholder."*

A promenade walkway extends along the top of the beach, with benches strategically placed along the way facing Little Sand Beach and the ocean.

Ellis Park, aka Ellis Short Sands Park and Short Sands Park, is a large, grassy area that contains a gazebo, a pavilion, and a playground with a basketball court. Free concerts and varied entertainment are scheduled in the Park during the summer by the Ellis Park Trustees.

The beach and park are owned by the Town of York and managed by the Ellis Park Committee (a private board of trustees).

LONG SANDS BEACH

LOCATION: York Beach (York County)

MAINE ATLAS & GAZETTEER: Map 1, B5

GPS PARKING: Metered parking along Long Beach Avenue

GPS LONG SANDS BEACH: 43.163710, -70.617793

GPS PUBLIC BATHROOMS: 43.164174, -70.618545

GPS LONG BEACH SUN & SURF RESTAURANT: 43.158906, -70.621079

HOURS: Consult website, https://www.yorkparksandrec.org, for specific details

FEE: *Parking*—Fee charged via kiosks; *Beach*—free

RESTRICTIONS: Regular beach rules & regulations apply; No domestic animals are allowed on the beach between the hours of 8:00 a.m. and 6:00 p.m., May 20th through September 20th. Between 6:00 p.m. and 8:00 a.m., domestic animals must be leashed.

ACCESSIBILITY: Near roadside

DEGREE OF DIFFICULTY: Easy

INFORMATION: Long Sands Beach, 189 Long Beach Avenue, York, ME 03909; (207) 363-1040

Seasonal lifeguards are present from the last week in June through Labor Day, 9:00 a.m. to 4:30 p.m. The public bathrooms are located midway along the beach. Kiosk-related parking is charged per hour from May 15th through October 15th, 8:00 a.m. until 10:00 p.m. For more information, consult https://www.yorkparksandrec.org/attractions/beaches.

Permit parking is allowed along the stretch of beach from Libby's Campground to Nubble Road in metered spaces. Permit Parking Sticker for residents, valid from May 15th through October 15th annually, can be obtained from the Town Clerk's Office, (207) 363-1003.

DIRECTIONS: From the center of Ogunquit (junction of U.S. 1/Main Street, Shore Road & Beach Street), drive south on U.S. 1 for ~4.3 miles.

At the junction of U.S. 1 & U.S. 1A, turn left onto U.S. 1A/Cape Neddick Road and head southeast for ~0.8 mile. When you converge onto U.S. 1A/Main Street, bearing right, head southwest for 0.6 mile. Continue south on Railroad Avenue, then Church Street for another 0.4 mile (both one-way streets). Then turn right onto U.S. 1A/Long Beach Avenue, heading southwest. As you drive along, you will see parking spaces along the street to your left. At some point, turn around, and then parallel park in an available space. You will end up next to the sidewalk and beach.

DESCRIPTION: Long Sands Beach encompasses 1.3 miles of course, gray sand and surf with some tide pools and groupings of rocks. It lies between the southwest corner of Cape Neddick (GPS: 43.168809, -70.600328), framed by  the Dover Bluffs, and Prebbles Point (GPS: 43.149718, -70.622328), to the south. Beyond Prebbles Point is 0.5-mile-long Lobster Cove, where Libby's Oceanside Camp (43.146606, -70.626103) and Camp Eaton (43.147416, -70.627405) are located between Prebbles Point and Roaring Rock Point.

On the south side of the Sun & Surf Restaurant (GPS: 43.158974, -70.621047) are two informational plaques. One provides detailed material on the Boon Island Light House; the other, on Long Sands Beach.

There is also an informational plaque by the public bathrooms entitled "Maine's Coastal Sand Dunes: The importance of natural coast barriers." In 2015, the Town of York built the new bath house, which you see today, when they moved U.S. 1A further away from the ocean, returning it to its pre-1940 alignment.

Boone Island (GPS: 43.121452, -70.476245), and its 133-foot-high lighthouse, lie nearly 8.0 miles offshore. It was automated in 1978. The island, measuring 450 feet long, 150 feet wide, and 14 feet above sea level, has been the scene of at least fifteen wrecks in the past.

YORK'S WILD KINGDOM

LOCATION: York (York County)

TENTH EDITION, NYS ATLAS & GAZETTEER: Map 1, B5

GPS PARKING: *1 Animal Park Road*—43.174727, -70.614780; *23 Railroad Avenue*—43.174353, -70.612236

GPS YORK'S WILD KINGDOM: 43.174970, -70.613826

HOURS: Check website, https://yorkswildkingdom.com, for specific details (Currently, the zoo opens at 10:00 a.m. and the rides start at 11:30 p.m.) Tickets can be purchased in advance on the website

FEE: Admission charged

ADDITIONAL INFORMATION: York's Wild Kingdom, 1 Animal Park Road, York, ME 03909; (207) 363-4911

DIRECTIONS: *U.S 1 Entrance*—From the center of Ogunquit (junction of U.S. 1/ Main Street, Shore Road & Beach Street), drive south on U.S. 1 for ~5.0 miles (or 0.7 mile past the junction with U.S. 1A). Turn left onto Animal Park Road and proceed southeast for <0.8 mile to the parking area, where no fee is charged.

Railroad Avenue entrance—From the center of Ogunquit (junction of U.S. 1/ Main Street, Shore Road & Beach Street), drive southwest on U.S. 1 for >4.0 miles.

When you come to the junction of U.S. 1 & U.S. 1A, turn left onto U.S. 1A/Cape Neddick Road and head southeast for ~0.8 mile. When you converge onto U.S.1A/Main Street, bearing right, head southwest for 0.6 mile. Continue south on Railroad Avenue (a one-way street) for 0.1 mile and park in a large area to your right. Be aware that this is a town parking lot, which means that a parking fee is required.

DESCRIPTION: York's Wild Kingdom is a privately owned zoo and amusement park that has been operating since 1980. You can spend the day on site observing and learning about a wide variety of animals, enjoy lunch, and have fun on the carnival rides. The Wild Kingdom is just a short distance away from Short Sands Beach.

HISTORY: York's Wild Kingdom is a family-owned business, which means that family are actively involved and take a personal interest in what goes on. The family's goal is to provide a safe, high-quality environment for the animals in their care and to give guests the opportunity to make memories each time they visit.

One question most frequently asked about the zoo is, "Where do the animals go in the winter?" The answer is that the majority of them stay right at the zoo, where they live in heated enclosures, cared for by dedicated zoo staff.

Feel free to ask staff if you have questions of your own about the animals.

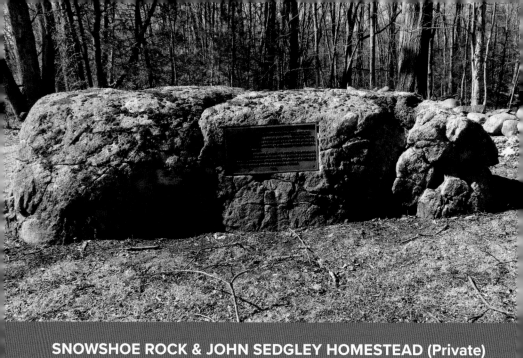

SNOWSHOE ROCK & JOHN SEDGLEY HOMESTEAD (Private)

LOCATION: York (York County)

MAINE ATLAS & GAZETTEER: Map 1, B4–5

GPS PARKING: *Snowshoe Rock*—43.169365, -70.663697; *Old Parish Cemetery*—43.143784, -70.653179

GPS DESTINATIONS: *Snowshoe Rock*—43.169393, -70.663844; *Cemetery marker & Old Parish Cemetery*—43.143986, -70.652641; *John Sedgley Homestead*—43.164712, -70.666685

HOURS: Dawn to dusk

FEE: None

ACCESSIBILITY: Near roadside

DIRECTIONS: *Snowshoe Rock*—From the center of Ogunquit (junction of U.S. 1/ Main Street, Shore Road & Beach Street), drive south on U.S. 1 for ~7.5 miles. At a traffic intersection where a blue sign points to I-95 and a green sign to the Maine Turnpike, turn right onto Spur Road that leads northwest for >0.4 mile. Instead of getting onto the Maine Turnpike/I-95, continue northwest for another 0.1 mile. Just before reaching the "Park & Ride" area near the end of Spur Road, bear right onto Chases Pond Road.

If you are approaching from the Maine Turnpike/I-95, get off at Exit 7 for The Yorks & Ogunquit. Drive to the northwest end of Spur Road and bear right onto Chases Pond Road.

Coming from either approach, head north on Chases Pond Road for >0.9 mile (or 225 feet past Old E. Scituate Road, which enters on your right). Opposite the house at 81 Chases Pond Road is a small space fenced in by a semi-circular stone wall. Park off on the left side of the road in front of the rock memorial.

Snowshoe Rock consists of a 3-foot-high, 5-foot-wide, and 10-foot-long boulder near the rear stone wall, with a commemorative plaque on its north side.

If you peer over the stone wall directly behind the boulder, you will notice that there is an unexpected 10–12-foot drop-off to the terrain below.

A line drawing of the rock is contained in Charles Edward Banks' *History of York Maine. Vol. I (1931).*

Cemetery Marker—From the junction of U.S. 1 and Spur Road leading to the Maine Turnpike/I-95, drive southwest on U.S. 1 for 0.3 mile. Turn left onto U.S. 1A/York Street and proceed southeast for 0.8 mile. When you come to Lindsay Road, turn right, and proceed southwest for 150 feet. The tombstone marker is directly to your left at the edge of the Old Parish Cemetery, aka Old York Cemetery, across from the Old School House.

John Sedgley Homestead—On the drive up along Chases Pond Road, look for the Sedley Homestead, now a private residence, to your left, 0.6 mile uphill from the Maine Turnpike Spur Road, just before Scituate Road comes in on your left.

DESCRIPTION: *Snowshoe Rock*—Snowshoe Rock marks the spot where a large party of Indian warriors led by a French missionary took off their snowshoes and readied themselves to attack a British settlement at York.

Charles Edward Banks quotes the first verse of a poem about the occasion written by a local, twentieth-century poet:

"They marched for two and twenty days,
All through the deepest snow;
And on a dreadful winter morn
They struck the cruel blow."

Tombstone Marker—This tombstone-like marker memorializes the many slain settlers in the early morning attack on the village.

Sedgley Homestead—The historic homestead is visible from the road.

HIGHLIGHTS:

- Historic boulder

- Historic tombstone marker

- John Sedgley Homestead (private)

HISTORY: What became known as the Candlemas Raid took place at dawn on January 24, 1692, during King William's War when Father Louise-Pierre Thury, a French missionary and secular priest, and Chief Madockawando, leader of the Penobscot, lead a party of 200–300 warriors into the village of York, killing 60–70 English settlers and burning many of the houses. The ~80 settlers who were captured were forced to walk to Canada where they were ransomed. Some did not survive the arduous journey. Others returned as long as ten years later.

Candlemas is a traditional celebration of the Christian "feast of the purification of the Virgin Mary."

Snowshoe Rock—The plaque on Snowshoe Rock reads, *"On Candlemas Day 1692 Abenaki Indians left their snowshoes on this rock and in the dawn of a January morning crept into York and captured or murdered three hundred sleeping inhabitants. In gratitude to William L. Grant who deeded this property to the Association for the Preservation of Historic Landmarks of York. This association will protect the monument in memory of the worst Indian attack in American history. 1949."*

A photograph of the historic rock, with a child standing next to it, can be seen in John D. Bardwell's *Old York: The Old Photographic Series* (1994).

Cemetery Marker—The tombstone marker reads: *"Near this spot are interred the remains of the victims of one of the worst massacres of colonial days. On Candlemas Day, 1691-2, in the dawn of a January morning, Abenaki Indians attacked the settlement of York, burning the houses and killing or capturing 300 of its inhabitants. About 40 were killed. The rest marched to Canada, many dying on the way.*

Erected to the memory of these hardy pioneers by the Society for the Preservation of Historic Landmarks." The cemetery marker was set in place by the Daughters of the American Revolution in 1976. However, there is no evidence to support the assertion that victims from the Candlemas Raid were buried here. Most likely, they were interred in mass in an unmarked grave at an unknown site.

Note: Figures given for the number of settlers killed and captured vary markedly according to sources.

John Sedgley Homestead—The Sedgley Homestead, built circa 1715 along what is now 44 Chases Pond Road, is considered to be the oldest homestead in Maine still resting on its original plot of land. In addition to the farmhouse, the homestead includes the Cape (a house), stables, carriage house, and outbuildings. It was listed on the National Register of Historic Places in 1976.

Jonathan Sedgley came to York from England as a young man and was a turner (a person skilled in turning wood on a lathe) by trade.

Since 1991, the Sedgley Homestead has been occupied by the Anthony Moore Painting Conservation, now called Northeast Painting Conservation.

ELIZABETH PERKINS HOUSE & SEWALLS BRIDGE

LOCATION: Kittery Point (York County)

MAINE ATLAS & GAZETTEER: Map 1, B5

GPS PARKING: 43.134946, -70.661765

GPS ELIZABETH PERKINS HOUSE: 43.135243, -70.661802

GPS SEWALLS BRIDGE: 43.135991, -70.660697

HOURS: Consult Elizabeth Perkins House Museum website for specific details

FEE: Admission charged

ADDITIONAL INFORMATION: Elizabeth Perkins House, 394 Southside Road, York, ME 03909

DIRECTIONS: From the center of Ogunquit (junction of U.S. 1/Main Street, Shore Road & Beach Street), drive south on U.S. 1 for ~8.0 miles.

When you come to the south junction of U.S. 1 & U.S. 1A, turn left onto U.S. 1A/York Street, and head southwest for >0.2 mile. Then bear right onto Organug Road, and proceed south, crossing the York River via Sewalls Bridge at 0.9 mile. Finally, turn right into the parking area for the Elizabeth Perkins House at 1.0 mile.

DESCRIPTION & HISTORY: The Elizabeth Perkins House is named for Elizabeth Perkins, who founded the Old York Historical Society and who, notably, spent time there with Samuel Clemens, i.e., Mark Twain, who summered across the river from the Perkins House. She purchased the house in 1898 along with her mother, Mary.

The Colonial-style house, dating back to 1730, overlooks the York River by Sewalls Bridge. The house was restored to the way it looked in the 1950s when Perkins summered there.

The Perkins house began as a small cottage with a chimney. In 1732, Joseph Holt added on the front part of the house and made other expansions too. The house still contains its original white oak beams, stenciled drawing room, and period furnishings, including a Simon Willard tall case clock.

Perkins and her mother are buried at the west edge of the lawn overlooking the York River. Tiny medallions set in the ground mark their resting spots.

In *An American Heritage Guide: Historic Houses of America* (1971), editors Beverley Hilowitz and Susan Eikov Green describe the Perkins House as an *"old frame Colonial house; the central part is the original small cottage and its chimney; the front part was built by Joseph Holt in 1732."*

Photographs of the home and its interior appear in John D. Bardwell's *The Old Photograph Series: Old York* (1994).

Sewalls Bridge—Two historic markers can be seen in the landscaped, triangular median (GPS: 43.136856, -70.660146) at the northeast end of the bridge. One recognizes Sewalls Bridge as a National Historic Civil Engineering Landmark; the second acknowledges the historical significance of the bridge.

The original Sewalls Bridge was built in 1761 by Major Samuel Sewall and was the first pile bridge (where the foundation consists of long poles) to be built in America. Sewall used multiple piles bound in a cluster at the top of an iron band. A pile from the old bridge is on display at the Old York Historical Society.

In James Phinney Baxter's *Agamenticus, Bristol, Georgiana, York* (1904), the author describes the construction of the bridge as follows: *"The method of construction was the erection of a whole section, or bent, at one time. This contained four piles of the proper length, the river bottom having been probed and marked for each requires length, then being capped by the cap still securely. This being done on the river bank, at the still of the tide, it was floated to its place and set upright. A large and lengthy oak log being fastened by tackle to a height of fifteen or more feet, and by the striking of the latch lock the tackle was released and the log fell with much force on the cap over each pile, and in time, the section was driven to the proper position."*

Sewall design was so successful that he and his associate, Captain John Stone, built a bridge of similar construction across the Charles River in Boston.

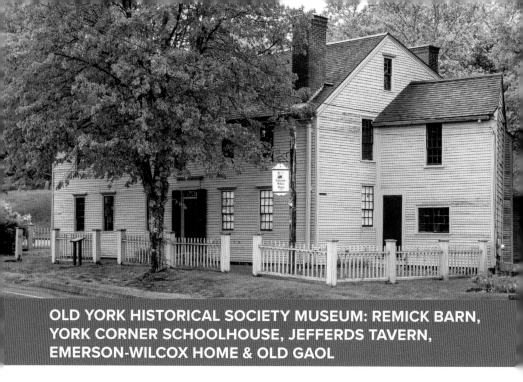

OLD YORK HISTORICAL SOCIETY MUSEUM: REMICK BARN, YORK CORNER SCHOOLHOUSE, JEFFERDS TAVERN, EMERSON-WILCOX HOME & OLD GAOL

LOCATION: York (York County)

MAINE ATLAS & GAZETTEER: Map 1, B5

GPS PARKING: 43.143784, -70.653179

GPS DESTINATIONS: *Remick Barn*—43.144353, -70.652980; *York Corner Schoolhouse*—43.144064, -70.652858; *Jefferds Tavern*—43.144223, -70.652854; *Emerson Wilcox Home Museum*—43.144087, -70.651930; *Old Gaol*—43.143727, -70.651694

HOURS: Consult website, https:oldyork.org, for specific details

FEE: Admission charged for museums

DEGREE OF DIFFICULTY: Easy

ADDITIONAL INFORMATION: Old York Historical Society Museum, 3 Lindsay Road, York, ME 03909; Visitor Center—(207) 363-1756

DIRECTIONS: From the center of Ogunquit (junction of U.S. 1/Main Street, Shore Road & Beach Street), drive south on U.S. 1 for ~8.0 miles.

When you come to the south junction of U.S. 1 & U.S. 1A, turn left onto U.S. 1A/York Street, and proceed southeast for 0.8 mile. At Lindsay Road, turn right, drive southwest for 200 feet, and bear right into the parking area for the Old York Historical Society Museum.

DESCRIPTION & HISTORY: *Old York Historical Society Museum*—The museum complex, which houses the visitor reception area, Virginia Weare Parsons Education Center, Remick Gallery, Jefferds Tavern, and York Corner Schoolhouse, is the starting point for visiting historical sites of interest near the north end of Lindsay Road. The museum center is also the home of the Old York Historical Society

Remick (Gallery) Barn—The 1834 Remick Barn, named for a family of farmers from Eliot, is the building closest to the intersection of U.S. 1/York Street and Lindsay Road. Beams from the old farm are part of the barn's internal structure. The Barn was erected here in 2004. Upstairs is the Remick Gallery, containing many historic artifacts and exhibits.

Jefferds Tavern—Next to the Visitor Center is Jefferds Tavern, which was built in 1750. The original owner was Dominicus Lord, who sold the house to Captain Samuel Jefferds, a prominent local innkeeper, who then converted it from a house into a tavern.

The tavern was located on the original King's Highway in Wells, ideally placed along a stage route between Portsmouth, New Hampshire, and Portland, Maine. Between 1939 and 1942, the tavern was dismantled, relocated, and reconstructed on U.S. 1 near the entrance to Rayden Road. In 1959, it was moved again to its present location in Old York through Elizabeth Perkins's advocacy under the guidance of architect Howard Peck.

An antique photograph of the old tavern can be seen in Kenneth Joy's *The Kennebunks: "Out of the Past"* (1967).

York Corner Schoolhouse—The York Corner Schoolhouse, fifteen feet south of Jefferds Tavern, is a one-room school that was built in 1745. It remains one of the oldest surviving schoolhouses in New England. The slates, wooden benches, quill pens and children's primers with the Lord's Prayer and Ten Commandments all harken back to an earlier period of York's history.

The schoolhouse was originally located near U.S. 1 and Route 9. It was moved to Organug Road in the 1850s where it was used as a home. In 1926, it

was moved to its present location after being purchased and restored by the Old York Historical Society. It was placed on the National Register of Historic Places in 1973.

Emerson-Wilcox Home—Although the Georgian-style Emerson-Wilcox House was completed in 1817, the small center chimney house around which the main house was built dates to 1742. There was an earlier house on the same spot dating back to the 1600s that was destroyed during the Candlemas Raid.

Over the years, the house has been used as a general store, stage tavern, tailor shop, post office, and residence.

In 1760, the house was expanded by Edward Emerson (a businessman and West Indies trader, and a relative of Ralph Waldo Emerson), creating the "L"-shaped look that defines the house today.

The last addition was made in 1817, which increased the number of rooms to fifteen.

The house is called the Emerson-Wilcox House both for Edward Emerson, who lived there in the eighteenth century, and for the Wilcoxes, a family of ship captains who lived in the house during the nineteenth century. Their descendants resided in the house until 1952.

It is presently under renovation and will remain closed for the time being after having been struck by an errant motorist in 2021.

Old Gaol—Old Gaol is a former, English royal prison atop Gaol Hill that is one of the oldest public buildings in Maine as well as one of the oldest prisons in the United States. The one-and-a-half-story prison was built in 1719/1720 using materials from the original 1656 jail. Further additions and improvements were made over time, the last one being in 1806.

Non-lethal punishment at the jail was delivered via a pillory, a whipping post, and a stock. The old jail features an austere stone cell on the first floor and debtor's prison on the second floor.

In the 1890s, the building became a schoolhouse.

In 1901, it was turned into the museum of colonial relics and has remained open to the public ever since.

Gaol is another word for "jail," a word more commonly used in the United Kingdom and Australia than in the United States.

The building was designated a National Historic Landmark in 1968.

WALK: *To reach the Emerson-Wilcox House*—From the Old York Historical Society Museum, walk north along the side of U.S. 1A/York Street for 250 feet, passing by the Old Burial Ground, on your right, owned by the First Parish Church, across the street. Take note of an informational plaque along the way entitled "Map of Old Burying Ground." The Emerson-Wilcox Home is immediately to your right.

To reach Old Gaol—From the Emerson-Wilcox House, walk across a second section of Lindsay Road (a one-way street) and then follow a stone slab path uphill for 100 feet to the top of the small hill where Old Gaol stands.

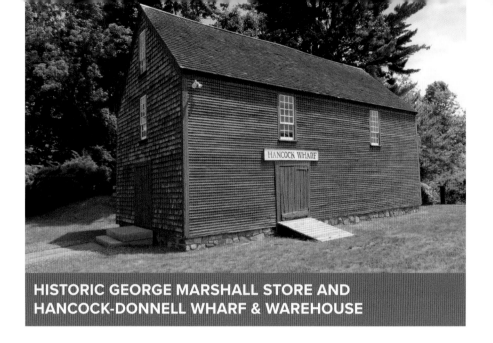

HISTORIC GEORGE MARSHALL STORE AND HANCOCK-DONNELL WHARF & WAREHOUSE

LOCATION: York (York County)

MAINE ATLAS & GAZETTEER: Map 1, B5

GPS PARKING: 43.136570, -70.657488

GPS LOCATIONS: *George Marshall Store (Gallery)*—43.136761, -70.657545; *Hancock-Donnell Wharf & Warehouse*—43.136620, -70.657174

ADDITIONAL INFORMATION: George Marshall Store, 140 Lindsay Road, York, ME 03909

DIRECTIONS: From the center of Ogunquit (junction of U.S. 1/Main Street, Shore Road & Beach Street), drive south on U.S. 1 for ~8.0 miles

When you come to the south junction of U.S. 1 & U.S. 1A, turn left onto U.S. 1A/York Street, and proceed southeast for 0.8 mile to Old York.

From Old York (junction of U.S. 1A & Lindsay Road), drive southwest on Lindsay Road for 0.6 mile. At the sign for the George Marshall Store Gallery and the Hancock-Donnell Wharf & Warehouse, turn left and park downhill in the public area behind the George Marshall Store next to the York River. A private parking area adjacent to the wharf is reserved for lobstermen.

DESCRIPTION & HISTORY: Both buildings are part of the Old York Historic District. *George A. Marshall Store*—In 1867, George A. Marshall purchased the Hancock-Donnell Warehouse and surrounding land and constructed a country store. According to an onsite informational plaque, "...*The structure was a center for mercantile activity along the York River for close to a century, selling not only a* *'general line' of goods, but also wood and coal, all unloaded at the wharf behind the building."*

It was acquired by the Society for the Preservation of Historic Landmarks in 1967.

The warehouse also likely served as the Custom House for the District Port of York, where taxes were collected on the cargo of incoming ships.

After 1954, the building served as a home for the York Art Association, as a gift shop, as offices and research library for the Old York Historical Society, and an art gallery for contemporary art in New England. Today, the Marshall Store gallery features artists from the New England area and is open to the public free of charge.

Hancock-Donnell Wharf & Warehouse—The Hancock-Donnell Wharf was built in the 1740s by John Donnell, a chair-maker and ferry owner. Goods shipped out to the West Indies and other ports of the world were initially stored in the warehouse, which more appropriately was called a chandlery, a place where supplies and equipment were kept and sold to boats and ships. It wasn't uncommon to see large schooners docked in front of the chandlery.

John Hancock's name became associated with the warehouse because a subsequent owner named Daniel Bragdon borrowed money from John Hancock and died in 1891 before paying off the loan. Hancock subsequently owned Bragdon's share of the property until his death in 1793.

The warehouse is the only surviving commercial building in York from the Colonial Period. It has undergone significant rehabilitation over the years, including the addition of a new foundation, but the majority of timbers and flooring are original.

Today, it represents York's maritime history in commerce, but is not open to the public.

STEEDMAN WOODS & WIGGLY BRIDGE

LOCATION: York Harbor (York County)

MAINE ATLAS & GAZETTEER: Map 1, B5

GPS PARKING: 43.136658, -70.647379 (limited)

GPS DESTINATIONS: *Informational plaque at start of causeway*—43.136469, -70.647693; *Barrells Millpond*—43.138435, -70.650696; *Wiggly Bridge*—43.136705, -70.649851; *Steedman Woods*—43.136943, -70.650349

HOURS: Daily, dawn to dusk

FEE: None

RESTRICTIONS: Check the Steedman Woods trailhead board for specific details; dogs must be leashed

ACCESSIBILITY: 0.8-mile walk

DEGREE OF DIFFICULTY: Easy

ADDITIONAL INFORMATION: Steedman Woods, 11 Lilac Lane, off Route 103, York, ME 03909

ADDITIONAL HIKES NEARBY: See chapters on Cliff Walk & Hartley Mason Reservation, York Harbor Beach, and Fisherman's Walk

DIRECTIONS: From the center of Ogunquit (junction of U.S. 1/Main Street, Shore Road & Beach Street), drive south on U.S. 1 for ~8.0 miles.

When you come to the south junction of U.S. 1 & U.S. 1A, turn left onto U.S. 1A/York Street, and head southeast for ~1.3 miles. At Route 103/Lilac Lane, bear right and head southwest for >0.1 mile. Limited parking is available on the left (east) side of the road. Most of it is permit-only, but several parking spots are for non-permit holders.

Parking is also available past the southeast end of the Route 103 Bridge (GPS: 43.133486, -70.648467), a short distance away.

DESCRIPTION: Steedman Woods is a forested area at the end of an island-like peninsula. It is connected to the southeast side of York Village by a dam with a walkway and the Wiggly Bridge. The pedestrian walkway was built on top of the foundation of the old dam.

The woods are considered to be the area occupied by one of the first English colonist (identity unknown).

HIKE: From the parking area on Lilac Lane, walk west across the dam for 0.1 mile to reach Steedman Woods, where you can either head clockwise or counterclockwise around a 0.7-mile-long loop trail that provides nearly continuous views of the waters of the York River and Barrells Millpond.

An informational plaque is located on the island at the west end of the Wiggly Bridge.

A short path from the west end of the loop trail leads to Mill Dam Road, a narrow residential street where no parking is available.

Walk east back across the dam to return to Lilac Lane/Route 103. If you wish to extend your walk further, a railed boardwalk heads south, paralleling Lilac Lane/Route 103, and leads to a dock (GPS: 43.135673, -70.648018) on the York River in 0.1 mile.

HISTORY: Steedman Woods is owned by the Old York Historical Society and looked after by volunteers. In 1978, the 17-acre woodland was donated to the Old York Historical and Improvement Society by C. Richard Steedman, a founding member of the Agamenticus Yacht Club.

According to Jan M. Collins and Joseph E. McCarthy in *Nature Walks in*

Southern Maine: Nature rich walks along the Maine Coast and Interior Hills (1996), "*An elaborate plan was drawn in 1890 to develop the land into villa sites, a huge hotel, and a wharf.*" Fortunately, the plans never came to fruition; elsewise, there would be no Steedman Woods to enjoy today.

Wiggly Bridge—The present Wiggly Footbridge was constructed in 1936 to connect a 0.1-mile-long, 12-foot-wide causeway dam to the mainland. The footbridge is 60-70 feet long, extending between two tiny green towers. It is said that the suspension bridge marks the spot where a number of eighteenth-century mills were located, which makes sense since this is where the sluiceway would most likely have been positioned. It is considered to be one of the smallest suspension bridges in the United States.

According to folklore, the name "Wiggly Bridge" came about in the 1940s when a group of girl scouts thought that the bridge seemed wiggly as they crossed it.

Barrells Pond, on the north side of the causeway dam, is a tidal pond that was created by nineteen early settlers who dammed Meeting House Creek (earlier known as the Agamenticus River, which meant, to Native Americans, "the little river which lies behind an island in its mouth") in 1726 with a 600-foot-long dam to power a sawmill and gristmill.

What's interesting is that the millpond powered an undershot waterwheel that utilized tidal currents to turn its paddlewheel. Although the novel concept of a tide mill may sound like a recent invention, it actually dates to Roman times, the earliest known tide mill being on the River Fleet in London.

Barrell Pond was named for Jonathan Sayward Barrell, who inherited the mill pond in 1784 from his grandfather, Jonathan Sayward.

FISHERMAN'S WALK

LOCATION: York Harbor (York County)

MAINE ATLAS & GAZETTEER: Map 1, B5

GPS PARKING: U.S. 1A/York Street—43.133766, -70.638459; Cul-de-sac at end of Harbor Beach Road—43.132956, -70.638742

GPS SIMPSON LANE WATERFRONT START: 43.133031, -70.641883

GPS DESTINATIONS: Wiggly Bridge—43.136705, -70.649851; Sayward-Wheeler House—43.135980, -70.646962

HOURS: Generally, dawn to dusk

FEE: Modest admission fee to tour the interior of the house

RESTRICTIONS: Dogs must be leashed

ACCESSIBILITY: 0.4-mile walk

DEGREE OF DIFFICULTY: Easy

ADDITIONAL INFORMATION: Sayward-Wheeler House, 9 Barrell Lane Ext., York, ME 03909

ADDITIONAL HIKES NEARBY: See chapters on Cliff Walk & Hartley Mason Reservation, York Harbor Beach, and Steedman Woods & Wiggly Bridge

DIRECTIONS: From the center of Ogunquit (junction of U.S. 1/Main Street, Shore Road & Beach Street), drive south on U.S. 1 for ~8.0 miles.

When you come to the south junction of U.S. 1 & U.S. 1A, turn left onto U.S. 1A/York Street and proceed southeast for ~1.8 miles.

Park either along U.S. 1A/York Street next to the Hartley Mason Reservation as you round the curve and begin heading east, or park in the cul-de-sac at the end of Harbor Beach Road if you have a permit.

During the tourist season, parking spaces can be scarce.

From where you parked, walk back (northwest) along U.S. 1A/York Street for several hundred feet and turn left onto Simpson Lane (a dead-end street that you passed on the drive in).

Walk southwest on Simpson Lane for 0.1 mile. At the end of the lane, turn right at the water's edge by the wrought iron railing, and begin walking west

along the riverside. When you come to Varrell Lane, walk across the street and continue through a tiny corridor bordered by a white fence on your left. A sign reads, *"Provided through the generosity of private landowners and the citizens of York for your enjoyment."* You will quickly come out to an open space where the cement walkway leads northwest along the shoreline and piers to Route 103.

Note: At the end of Simpson Lane, you can also turn left and walk east for 0.1 mile past the Agamenticus Yacht Club on your right. When you come to a large, green space, walk across it to Stage Neck Road and follow Stage Neck Road north uphill to Harbor Beach Road. In all likelihood, this small part of Fisherman's Walk is typically used by guests staying at the Stage Neck Inn (GPS: 43.130844, -70.638697).

DESCRIPTION: This pretty walk takes you along the shoreline of the York River past a series of docks and piers to where the Wiggly Bridge/Steedman Woods hike continuation can be accessed.

HIGHLIGHTS:

- Views of York Harbor and its islands
- Sayward-Wheeler House

WALK: From the end of Simpson Lane, follow the Fisherman's Walk northwest along the North Basin of the York River.

The islands to your left consist of Harris Island (partly concealed behind Bragdon Island), Bragdon Island, which Route 103 crosses over, and then Pine Island. All are interconnected except the separated part of Bragdon Island.

At 0.3 mile, you will come to the cul-de-sac terminus of Barrell Lane Ext. Continue northwest, now on Barrell Lane Ext., for another 250 feet and turn left onto a paved walkway where the railing on Barrell Lane Ext. begins.

If you wish to first see the Sayward-Wheeler Home, walk north up Barrell Lane Ext. for ~100 feet for a head-on view of this historic house, on your left.

Return to the paved walkway, turn right, and head northwest for 250 feet to Route 103/Lilac Lane. Along the way, you will pass by an informational plaque that provides details about the Sayward-Wheeler House. A photograph of the house can be seen in James Phinney Baxter's *Agamenticus, Bristol, Georgiana, York* (1904).

From here, the Steedman Woods/Wiggly Bridge hike can be undertaken.

HISTORY: *Sayward-Wheeler House*—The Sayward-Wheeler House on 9 Barrell Lane Extension was built in ~1718 by Noah Peck and sold in 1720 to John Sayward, a mill-wright, merchant, judge, and representa-tive to the Massachusetts General Court. The Sayward family and descendants lived there until 1977. The last occupant was Elizabeth Cheever Wheeler, who had

purchased the house in 1900 as a vacation retreat for herself and her family, as well as to preserve the home as part of her family heritage. It is said that the house contains one of the best-preserved colonial interiors in the country.

Wheeler's heirs, Bancroft Cheever, Leonard Wheeler, Eunice Wheeler, and Nathaniel Wheeler presented the house to Historic New England, and it opened to the public in 1978.

Consult *Historic New England's* website, https://www.historicnewengland. org/property/sayward-wheeler -house, for specific details about touring the house.

York River—The York River is 13 miles long, with half of it being tidal. Rising from York Pond (GPS: 43.188514, -70.765541) in Eliot, it is fed by a watershed of 32 square miles.

York Harbor—During the eighteenth century, York Harbor, aka Lower Town, was a flourishing seaport lined with wharves and warehouses. In *Old York: Proud Symbol of Colonial Maine. 1652–1952* (1952), Edward M. Marshall writes that mass transportation became the travel norm during the late 1800s to early 1900s. The York Harbor & Beach Railway operated from 1887 to 1925, and the Portsmouth, Kittery & York Beach Street Electric Railway ran from 1897 to 1920.

With the infusion of mass transportation, York Harbor became a fashion-able summer resort with exquisite mansions and large hotels like the Marshall House (which was destroyed by fire in 1916, rebuilt in brick in 1918, and then demolished in 1972), and the Albracca Hotel (which was partially destroyed by fire in 1924 and brought back to life in 2020). Today, most of the old hotels are gone, replaced by condominiums and year-round residences.

YORK HARBOR CLIFF WALK & HARTLEY MASON RESERVATION

LOCATION: York (York County)

MAINE ATLAS & GAZETTEER: Map 1, B5

GPS PARKING: *York Harbor Cliff Walk*—43.133138, -70.639451; *Hartley Mason Reservation*—43.133785, -70.638477

GPS YORK HARBOR CLIFF WALK: *Cul-de-sac start*—43.132956, -70.638742; *York Harbor Reading Room*—43.133649, -70.636799; *Overlook*—43.133475, -70.634150; *Milbury Lane terminus*—43.134902, -70.630162

GPS HARTLEY MASON RESERVATION ENTRANCES: *U.S. 1A*—43.133766, -70.638459; *Harbor Beach Road*—43.133353, -70.639567; *From Cliff Walk*—43.133332, -70.637868

GPS HARTLEY MASON RESERVATION DESTINATIONS: *Pleasure Ground*—43.133738, -70.637361; *Informational plaques*—43.133644, -70.638398 & 43.133916, -70.637112; *York's Fisherman's Memorial*—43.133330, -70.638029; *Lighthouse Memorial*—43.133338, -70.638034

HOURS: Daily, sunrise to sunset

FEE: None

RESTRICTIONS: *York Harbor Cliff Walk*—For pedestrians only. Dogs are not allowed on the trail. Rules & regulations are posted.

ACCESSIBILITY: *York Harbor Cliff Walk*—0.5-mile hike (1.0-mile hike round trip); *Hartley Mason Reservation*—0.2-mile walk

DEGREE OF DIFFICULTY: *York Harbor Cliff Walk*—Moderate, best undertaken between late April and October; *Hartley Mason Reservation*—Easy

ADDITIONAL INFORMATION: Hartley Mason Reservation, 481 York Street, York, ME 03909; York Harbor Reading Room (private), 491 York Street, York Harbor, ME 03911; (207) 363-2450

Paddling & Biking Adventures along coast of southern Maine—Harbor Adventures, PO Box 345, York Harbor, ME 03911; (207) 363-8466; www.HarborAdventures.com

ADDITIONAL HIKES NEARBY: See chapters on York Harbor Beach, Fisherman's Walk, and Steedman Woods & Wiggly Bridge

DIRECTIONS: From the center of Ogunquit (junction of U.S. 1/Main Street, Shore Road & Beach Street), drive south on U.S. 1 for ~8.0 miles.

When you come to the south junction of U.S. 1 & U.S. 1A, turn left onto U.S. 1A/York Street, and proceed southeast for ~1.8 miles.

York Harbor Cliff Walk—As U.S. 1A/York Street veers left, bear right onto Harbor Beach Road, going past the road that leads to the Stage Neck Inn (at one time the site of the old Marshall House), to the cul-de-sac parking area facing York Harbor Beach in 0.1 mile. Be sure to have a parking permit if you expect to park here. Otherwise, park along U.S. 1/York Street.

Hartley Mason Reservation—Follow U.S. 1A/York Street as it veers left from Harbor Beach Road. There is 2-hour, parallel parking immediately to your right, directly next to the Hartley Mason Reservation.

DESCRIPTION: *York Harbor Cliff Walk*—The cement and crushed gravel surfaced Cliff Walk takes you above York Harbor Beach, past the York Harbor Reading Room (on your left), and past a series of grand, nineteenth-century mansions

(also on your left)—all the time with continuous views to your right of Maine's southern coastline with its rocky cliffs, some nearly as high as 50 feet. Some walkers might consider it a more rustic version of Ogunquit's Marginal Way.

Hartley Mason Reservation—The 4-acre reservation, aka Hartley Mason Reserve and Hartley Mason Park—once a private seaside estate—offers a 0.3-mile-loop walk with continuous views of York Harbor. There are numerous monuments and informational plaques scattered throughout the reservation.

HIKE: *York Harbor Cliff Walk*—The Cliff Walk starts from the east side of the cul-de-sac and ends up at Milbury Lane (from which the offshore Millbury Ledge gets its name) before returning via the same route. It begins as a paved walkway but quickly turns into a narrow, dirt path on a rocky terrain. There are several flights of stone steps. At >0.1 mile, you will pass by the historic York Harbor Reading Room, on your left where there is a gated entrance. Along the trek, the path is lined with beach roses (rosa rugosa).

During the first half of the hike, views of the estates to your left are particularly obscured by high cement walls.

In <0.3 mile, you will come to an overlook on your right that provides views, looking back, of York Harbor.

The trail ends along a Town right-of-way at the end of Milbury Lane.

Hartley Mason Reservation—The Preserve can be entered from York Street/U.S. 1A, the cul-de-sac road, 0.1 mile before the end of the road, or from the Cliff Walk, 0.1 mile from the start. There are nearly 0.2 mile of walkways in the park, taking you by sculptures, benches, informational plaques and, of course, impressive views of York Harbor Beach and the Atlantic Ocean.

HISTORY: *Hartley Mason Reservation*—The reservation, established in 1993, is dedicated to sailors who have perished at sea. The Park land was donated to the Town of York by Hartley Mason, a haberdashery entrepreneur, industrialist, and philanthropist.

The Park's gardens were made possible through the Hartley Mason Reservation Trust with support from the Nathan Wheeler Trust.

Pleasure Ground is an art piece consisting of 1-foot-tall, bronze-cast figures engaged in various activities mounted

on top of an 8-foot by 4-foot, 3-ton rock. The art piece was created in 2001 by Sumner Winebaum, a sculptor, Portsmouth businessman, and philanthropist. The artist states that his goal was to depict people enjoying the park.

In the 1880s, the top part of the Hartley Mason Reservation, now natural looking, was occupied by six summer houses. It's always amazing to realize just how much things can change over time.

York's Fisherman's Memorial— The memorial, dedicated to Captain Daniel A. Donnell who died at sea while hauling in traps, is also "Dedicated to those who lost their lives at sea & for those who work and love the ocean."

York Harbor Reading Room— This exclusive club was founded in 1897 by a small group of summer residents. The present building opened in 1910.

YORK HARBOR BEACH

LOCATION: York Harbor (York County)

MAINE ATLAS & GAZETTEER: Map 1, B5

GPS PARKING: 43.132956, -70.638742

GPS YORK HARBOR BEACH: 43.132641, -70.638134

GPS DESTINATION: *Public Restrooms*—43.133112, -70.638999

HOURS: Check website, https://www.yorkparksandrec.org, for specific details

FEE: None

RESTRICTIONS: Regular beach rules & regulations apply; Domestic animals are not allowed on the beach between 8:00 a.m. and 6:00 p.m. from May 20th through September 20th. Pets must be leashed between 6:00 a.m. and sunrise from May 20th to September 20th.

ACCESSIBILITY: Next to the cul-de-sac

ADDITIONAL INFORMATION: York Harbor Beach, Harbor Beach Road, York, ME 03909

Public restrooms are open daily from the first weekend in May through Columbus Day.

Parking at the cul-de-sac is limited and requires a resident permit parking sticker from the Town Clerk's Office at 186 York Street. Additional parking, limited to 2 hours, is available along Route 1A.

Lifeguards are on duty seasonally from Memorial Day weekend through Labor Day weekend.

For further information, consult https://www.yorkparksandrec.org/attractions/beaches.

ADDITIONAL HIKE NEARBY: See chapters on Cliff Walk & Hartley Mason Reservation, Fisherman's Walk, and Steedman Woods & Wiggly Beach.

DIRECTIONS: From the center of Ogunquit (junction of U.S. 1/Main Street, Shore Road & Beach Street), drive south on U.S. 1 for ~8.0 miles.

When you come to the south junction of U.S. 1 & U.S. 1, turn left onto U.S. 1A/York Street, and proceed southeast for ~1.8 miles.

As U.S. 1A/York Street veers left, bear right onto Harbor Beach Road, immediately passing by the road to Stage Neck Inn. You will come to the cul-de-sac parking area facing York Harbor Beach in 0.1 mile.

DESCRIPTION: York Harbor Beach is a 0. 2-mile-long stretch of sand nestled between the rocky bluffs to the south of Fort Point (GPS: 43.130847, -70.637511), named for a fort that once stood near the site of the former 325-guest Marshall House (now the Stage Neck Inn), and rocky bluffs to the northeast towards East Point (GPS: 43.133850, -70.623224). The entire island is called Stage Neck Island or, simply, the "Neck." The word "neck" takes on an ironic twist when you realize that it was here that prisoners were executed on gallows.

Most of the York Harbor Beach is sandy with an occasional tide pool, but there are a couple of small areas of rocks and pebbles.

Before the present-day restrooms were built by the cul-de-sac, the spot was occupied by a pavilion with 400 changing rooms. The pavilion, called the Sea Urchin Bathhouses, was built in 1893 and lasted until 1978 when it was destroyed by a fierce winter storm.

York Harbor Beach is known locally as Mothers Beach because the rocky bedrock on both sides, like a playpen, serves to keep toddlers and youngsters within a defined area.

{4}

KITTERY & KITTERY POINT

Kittery and Kittery Point occupy the extreme southeast corner of Maine. For this reason, Kittery is often referred to as the gateway town into Maine.

Kittery was incorporated in 1647, making it the oldest town in Maine. It was likely named for Kittery Manor, the manor of Alexander Shapleigh (a founder of Kittery) who came from Kingswear, Devon England in 1635. Kittery is home to the 200+year-old Portsmouth Naval Shipyard.

Kittery Point was first settled in 1623. According to W. Woodford Clayton, in *History of York County, Maine: With illustrations and biographical sketches of its prominent men and pioneers* (1880), Kittery Point "*occupies a peninsula a mile and a quarter in length...*" and "*...from a quarter to half a mile wide.*"

FORT MCCLARY
Fort McClary State Historic Site

LOCATION: Kittery Point (York County)

MAINE ATLAS & GAZETTEER: Map B4-5

GPS PARKING: 43.082084, -70.709226

GPS DESTINATIONS: *Bastion* (a projecting part of the fort)—43.082091, -70.709664; *Blockhouse*—43.081753, -70.709234; *Magazine*—43.081859, -70.709339; *Rifleman's House*—43.081892, -70.709228; *Hiking area*—43.082188, -70.708663

HOURS: Daily, 10:00 a.m. to 8:00 p.m.

FEE: Modest charge

RESTRICTIONS: Regular Park rules & regulations apply

ACCESSIBILITY: *Grounds*—Open daily; *Museum*—Open Memorial Day to Columbus Day

DEGREE OF DIFFICULTY: Easy

ADDITIONAL INFORMATION: Fort McClary, 103 Pepperrell Road, Kittery Point, ME 03905; (207) 490-4079

DIRECTIONS: From the center of Ogunquit (junction of U.S. 1/Main Street, Shore Road & Beach Street), drive south on U.S. 1 for ~12.0 miles.

When you come to the junction of U.S. 1 & Haley Road, turn left onto Haley Road and head southeast for ~3.0 miles. At Route 103/Pepperrell Road, turn right and proceed west for ~0.8 mile. Finally, turn left into the park entrance, marked by a huge stone with the fort's name carved in it.

DESCRIPTION: Fort McClary is a restored coastal fortification. In *Old Kittery and her Families* (1903), Everett Schermerhorn Stackpole describes how the grounds looked before being restored: *"Huge blocks of granite lying about show that the government once planned an extensive fortress here, but the old methods of defense are now obsolete, and the fort is of little worth except as an ancient landmark."*

The granite wall facing south toward the ocean is dated 1808-1844. The bastion fronting the parking area is dated 1864-1868.

John Eldridge Frost, in *Colonial Village* (1947), adds that *"An enormous granite wall was commenced about the fort. While work was in progress, the [Civil] war came to a close, and soon all building ceased. Great piles of unused granite lay about. The enlisted men's quarters, the kitchen, the blockhouse, the chapel, the magazine, the hospital and the guard house were standing in 1870."*

Frost notes that some historians believe that four forts were built on this site, in 1690, 1721, 1812, and 1864—one on top of the other. As to the exact number, it may all depend upon one's definition of what constitutes a fort.

The pentagonal walls of the fort were never completed.

Slightly southeast of the fort next to Pepperrell Cove are huge stone blocks, obviously intended for the fortification but, in the end, never used.

Pepperrell Cove (GPS: 43.079776, -70.699577), Phillips Island (GPS: 43.081374, -70.698885), Gooseberry Island (GPS: 43.079053, -70.698189), and Fishing Island (GPS: 43.076525, -70.701989) are visible from the fort.

There are also distant views of Fort Point (GPS: 43.071456, -70.709563) in New Hampshire, 0.6 mile due south. Fort Point, located on the northeast corner of Great Island, is the oldest continuously occupied military site in the United States.

HISTORY: Fort McClary was founded in 1809 but was preceded by other coastal defenses. Around 1689, a simple earthwork or primitive blockhouse was constructed on land owned by William Pepperrell, for whom Pepperrell Cove is named. At the time, the site came to be known as Battery Pasture.

Around 1720, an actual fort was erected on Battery Pasture. It was named Fort William in honor of William Pepperrell. In 1779, near the end of the Revolutionary War, Fort William was abandoned.

In 1808, a new fort was built on the same site and named Fort McClary this time in honor of Major Andrew McClary, a soldier who died at the Battle of Bunker Hill on June 17, 1775; the honor perhaps bestowed on McClary because he was the last American soldier to die on the battlefield.

A large hexagonal blockhouse was built in 1844-1846.

Two years later, the fort was deactivated and then re-garrisoned during the Civil War with four 32-pounder naval guns. The fort subsequently remained active during the Spanish-American War and World War I.

In 1918, Fort McClary was again deactivated and, six years later, the bulk of the property was transferred to the State of Maine.

In 1969, the fort was placed on the National Register of Historic Places.

Much of what can be seen today is a replica of the fort as looked over a century ago.

HIKE: A small trail system for hiking can be found near the northeast end of the parking area.

LADY PEPPERRELL HOUSE (Private)

LOCATION: Kittery Pointy (York County)

MAINE ATLAS & GAZETTEER: Map 1, B4

GPS PARKING: 43.081540, -70.715840

GPS LADY PEPPERRELL HOUSE: 43.081656, -70.716182

ACCESSIBILITY: Private residence

ADDITIONAL INFORMATION: Lady Pepperrell House, Route 103, Kittery Point, ME 03905

DIRECTIONS: From the center of Ogunquit (junction of U.S. 1/Main Street, Shore Road & Beach Street), drive south on U.S. 1 for ~12.0 miles

When you come to the junction of U.S. 1 & Haley Road, turn left onto Haley Road, and head southeast for ~3.0 miles.

At Route 103/Pepperrell Road, bear right and proceed southwest for >1.0 mile. Pull into a small off-road area on your left in front of the First Congregational Church Cemetery, just before Route 103/Pepperrell Road makes a right angle turn in front of the Pepperrell House.

DESCRIPTION & HISTORY: The Georgian-style house, with its hip roof [a roof with inclined ends], four interior end chimneys, modillion [bracketed] cornices, center projecting pavilion, columned and balustraded [railed] side porch, was constructed in 1760 by Lady Mary (Hirst) Pepperrell as a memorial to her late husband, Sir William Pepperrell, who died in 1759. She purposefully had the house built at its present location to be close to her daughter. A pair of dolphins graces the front door, symbolic of the ocean from where the Pepperrell's fortune was made. A photograph of the exterior and interior of the house can be seen in Everett S. Stackpole's *Old Kittery and her Families* (1903).

Sir William Pepperrell was a successful merchant who was declared a Baronet by King George II for his leadership against a French fortress on Cape Breton Island in Nova Scotia. His father, Colonel William Pepperrell is remembered by a tomb that can be seen behind a parking lot across the street from Bistro 1828 (formerly Frisbee's Market). The GPS for the tomb is 43.083955, -70.703866. A plaque on a boulder near the tomb reads, "*In commemoration of the courage and wisdom of Col. William Pepperrell. Born in Devonshire 1646. Died in Kittery 1734. And of his son Sir William Pepperrell, Bart. Born in Kittery 1696, Died in Kittery 1759. Chief Justice of Common Pleas, President of the Council of Massachusetts, he commanded the Colonial forces at the successful siege of Louisburg 1745. And in recognition of his service was made a Baronet and General in the British Army, honors never before conferred on a colonist. Erected by the Pepperrell Association 1905.*"

The Pepperrell House, a private residence dated 1682, stands next to the Bistro at a GPS of 43.083004, -70.702979.

The Lady Pepperrell's house was designated a National Historic Landmark in 1960. It remains in private ownership but has, on occasion, been open to the public.

The house stands virtually opposite the historic First Congregation Church [GPS: 43.081728, -70.715341), built in 1729. The 2½-story parsonage was constructed in 1733 for Rev. John Newmarch and his family. Lady Pepperrell was very religious, which is why her home lies diagonally across the road from the church.

The adjacent cemetery was established in 1833 and contains the graves of many Revolutionary War veterans. If you walk through the graveyard, you will encounter the tomb of Levi Thaxter, husband of poet Celia Thaxter [see chapter on Seapoint Beach & Crescent Beach]. The epitaph was written specifically for Thaxter by Robert Browning, an English poet and playwright.

FORT FOSTER
Fort Foster Park

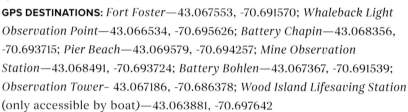

LOCATION: Kittery Point (York County)

MAINE ATLAS & GAZETTEER: Map 1, C4

GPS PARKING: *Area 1*—43.068473, -70.691062; *Area 2*- 43.067291, -70.693192; *Area 3*—43.065667, -70.687948; *Area 4*—43.067901, -70.684805; *Front of Gatehouse*—43.070635, -70.686684

GPS DESTINATIONS: *Fort Foster*—43.067553, -70.691570; *Whaleback Light Observation Point*—43.066534, -70.695626; *Battery Chapin*—43.068356, -70.693715; *Pier Beach*—43.069579, -70.694257; *Mine Observation Station*—43.068491, -70.693724; *Battery Bohlen*—43.067367, -70.691539; *Observation Tower*- 43.067186, -70.686378; *Wood Island Lifesaving Station* (only accessible by boat)—43.063881, -70.697642

HOURS: Consult website, https://www.kitteryme.gov/fort-foster-park, for details

FEE: Per vehicular charge for admission; credit card-only; an identical fee is charged to walkers and bicyclists.

ACCESSIBILITY: Mileages are variable, but none are of any substantial length. The pier walk is 0.1 mile long

DEGREE OF DIFFICULTY: Moderately easy

ADDITIONAL INFORMATION: Fort Foster Park, 51 Pocahontas Road, Kittery Point, ME 03905; (207) 439-2182; *Park map*—fortfoster.weebly.com/maps--trails.html; *Park map* (color)— fortfoster.weebly.com/uploads/3/0/9/3/30934187/fortfoster_ 11x17_20190531.pdf

DIRECTIONS: From the center of Ogunquit (junction of U.S. 1/Main Street, Shore Road & Beach Street), drive south on U.S. 1 for ~12.0 miles.

When you come to the junction of U.S. 1 & Haley Road, turn left onto Haley Road, and head southeast for ~3.0 miles. At Route 103/Tenney Hill Road, turn left, go east for >0.2 mile, and then right onto Chauncey Creek Road. After traveling east on Chauncey Creek Road for 0.5 mile, turn right onto Gerrish Island Lane and proceed south for 0.1 mile, crossing over Chauncey Creek in the process. You are now on Gerrish Island. Turn right onto Pocahontas Road (named for a vanished hotel), head south for ~1.1 miles, and then right into the entrance to Fort Foster, reaching the contact station in 0.1 mile.

DESCRIPTION: Fort Foster was a defensive battery fortification that helped to guard the Maine coastline from enemy attack. It served its purpose from 1901 to 1946.

DRIVE: Roads extend through the park, taking you from one site to the next. A 0.2-mile-long road leads across the wetlands in the middle of the island.

Pier Beach is located on the west side of the Park, north of the playground.

HIKE: The >1.0-mile-long shoreline path takes you along the south shoreline next to Windsurfer's Beach (GPS: 43.065754, -70.689639), aka Whaleback Beach, and then northeast along the east shore by Scuba Beach (GPS: 43.068232, -70.682753), aka Rocky Beach, and then west towards the gatehouse.

HISTORY: Fort Foster, occupying 88 acres of land on the southwest tip of Gerrish Island, was constructed in 1898–1901 as part of a coastline defense for America. The fort was equipped with two gun-batteries: Battery Bohlen with three 10-inch M1895 disappearing guns, and Battery Chapin with two 3-inch M1902 guns on pedestal mounts. Battery Bohlen was named for Brigadier General Henry Bohlen, and Battery Chapin for Brigadier General Edward Payson Chapin, both of whom had fought and died in the Civil War. Bolen was the first foreign-born Union General to serve in the Civil War; Chapin, who was twice wounded on the same day, was posthumously promoted to Brigadier General following his death.

In 1942, a six-story fire control tower for spotting potential targets was constructed. It was used until 1944, and still stands.

In 1946, the remaining batteries were deactivated, and the site closed as a fort in 1948. For a few years it was used as a recreational area by personnel from the Portsmouth Naval Shipyard until the land was transferred to the Town of Kittery's Public Works Department. According to *North American Forts* (https://www.northamericanforts.com/East/Maine/Fort_Foster/history.html) *"The Kittery Parks Division had the lower level of Battery Bolen sealed and filled-in with soil in the late 1980s, along with sealing other structures. Battery Chapin's earthen berm was removed much earlier, probably by the Navy in the 1950s."*

The park is managed today by the Town of Kittery.

The 75-foot-high Whale Back Light, guarding the entrance to Portsmouth Harbor, can be seen from the fort. The current lighthouse was built in 1872 and automated in 1963.

CUTTS ISLAND TRAIL & CHAUNCY CREEK PADDLE
Part of the Rachel Carson National Wildlife Refuge

LOCATION: Kittery Point (York County)

MAINE ATLAS & GAZETTEER: Map 1, B4

GPS PARKING: 43.087867, -70.675647

GPS CUTTS ISLAND TRAILHEAD: 43.087820, -70.675585

GPS LAUNCH SITE: 43.087987, -70.675762

GPS DESTINATION: *Stone wall*—43.094718, -70.672077; *End of peninsula*—43.097058, -70.667339

HOURS: Sunrise to sunset

FEE: None

RESTRICTIONS: Regular Park rules & regulations apply; dogs allowed on leash

ACCESSIBILITY: >1.8-mile-loop trail

DEGREE OF DIFFICULTY: Moderately easy

ADDITIONAL INFORMATION: Cutts Island Trail, Seapoint Road, Kittery, ME 03905
Dogs are not permitted on the trails.
A restroom is located at the trailhead.

DIRECTIONS: From the center of Ogunquit (junction of U.S. 1/Main Street, Shore Road & Beach Street), drive south on U.S. 1 for ~12.0 miles.

When you come to the junction of U.S. 1 & Haley Road, turn left onto Haley Road, and head southeast for 3.0 miles. Then turn left onto Route 103/Tenney Hill Road and proceed northeast for ~0.9 mile. At Cutts Island Lane/Seapoint Road, turn right and head southeast for 0.4 mile. Finally, turn left into the roadside pull-off as soon as you cross over the Chauncy Creek Bridge.

The trail starts by the kiosk. Next to it is a wooden restroom. The Orange Loop Trail and short, connecting spur trail constitute a hike of 1.8 miles.

HIKE: The hike takes you primarily through a wooded area with an elevation change of <50 feet. We will assume that you are following the trail system clockwise, with Chauncy Creek, a tidal river, constantly to your west (left). In <0.1 mile, you will come to the first informational plaque. From here, in another <0.2 mile you will reach a junction. The path to your right connects the two main trails. Turn left at this point and continue following the main trail as it takes you along the west shore of the island. In another 0.3 mile, you will come to a second junction. A faded plaque tells you your present location. Continue north for another 200 feet to reach a second informational plaque adjacent to a rock wall. It always comes as a pleasant revelation to realize that the land, seemingly so uninhabited, was used for other purposes in the past. From here, continue northeast, no longer on the loop-trail system, for another 0.4 mile until you arrive at the end of the peninsula. You will be gazing across a vast area of marshland that is part of the 7,500-acre Brave Boat Harbor. An informational plaque provides information about the salt marshes of Maine.

Retrace your steps for 0.4 mile. When you come back to the junction, veer left and follow the trail as it takes you along the east side of the island. There is not as much to see here except a vague area of marshland to your left. In 0.3 mile, you will come to the east end of the path that connects the two main trails. An informational plaque by this junction talks about the forest and its creatures. Continue south on the main trail for another 0.3 mile to end up back at your starting point.

We spoke with Ranger Thomas Wall, Visitor Services Manager at Rachel Carson National Wildlife Refuge, who asked that visitors be respectful of the property and not vandalize the trees, which have been under constant assault.

PADDLE: Because the trailhead parking area is located next to Chauncy Creek, it also affords an excellent launch site for paddlers wishing to follow the creek upstream through a marshy area between the west side of Cutts Island and Brave Boat Harbor Road.

Paddlers can also go under the Cutts Island Lane Bridge and then head southwest downstream for ~1.1 miles, passing by a row of old pier posts in <0.1 mile, and going under the Gerrish Island Lane Bridge in 0.4 mile. Hoyts Island (GPS: 43.083183, -70.696065) or Phillips Island (GPS: 43.081345, -70.698729) might both be natural turn-around points before you venture too far out towards the body of the ocean.

HISTORY: Chauncy Creek is likely named for Charles Chauncy who resided on the creek at a point near its junction with the outlet of Deering's Guzzle.

During President Thomas Jefferson's embargo of 1807, which crippled most of New England's shipping business except for those who became privateers during the War of 1812. Capt. Joseph Cutts safeguarded his vessels by sailing up Chauncy Creek and anchoring them behind Gerrish Island. Unfortunately, the vessels were never returned to their original location and eventually rotted away.

Joseph's wife was the former Mary Chauncy, another connection with the name of the creek. Mary was also the great-niece of Lady Pepperrell [see Lady Pepperrell House chapter], just as Joseph was the great-nephew of Sir William Pepperrell.

Cutts Island is named for Robert Cutts, a shipbuilder, and his son, Richard.

SEAPOINT BEACH & CRESCENT BEACH

LOCATION: Kittery Point (York County)

MAINE ATLAS & GAZETTEER: Map 1, B5

GPS PARKING: *Seapoint Road*—43.090641, -70.666130 (non-residents); *Beach area*—43.090412, -70.662909 (residents-only)

GPS DESTINATIONS: *Seapoint Beach*—43.088799, -70.662185; *Seapoint*—43.085816, -70.660393; *Crescent Beach*—43.085080, -70.663034; *Thaxter Memorial boulder*— 43.086170, -70.66043 (estimated)

HOURS: Dawn to dusk

RESTRICTIONS: Regular beach rules & regulations apply; Kittery residents must display a Kittery dump sticker on their vehicle

ACCESSIBILITY: 0.2-mile walk to beach

DEGREE OF DIFFICULTY: Easy

ADDITIONAL INFORMATION: Seapoint Beach, Seapoint Road, Kittery Point, ME 03905

The beach and parking area are closed from 11:00 p.m. to 3:00 a.m. from May 15th to September 30th.

Dogs are not allowed on the beach from 10:00 a.m. to 5:00 p.m., Memorial Day to Labor Day. On all other days, dogs must be on leash.

DIRECTIONS: From the center of Ogunquit (junction of U.S. 1/Main Street, Shore Road & Beach Street), drive south on U.S. 1 for ~12.0 miles.

When you come to the junction of U.S. 1 & Haley Road, turn left onto Haley Road, and head southwest for ~3.0 miles. Then turn left onto Route 103/Tenney Hill Road and proceed northeast for ~0.9 mile. When you reach Cutts Island Lane/Seapoint Road, turn right and head southeast for ~1.4 miles.

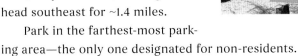

Park in the farthest-most parking area—the only one designated for non-residents.

From here, walk >0.2 mile along Seapoint Road to the beach. You will pass by several roadside pull-offs for residents of Kittery Point, as well as a small parking area at the end of Seapoint Road, which is also for residents of Kittery Point only.

DESCRIPTION: *Seapoint Beach* is a 0.4-mile-long expanse of pebbly beach and soft sand between a rocky area to the north and the Seapoint peninsula (GPS: 43.085777, -70.659829), to the south. There are occasional patches of rocks in between both ends, but most of the beach is sandy.

Crescent Beach is a 0.2-mile-long stretch of sand between Seapoint, to the northeast, and the northeast end of Gerrish Island with its private mansions, to the south along Tower Road and Goodwin Road. It is one of several beaches in Maine that are named Crescent Beach because of their curved shape.

HIKE: Crescent Beach can be reached from Seapoint Beach by scampering up a sloping, 5-foot-high, rocky mound that hugs the shoreline near the south end of the beach. Once on top, you can follow a 0.3-mile-long rock-strewn path that takes you around the spit of rocky land between the two beaches. Along the way, you will encounter a plaque mounted on a medium-sized boulder that reads, "*Seapoint. Given to the Kittery Land Trust by Eliot and Margaret Hubbard in memory of Rosamond Thaxter. 1895–1985, whose love for this town and its environs expressed itself in many acts of generosity. 1998.*"

HISTORY: Seapoint is a 3.0-acre spit of land that separates Seapoint Beach from Crescent Beach. It is conserved by the Kittery Land Trust (https://

kitterylandtrust.weebly.com), part of the Maine Land Trust Network (https://www.mltn.org). The land was donated to the Land Trust by the Hubbard family in memory of Rosamond Thaxter, author of the biography *Sandpiper: the life and letters of Celia Thaxter* (1999).

Gerrish Island is named for Timothy Gerrish and, later, Joseph Gerrish, who lived in a two-story, Georgian-style house that fronted the ocean. The house, like the one on Cutts Island owned by the Cutts, no longer exists.

In the 1600s, the island was known as Champernowne Island for Capt. Francis Champernowne, a seventeenth-century adventurer who had a farm at Strawberry Bank in Portsmouth, New Hampshire.

ADDITIONAL SITS MANAGED/OWNED BY THE KITTERY LAND TRUST:

- Clayton Lane (8.5 acres), end of Clayton Lane (daytime parking only). Kittery, ME; GPS: 43.135981, -70.732509; no trails

- Norton Preserve (170 acres), end of Norton Road past yellow farmhouse, Kittery, ME; GPS: 43.118563, -70.695553

- Remick Preserve (70 acres), Fernald Road, Kittery, ME; GPS: 43.117295, -70.757184

- Nooney Farm (30 acres), Stevenson Road, Kittery, ME; GPS: 43.114878, -70.747062

- Fairchild easement (17 acres), 8 Pocahontas Road trailhead, Kittery, ME; GPS: 43.082219, -70.692648 (general)

BRAVE BOAT HEADWATERS PRESERVE TRAIL
Kittery Land Trust

LOCATION: North of Kittery Point (York County)

MAINE ATLAS & GAZETTEER: Map 1, B4

GPS PARKING: 43.108713, -70.673379

GPS DESTINATIONS: *Vernal Pool*—43.108990, -70.673457 (estimated); *Cranberry Lane entrance to trail system*—43.111463, -70.684323

HOURS: Daily, dawn to dusk

FEE: None

RESTRICTIONS: Regular Park rules & regulations apply; leashed pets allowed

ACCESSIBILITY: 0.7-mile hike on main trail (estimated); 0.7-mile hike along loop trail

DEGREE OF DIFFICULTY: Moderately easy

ADDITIONAL INFORMATION: Brave Boat Headwaters Preserve Trail, 185 Brave Boat Harbor Road, Kittery Point, ME 03905

Kittery Land Trust, PO Box 467, 120 Rogers Road, Kittery, ME 03904-0467; (207) 439-8989; info@kitterylandtrust.org

Trail map—https://kitterylandtrust.weebly.com/uploads/1/0/8/9/108953385/brave-boat-headwaters-trail-map.pdf

DIRECTIONS: From the center of Ogunquit (junction of U.S. 1/Main Street, Shore Road & Beach Street), drive south on U.S. 1 for ~12.0 miles.

When you come to the junction of U.S. 1 & Haley Road, turn left onto Haley Road and head southeast for ~3.0 miles. Bear left onto Route 103/Tenney Hill Road/Brave Boat Harbor Road, go northeast for ~2.4 miles and turn left into the parking area, opposite Salt Marsh Lane.

DESCRIPTION: The Brave Boat Headwaters Preserve Trail leads through a forested area west of Brave Boat Harbor following old roads and paths.

HIKE: From the kiosk, hike northeast, following the white-marked trail/road. You will pass by a vernal pool (a seasonal pool of water) on your left in >0.05 mile. The trail begins to descend, with rock walls appearing on your left, and then, switching over to your right. The trail becomes less road-like at this point. Soon, you will cross over a tiny stream via a boardwalk and then cross over three stone walls in succession, gradually continuing to descend. When you come to a Land Trust Bench on your left, you have arrived at a junction. A 0.7-mile-long, red-marked trail goes off to your left, eventually circling back to the main trail further ahead.

Continue straight ahead on the white-marked trail. More stone walls are seen as the trail continues its gradual descent. At a low point, you will come to a junction where the red-marked trail returns on your left. The white-marked trail, now called the Sawyer Farm Trail, parallels a pasture, which is visible through the woods to your right. The trail crosses over a stream via a board-walk and then climbs uphill, now closer to the pasture. Within a few more minutes, the trail ends at Cranberry Lane (an offshoot of Bartlett Lane) next to a telephone pole marked 42/84/42.

You can retrace your steps to the parking area or follow the red-marked Loop Trail along the way back to add a little variety to your hike.

HISTORY: The headwaters Preserve, when completed, will encompass 150 acres of land, 100 of which are or will be accessible to the public. It is a patchwork of public lands and private lands with conservation easements in place. For this reason, it is important that hikers remain on the trails and not wander off.

Brave Boat Harbor, southeast of the Brave Boat Headwaters Preserve Trail, was presumably named for the harbor's tricky entrance, where only captains of brave boats dared enter when the weather worsened and produced danger-ous surf across the passageway.

AMBUSH ROCK

LOCATION: Eliot (York County)

MAINE ATLAS & GAZETTEER: Map 1, B3

GPS PARKING: Pull-off next to historic rock

GPS AMBUSH ROCK: 43.163648, -70.797236

ACCESSIBILITY: Roadside

ADDITIONAL INFORMATION: Ambush Rock, 786 Goodwin Road, Eliot, ME 03903

DIRECTIONS: From the center of Ogunquit (junction of U.S. 1/Main Street, Shore Road & Beach Street), drive south on U.S. 1 for ~12.7 miles (or 0.2 mile after crossing over Spruce Creek). At a traffic intersection with Route 101/Wilson Road/Goodwin Road, turn right onto Route 101/Wilson Road/Goodwin Road and head northwest for >5.5 miles (or 0.6 mile past Depot Road, which enters on your left). Look for the roadside memorial on your right.

DESCRIPTION: In *Kittery and her Families* (1908), Everett S. Stackpole writes, "*...The night after [Major Charles] Frost's burial the Indians opened up his grave, took out the body, carried it to the top of Frost's Hill and suspended it upon a stake. His resting place was marked some years later with a flat stone, on which is a rudely chiseled inscription: 'Here lyeth intrrd ye body of Mj. Charles Frost age 65 years. Dead July ye 4th 1697'.*" An old photograph of the rock can be seen in Stackpole's book.

Frost's gravesite is on the old Berwick Road, between South Berwick and Portsmouth.

The plaque on Ambush Rock reads: "*Here on Sunday July 4, 1697, Major Charles Frost, Phebe Littlefield, wife of John Heard, Dennis Downing, were killed by Indians while returning on horseback from the meeting house in the Parish of Unity in the Precinct of Berwick where they had attended Divine Service.*"

HISTORY: On July 4th, 1897, the newly formed Eliot Historical Society met at the rock to hold a commemoration ceremony marking the 200th anniversary of the murders. This was their first public event as an organization.

The plaque facing the road was set into the rock by Ralph Bartlett in 1915. At one time an old stone wall crossed over the center of the rock, paralleling the road.

As an interesting historical footnote, Charles Frost was the 5th great-grandfather of the poet Robert Frost.

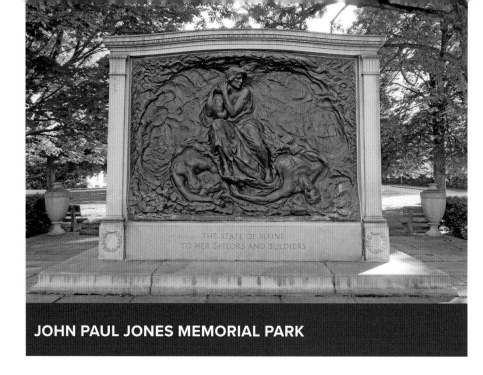

JOHN PAUL JONES MEMORIAL PARK

LOCATION: Kittery (York County)

MAINE ATLAS & GAZETTEER: Map 1, B3–4

GPS PARKING: Park on side streets as close to the park as possible

GPS JOHN PAUL JONES MEMORIAL PARK: 43.084739 -70.750662

HOURS: Dawn to dusk

FEE: None

RESTRICTIONS: Regular Park rules & regulations apply

ACCESSIBILITY: 0.1-mile walk from one end of the park to the other

DEGREE OF DIFFICULTY: Easy

ADDITIONAL INFORMATION: John Paul Jones State Historic Site, U.S. 1, Kittery, ME 03904

DIRECTIONS: From the center of Ogunquit (junction of U.S. 1/Main Street, Shore Road & Beach Street), drive south on U.S. 1 for ~14.5 miles. (Note: Along the way, stay on U.S. 1 as it becomes State Street and avoid U.S. 1 BYP/Bypass).

As soon as you cross over Government Street, U.S. 1 becomes a one-way street: U.S. 1/Newman Street takes you south and U.S. 1/Hunter Avenue takes you north. Each street has a sidewalk.

You will need to park on a side street or anywhere in the vicinity where parking is legal.

One other parking option for those who wish to combine visiting the Park with enjoying a meal is to park at Warren's Lobster House (GPS: 43.083892,

-70.750200) located on Water Street, just before you come to the Piscataqua River Bridge that leads onto Badger's Island and then over into New Hampshire.

DESCRIPTION: The site commemorates John Paul Jones, one of the founders of the U.S. Navy, and his ship, the U.S.S. Ranger, which was built nearby and launched in 1777.

The large, bronze, bas (low) relief framed in granite is unique in that instead of featuring soldiers and weapons, it displays a woman holding a child.

Two plaques can be seen at the site, one for John Paul Jones; the other for Maine soldiers and sailors.

HISTORY: John Paul Jones Memorial Park is trapezoidal in shape and encompasses 2 acres of land bounded by streets and private residences. It was established in 1926 and officially named for John Paul Jones in 1927.

The four urns surrounding the memorial have an interesting history. During the 1940s and World War II, they were removed to safeguard them and later dumped into the river. During the 1999 restoration project, the urns were retrieved from the river, refurbished, and replace around the monument,

The *Maine Sailors and Soldiers Memorial*, at the south end of the Park, was erected in 1924–1926. It was sculpted by Bashka Paeff who, earlier in her career, was known as the Subway Sculptor.

The *Province of Maine Monument*, set into place in 1931, memorializes Sir Ferdinando Gorges who was chartered the Province of Maine in 1635.

The *Sloop Ranger Monument* near the northwest end of the Park, was originally erected on nearby Badger's Island (named for William and Robert Badger, master shipbuilders) in 1905. In 1963, it was moved to its present location. The monument commemorates the U.S.S. Ranger, Jones' first command.

It was from Badger's Island (GPS: 43.082159, -70.752462) that John Paul Jones and his crew set sail on the U.S.S. Ranger in 1777, bringing word to France of America's victory over the British at the Battle of Saratoga. Two months later, Jones went on to raid British waters.

Interesting, John Paul Jones was born John Paul. It wasn't until later in life that he assumed the surname Jones in addition to his original surname. He is famous for saying "I have not yet begun to fight!" when he was up against the more heavily armed British warship Serapis. It is said that his memoirs inspired writers like James Fenimore Cooper and Alexandre Dumas to write adventure novels.

For those wishing to visit the John Paul Jones House (GPS 43.075212, -70.760290), it is located nearby on 43 Middle Street, Portsmouth, NH 03801; (603) 436-8420.

{5}

NORTH BERWICK AREA

North Berwick was set off from Berwick in 1831. It was first settled in 1693 by a Quaker named John Morrell.

Berwick was named after Berwick-upon-Tweed, England.

The Falls Chamber of Commerce covers the area of Berwick, North Berwick, South Berwick, Somersworth, and Rollinsford. They can be reached at 472 High Street, Somersworth, NH; (603) 749-7175 or at https://gscdtfc.wildapricot.org.

HILTON-WINN PRESERVE
York Land Trust

LOCATION: West of Ogunquit (York County)

MAINE ATLAS & GAZETTEER: Map 2, E5

GPS PARKING: 43.257267, -70.652564

GPS DESTINATION: *Head-on view of Ogunquit River by old bridge abutment*—43.261015, -70.650930; *Powerline corridor*—43.262549, -70.651343; *Cascade*—43.262451, -70.650116; *Old dam/sawmill site*—43.263130, -70.650412

HOURS: Dawn to dusk

FEE: None

RESTRICTIONS: Regular Park rules & regulations apply; day-use only; dogs must be leashed and cleaned up after

ACCESSIBILITY: 0.3-mile hike to head-on view of Ogunquit River; 1.5 miles of trails

DEGREE OF DIFFICULTY: Easy

ADDITIONAL INFORMATION: Hilton-Winn Preserve, 174 Ogunquit Road, York, ME 03902; https://yorklandtrust.org/explore/hilton-winn-preserve
    Trail maps—https://yorklandtrust.org/wp-content/uploads/Hilton-Winn.pdf
    https://yorklandtrust.org/wp-content/uploads/Current-Hilton-Winn-Preserve-Trail.pdf

DIRECTIONS: From the center of Ogunquit (junction of U.S. 1/Main Street, Shore Road & Beach Street), drive north on U.S. 1/Main Street for 0.1 mile. Turn left onto Berwick Road/Ogunquit Road and head west for ~3.0 miles. Then turn right into the preserve's parking area immediately after crossing over a short bridge spanning the Ogunquit River.

DESCRIPTION: The hike takes you along the upper part of the Ogunquit River, long before the stream descends from the hills and flows into the Atlantic Ocean. A small cascade is seen along the hike.

HIKE: Follow the white-blazed Boardwalk Trail north, walking along a section of boardwalks through a semi-marshy area for 0.1 mile. After another <0.1 mile, the trail goes slightly uphill, crosses over a section of exposed bedrock, and then descends slightly to a lower level. In another 0.1 mile, you will pass by a spur path to Hilton Lane, which enters on your left.

Within 0.05 mile farther, the Boardwalk Trail turns dramatically left. First, bear right at this "T" junction, following a wide path that leads to the Ogunquit River in ~75 feet. This will be your first opportunity to actually stand facing the river (not counting, of course, the bridge crossing before the trailhead).

The Ogunquit River is ~30 feet wide here, narrowing significantly as it flows past where you are standing. Look across to the opposite side of the river to see an old stone wall, perhaps a bridge abutment, part of an old dam, or the wall of a vanished mill. Take note that a stone wall supports the south side of the land where you are standing.

Return to the main trail and follow it west for <0.1 mile. When you come to Hilton Lane (an old woods road), bear right and proceed north, quickly

walking across a powerline corridor. Once you are in the woods again, turn right and follow the red-blazed Loop Trail. In >0.05 mile, the trail takes you to a 6-foot high, elongated cascade on the Ogunquit River. The trail continues on the other side of the stream, but there is no handy footbridge crossing (at least at this time). Presently, a 3-inch-wide tree limb stretched across the river, with a handline above to help with balance, provides the only way to cross the river to continue on the red-blazed Loop Trail.

About 200 feet downstream from the cascade, close to Hilton Lane, is the site of an old sawmill or gristmill, which disappeared from maps beginning in 1856 according to the Land Trust website. When the foliage is sparse, you can look downstream from the cascade and see a wide, breached dam 200 feet away. To reach the dam, merely follow the Ogunquit River downstream for 200 feet.

If instead of taking the red-blazed Loop Trail from Hilton Lane, continue north on Hilton Lane for another <0.05 mile and you will come to an impasse where a stone bridge of some kind once existed. For those with good balance, it seems feasible to rock-hop across the stream next to the bridge abutments if you wish to follow Hilton Lane farther north. The defunct bridge lies virtually next to the confluence of the Ogunquit River and Tatnic Brook.

HISTORY: The Hilton-Winn Preserve encompasses 195 acres of land and is part of the "Mt. Agamenticus to the Sea Conservation Region." The land was originally inhabited by the Armouchiquois tribe, Algonquian-speaking Native Americans. Around 1640, an English settler named Edward Winn began farming the land after receiving a royal land grant. Over the next four centuries, the land was farmed by eight generations of Winns and grew to encompass over 200 acres.

In the 1940s, Clifford Hilton, who was Ada Winn's son, purchased the farm; hence the Preserve's name Hilton-Winn.

In 1999, the land was donated to the York Land Trust (yorklandtrust.org) by Ethel Hilton, Clifford Hilton's wife.

The property connects with the Kimball Farm North Preserve [see next chapter].

ADDITIONAL YORK LAND TRUST SITES:

- Highland Farm Preserve (151 acres), 321 Cider Hill Road/Rout 91, York, ME; GPS: 43.171863, -70.716557

- McIntire Highlands Preserve (458 acres), Kittery Water District Access Road (off of Linscott Road), York, ME; GPS: ~43.191106, -70.728381

- Smelt Brook Preserve (300 acres), Cider Hill Road, York, ME; Park at Highland Farm Preserve lot. Trailhead on opposite side of Cider Hill Road from Highland Farm Preserve; GPS: 43.171687, -70.717370

- McFeely Preserve (38 acres), Marsh Brook Lane (0.25 mile from Clay Hill Road), York, ME; GPS: ~43.227810, -70.632002

- Fuller Forest Preserve (220 acres), Bartlett Road, York, ME; GPS: ~43.130378, -70.668961

KIMBALL FARM NORTH PRESERVE
Great Works Regional Land Trust

LOCATION: West of Ogunquit (York County)

MAINE ATLAS & GAZETTEER: Map 2, E5

GPS PARKING: 43.258574, -70.656972

GPS DESTINATIONS: *Pride Rock*—43.259031, -70.657433; *Split Rock*—43.262318, -70.661083; *Tatnic Brook*—43.262923, -70.657121; *Powerline corridor*—43.263296, -70.653956; *Washed out bridge crossing*—43.263683, -70.650474

HOURS: Dawn to dusk

FEE: None

RESTRICTIONS: Regular Park rules & regulations apply

ACCESSIBILITY: Variable depending upon paths taken; 3.0 miles of trails

DEGREE OF DIFFICULTY: Moderately easy

ADDITIONAL INFORMATION: Kimball Farm North Preserve, Ogunquit Road, South Berwick, ME 03907

  Trail map—https://gwrlt.org/kimball-farm-north-preserve

DIRECTIONS: From the center of Ogunquit (junction of U.S. 1/Main Street, Shore Road & Beach Street), drive north on U.S. 1/Main Street for 0.1 mile. Turn left onto Berwick Road/Ogunquit Road and proceed west for ~3.3 miles. Turn right into the parking area.

DESCRIPTION: The trail passes by glacial erratics, including one particularly large split rock, vernal pools, and Tatnic Brook.

According to Charles Edward Banks, in the *History of York, Maine. Vol. II* (1935), *tatnic* is the Native American word for "to shake or tremble," a reference to the shaky footing on toussocks of marshy land.

HIKE: From the kiosk, follow the green-blazed Breen Norris Farm Trail northwest. Within 100 feet, the trail divides momentarily, passing around two medium-sized boulders. A trailside sign identifies the boulder(s) as "Pride Rock."

In >0.05 mile, turn left onto the blue-blazed River Trail. Quickly, several near-trailside boulders are passed, the largest being 7 feet in height.

In >0.2 mile, turn left onto the 0.5-mile-long, red-blazed Split Rock Trail. In 0.2 mile, you will pass by an 8-foot-high boulder on your right, 15 feet from the trail. But the best is yet to come. In another 100 feet, the trail takes you through a 3-foot-wide gap in a massive split rock. The smaller section of this glacial erratic, to your right, is ~8 feet high and equally as long. The portion of the rock to your left is far larger. It stands ~8 feet high and is irregular in shape, with a length of >25 feet.

In 0.4 mile you will pass by a 4-foot-high boulder on your left and then reach the end of the Split Rock Trail at ~0.5 mile.

Turn left onto the blue-blazed River Trail, passing immediately by the Breen-Morris Farm Trail as it enters on your right. In <0.2 mile, walk across a boardwalk and then, within 0.05 mile, across an open field. As soon as you are in the woods again, immediately stepping over a stone wall, you will notice that the trail now parallels Tatnic Brook, a tributary of the Ogunquit River, to your left. The name, River Trail, finally makes sense. The trail goes up and then down as you pass through a powerline corridor, and then heads northeast to eventually reach the yellow-blazed Hilton Lane (a rural road from 1785) in the adjoining Hilton-Winn Preserve. If you turn left onto Hilton Lane, you will immediately see that the old road abruptly ends where an old stone bridge has been washed out. For determined hikers, it is possible to rock hop across the stream next to the bridge abutments and continue following the 1,4-mile-long Hilton Lane as it proceeds farther northwest.

Refer to the previous chapter on the Hinn-Winn Preserve for descriptions of an old dam/mill site, and cascade on Ogunquit Creek, just east of Hilton Lane.

HISTORY: The Kimball Farm North Preserve connects with the Hilton-Winn Farm Preserve and the Hilton-Winn Farm.

The Preserve encompasses 37 acres of land and is part of the Great Works Regional Land Trust. The land was once farmed by the Winn and Hilton families for two centuries.

Adjacent to the Preserve is the 48-acre Hilton-Winn farm (GPS: 43.258819, -70.654806), now home to the Youth Enrichment Program run by Nancy Breen, owner of the farm. The goal of the Preserve is "to provide a county-farm experience to enrich the hearts, minds and spirits of children."

KENYON HILL PRESERVE
Great Works Regional Land Trust

LOCATION: South Berwick (York County)

MAINE ATLAS & GAZETTEER: Map 2, E4

GPS PARKING: 43.262150, -70.678797

GPS DESTINATIONS: *High Wall*—43.260512, -70.681603; *Rock shelter/Crevice hideout*—43.259941, -70.683196; *Foundation ruins*—43.257633, -70.681146; *Split Rock*—43.260305, -70.679686

HOURS: Daily, dawn to dusk

FEE: None

RESTRICTIONS: Regular Park rules & regulations apply; dog-friendly, but pet must be controlled by leash or verbal commands

ACCESS: 1.0-mile loop trail

DEGREE OF DIFFICULTY: Moderate

ADDITIONAL INFORMATION: Kenyon Hill Preserve, 110 Ogunquit Road, South Berwick, ME 03908; https://gwrlt.org/kenyon-hill-preserve

Trail map—https://mainebyfoot.com/ kenyon-hill-preserve-south-berwick

DIRECTIONS: From the center of Ogunquit (junction of U.S. 1/Main Street, Shore Road & Beach Street), drive north on U.S. 1/Main Street for 0.1 mile and turn left onto Berwick Road. Head northwest on Berwick Road/Ogunquit Road for

<4.5 miles and turn left into the Kenyon Hill parking area, marked by a wooden sign. If you come to Bennett Lot Road on your left, then you have gone too far by 0.1 mile.

DESCRIPTION: Split Rock is a 15-foot-high boulder that has cracked into two halves that lie close together. The total length of the two pieces is ~15 feet.

There is a large boulder opposite split rock, looming at a height of 20 feet, with a length of ~20 feet.

According to the Great Works Regional Land Trust, a significant number of house-sized glacial erratics (boulders that differ from the surrounding rock because they were pushed to their present location by glaciers) are found in the Preserve.

HIKE: In *Erratic Wandering: An Explorer's Hiking Guide to Astonishing Boulders in Maine, New Hampshire and Vermont* (2018), Massachusetts-based photographer and explorer Christy Butler writes, "*From the parking area, a painted blue-blazed 1.0-mle-loop trail readily allows a hike which will pass by some classic New England stone walls, remarkable stone ledges, and between some massive glacial erratic boulders.*" If you love large rocks, this Preserve has it all.

We will assume that you follow the blue-blazed loop trail counter-clockwise, leaving the best for last. The hike takes you along the base of some high cliffs, one of which is over 100 feet long and 25 feet high. For purposes of a GPS listing, we have given it the name "High Wall."

At the end of this extended high rock wall, pay attention, for the blue-blazed trail makes an acute turn here, almost doubling back momentarily.

Soon, the trail takes you to another area of towering rock, where a small shelter cave can be seen on the right side of the rock formation. Look for a

crevice in the rock that can be climbed up and into a tiny rock-created room. Hikers have put branches on top of this space to make it feel even roomier.

All in all, this part of the hike goes through a very dynamic area, filled with hillocks of rock and ledges, and plenty of interesting places for children to explore or play hide-and-go-seek.

Continuing, you will pass by an orange-blazed trail that comes in on your left.

For the next 0.4 mile or so, the hike becomes fairly straight-forward with no surprises until you come to a noticeable spur path on your right that leads in 50 feet to the stone foundation of a former house.

Continuing on the main trail, you will pass by the orange-blazed trail as it re-enters on your left.

From here, the path, now more road-like, passes between two large boulders in <0.1 mile. One is a large, 15-foot-high split rock; the other is an enormous, 20-foot-high boulder that is even larger and longer than the split rock.

Continue for another 0.1 mile back to the parking area.

HISTORY: The 108-acre Kenyon Hill Preserve, owned by the Great Works Regional Land Trust, was established in 2002. In addition to enormous granite boulders, two foundations and a dug well are evident.

Boulderers (rock-climbers who scale boulders) frequent the Preserve and have given names to four of the large rocks—*Pyramid Boulder* (GPS: 43.261, -70.681), *The Clubhouse* (GPS: 43.26, -70.682), *Two and a half Bouldermen* (GPS: 43.261, -70.68), and *Batman's Lair* (GPS: 43.261, -70.681), the huge cliff face. This information was obtained from the Mountain Project website, https://www.mountainproject.com/area/120402887/kenyon-hill- preserve.

Note: This is just one of eighteen (and counting) preserves overseen/protected by the Great Works Regional Land Trust (https://gwrlt.org/preserves/).

ADDITIONAL GREAT WORKS REGIONAL LAND TRUST PRESERVES::

- Newichawannock Woods (83 acres), 76 Route 236, Berwick, ME; GPS: 43.261772, -70.846736

- Keay Brook Preserve (102 acres), 251 Hubbard Road, Berwick, ME; GPS: 43.307377, -70.901057

- Goodwin Forest (81 acres), 870 Goodwin Road/Route 101, Eliot, ME; GPS: 43.168500, -70.801780

- Douglas Memorial Woods (25 acres), 1412 State Road, Eliot, ME; GPS: 43.127024, -70.795543

- Grant Meadow at Beaver Dam Heath (181-acre), Diamonds Hill Road, North Berwick, ME; GPS: 43.308, -70.79

- Tatnic Woods Preserve (26 acres), 2460 Tatnic Road, Wells, ME; GPS: 43.283133, -70.691538

- Perkinstown Common (289 acres), Thompson Road cul-de-sac off Perry Road, Wells, ME; GPS: 43.325433, -70.701683

- Desrochers Memorial Forest (135 acres), Town Forest Road, South Berwick, ME; GPS: 43.249806, -70.761329

- Rocky Hills Preserve (200 acres), Punkintown Road, South Berwick, ME; GPS: 43.198327, -70.791451

- Savage Wildlife Preserve (26 acres), 15 Dover-Eliot Road, South Berwick, ME; GPS: 43.182816, -70.815128

- Payeur Preserve (35 acres), Spring Hill Road, Ogunquit, ME; GPS: 43.249876, -70.616948

- Bauneg Beg Mountain Conservation Area (89 acres), 281 Fox Farm Hill Road, North Berwick, ME; GPS: 43.394330, -70.781838

- Grover-Herrick Preserve (52 acres), West Fifth Street, North Berwick, ME; GPS: 43.371176, -70.743653

- Negutaquet Conservation Area (100 acres), 219 Lebanon Road, North Berwick, ME; GPS: 43.319814, -70.753234

ORRIS FALLS CONSERVATION AREA
Great Works Regional Land Trust

LOCATION: South Berwick (York County)

MAINE ATLAS & GAZETTEER: Map 2, E4

GPS PARKING: *Emerys Bridge Road*—43.268615, -70.700362; *Thurrell Road*—43.279867, -70.720246

GPS DESTINATIONS: *Orris Falls*—43.275697, -70.711345 (Google Earth); *Great Balancing Rock of Tatnic*—43.271000, -70.701750; *Split Rock* -43.270944, -70.700361; *Tatnic Ledges*—43.273096, -70.702689 (Google Earth); *Big Bump*—43.279442, -70.710022; *Littlefield Homestead foundation*—43.276174, -70.710943; *Lachance Point*—Not taken; *Orris cemetery*—43.275514, -70.711581

HOURS: Dawn to dusk

FEE: None

RESTRICTIONS: Be respectful of property boundaries along the right-of-way that crosses private lands; dogs must be leashed at all times

ACCESSIBILITY:

From Emerys Bridge Road—*Balanced Rock & Split Rock area*—0.4-mile hike; *Tatnic Ledges*—0.7-mile hike; *Littlefield Homestead Foundation*—>1.0 mile; *Orris Falls*—1.1-mile hike; *Big Bump*—1.4-mile hike; *Thurrell Road*—1.8-mile hike

From Thurrell Road—*Littlefield Homestead Foundation*—0.7-mile hike; *Orris Falls*—<0.8-mile hike; *Balanced Rock & Split Rock area*—1.4 mile-hike; *Emerys Bridge Road*—1.8-mile hike

DEGREE OF DIFFICULTY: Moderate

ADDITIONAL INFORMATION: *Orris Falls Conservation Area: Emerys Bridge entrance*—551 Emerys Bridge Road, South Berwick, ME 03908; *Thurrell Road entrance*—100 Thurrell Road, South Berwick, ME 03908

Trail map—https://www.mainetrailfinder.com/ trails/trail/ orris-falls-conservation-area

DIRECTIONS: *Emerys Bridge Road parking*—From the center of Ogunquit (junction of U.S. 1/Main Street, Shore Road & Beach Street), drive north on U.S. 1/Main Street for 0.1 mile and turn left onto Berwick Road, heading northwest on Berwick Road/Ogunquit Road for ~5.5 miles. Turn left onto Emerys Bridge Road and proceed southwest for 0.7 mile (passing by the old parking entrance at 0.4 mile). Then turn right into the new parking area.

Thurrell Road Parking—Instead of turning left onto Emerys Bridge Road, continue northwest on what is now Boyds Corner Road for another ~1.4 miles. When you come to Thurrell Road, turn left and head southwest for >0.7 mile to 100 Thurrell Road. The tiny parking area is on your left.

DESCRIPTION: *Balanced Rock, aka Great Balancing Rock of Tatnic*—In "Maine Geologic Facts and Localities April 2012: Orris Falls Conservation Area and the Great Balancing Rock of Tatnic"—a 19-page paper written by Thomas K. Weddle for the Maine Geological Survey, Department of Agriculture, Conservation & Forestry—the author writes: *"Balancing Rock is noteworthy for several reasons; it is a large stone (20x12x15 feet in dimensions) and it is a perched boulder. Also, its shape is distinctive; glacial geologists would call it a 'bullet stone' in reference to its shape. It is believed that as the bullet stone was transported in the ice, the ice flowed from the smooth, narrow end toward the thicker blunt end. The deposition of the stone from the ice occurred later, when the ice in the region was wasting away. The final resting position of the stone may have had less to do with ice flow, and more likely was controlled by local ice-stagnation and down wasting at the glacier*

margin when the front of the ice sheet was positioned at the southern edge of the Tatnic Hills, about 15,500 years ago."

For the sake of contrast, the largest boulder in Maine is the 25-foot-high, 30-foot-wide, 100-foot-long Daggett Rock (44.848373, -70.304900) that is estimated to weigh 8,000 tons. It is located off of Wheeler Hill Road in Phillips, farther north.

Split Rock is a massive, 14-foot-high glacial boulder that has split into two large halves with a gap in between wide enough to walk through.

Orris Falls is a 12-foot-high cascade formed in an impressively steep, 90-foot-deep gorge on a tiny tributary of Boyd Brook and the Great Works River. This is a seasonal waterfall and best viewed in the early spring or following bouts of heavy rainfall.

Big Bump is a huge outcrop made of igneous rock that overlooks beaver-created wetlands to the east.

Tatnic Ledges consist of a ledge overlook.

HIKE: *Emerys Bridge Road approach*—The directions given here start from the new Emerys Bridge Road parking area. Follow the orange-blazed trail for 0.5 mile, initially through a right-of-way, to an area flush with glacial erratics (rocks moved by glaciers), including Balancing Rock and Split Rock. Balancing Rock can be reached by its own loop trail, to your left, indicated by a sign that states, simply, "balancing rock."

From Balancing Rock, continue northwest for another >0.2 mile to reach the Tatnic Ledges Lookout, on your left. You will see a wide spur path on your left that loops to the Tatnic Ledges Lookout and back to the main trail. Unless the foliage is sparse, you will probably see very little.

Resume your course northwest, immediately passing by a unique looking, 10-foot-high boulder on your left, and then heading downhill. Eventually, you will see a body of water to your right. The trail turns sharply left here and soon

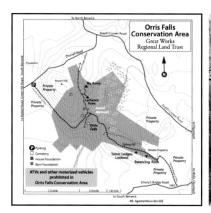

crosses a tiny creek. In another moment, a footbridge takes you over the outlet stream from the pond you had earlier glimpsed. Beavers have created a small dam next to the footbridge. As soon as you cross over the footbridge, turn left at a sign that states "Orris Falls" onto a short trail that takes you south, following the stream as it begins to deepen into a gorge. In >0.05 mile, a path to your left takes you down into the gorge to the top of Orris Falls.

There appears to be no obvious or easy way to get down to the base of the falls from this side of the gorge for a head-on shot, so, hopefully, you will be satisfied with the view from the top.

Return to the top of the gorge. Just ahead is a bench that overlooks the gorge. If you reach this bench, then you have gone too far.

Return to the main trail. In 100 feet you will see, to your right, an informational plaque that provides details about the Littlefield Homestead, as well a photograph of the house. Directly behind the historical marker are the foundation ruins of the old homestead, which are surprisingly intact and extensive.

The homestead is at the junction of the main road/trail (an old colonial road), and a second road/trail. Turn right, passing by the homestead foundations on your right and the barn foundation on your left, which lies virtually opposite the homestead.

Big Bump—Continue on this road/trail for 0.3 mile. Disregard the first trail to your right that takes you up to Big Bump on an impossibly steep trail. In another several hundred feet, you will come to a second spur path on your right that takes you uphill to the top of Big Bump gently. Be prepared for limited views unless the foliage is sparse.

Return to the junction by the homestead foundation. If you continue straight ahead, the trail will take you past the old Littlefield Cemetery on your right, where Daniel, Mercy, Eunice, and Henrietta Littlefield are buried, and eventually to the Thurrell Road Parking area.

Thurrell Road approach—The hike from Thurrell Road is a much easier approach than from Emerys Bridge Road if your goal is to visit only Orris Falls and the homestead ruins. Follow the wide, old woods road southeast for >0.6 mile. You will come to a junction fronted by a large sign. The main road, marked with orange blazes, leads to the left and takes you past the Orris cemetery and then to the central junction where Orris's homestead was located. From here, it is a quick jaunt to the waterfall by following the trail leading down from the pond to the cascade.

The blue-blazed trail to your right, sponsored by Carol West, takes you along Orris Falls Gorge and past the waterfall. Both the orange-blazed and blue-blazed routes to the waterfall are approximately the same length.

If you wish to see the Balancing Rock, cross the footbridge spanning the pond's outlet scream and proceed southeast on the main trail for ~0.7 mile. Look for a sign on your right indicating the spur path loop to Balancing Rock.

HISTORY: The 213-acre Orris Falls Conservation Area in the Tatnic region of South Berwick contains a number of impressive boulders as well as a medium-sized waterfall contained in a 90-foot-deep gorge. Conservation efforts began in 1999.

The Tatnic Ledges is a 15-acre parcel that connects the Orris Falls parcel with the Balancing Rock parcel.

Orris Falls is named for Orris & Mercy Littlefield, who lived here in the late nineteenth century. The stone foundations of their home and barn have survived the passage of time and stand next to the trail heading towards Big Bump and Lachance Point.

ELROY DAY CANOE LAUNCH

LOCATION: North Berwick (York County)

MAINE ATLAS & GAZETTEER: Map 2, E4

GPS PARKING: 43.309779, -70.734488

GPS LAUNCH SITE: 43.310317, -70.735151

HOURS: Dawn to dusk

FEE: None

ACCESSIBILITY: 250-foot carry to put-in

ADDITIONAL INFORMATION: Elroy Day Canoe Launch, Great Works Estate Road, North Berwick, ME 03906

DIRECTIONS: From the center of Ogunquit (junction of U.S. 1/Main Street, Shore Road & Beach Street), drive north on U.S. 1/Main Street for 0.1 mile, turn left onto Berwick Road/Ogunquit Road/Boyds Corner Road/Main Street, and head northwest. After ~9.0 miles, you will reach North Berwick.

Turn right onto Wells Street/Route 9 and proceed northeast for 0.2 mile. When you come to Great Works Estates Road (unnamed) opposite Burma Road, turn left at the sign for Pratt & Whitney and the Elroy Day Canoe Launch and drive northwest for 0.1 mile. Finally, bear left onto a dirt road that leads to the parking area in 100 feet.

From the parking area, carry your watercraft 250 feet to the dock put-in on the Great Works River.

PADDLE: *Downstream*—It is only possible to paddle downstream for 0.3 mile before approaching the Great Works River Reservoir and dam, where the Johnson Monument Company is located. It is the dam that backs up enough water to make paddling on this part of the Great Works River possible.

Upstream—Heading upstream provides more options. In >0.1 mile, you will come to a fork. Bearing right takes you east on West Brook for 0.4 mile to the dam at Pratt & Whitney (a company that designs, manufactures and services aircraft engines and auxiliary power units). Along the way, you will pass under two bridges, one that leads to a private residence and the other along the Great Works Estates Road.

Bearing left takes you farther north up the Great Works River towards a remote, forested area.

HISTORY: *The Great Works River* is a ~24.5-mile-long river that rises west of Sanford and flows generally south to its confluence with the Salmon Falls River, earlier called Hog Point Brook. The Great Works River's unusual name comes from a 1651 sawmill that operated on the river with 20 saws. The mill was called the "Great Mills Workes," a name, later foreshortened, that came to be applied to the river. In *History of York County, Maine: with illustrations and biographical sketches of its prominent men and pioneers* (1880), W. Woodford Clayton expands a bit on what the Great Works were like. "*Great Works is a factory hamlet of thirty buildings, surrounded by a broken but well-improved farming community. There are here the factory of the Newichawannock Company...*" Clayton mentions that the hamlet is "*...about a mile above the confluence with the Piscataqua...The total fall is 60 feet, divided in its descent into three pitches, by as many dams...At the lower dam stands the brick mill, 40 by 80 feet, five stories high, built in 1859; and a few rods [1 rod = 16.5 feet] above, at the next dam, is the other mill, of wood, 30 by 130 feet, two stories high, built in 1860. Ten sets of machinery are in operation.*" (GPS: 43.219338, -70.797039).

The Preserve is named for Elroy Kenneth Day who was born in South Berwick in 1913 and died in 2000.

West Brook is a tributary of the Great Works River, rising in the hills northeast of North Berwick.

HACKMATACK FARM PLAYHOUSE

LOCATION: Berwick (York County)

MAINE ATLAS & GAZETTEER: Map 2, E3

GPS PARKING: 43.288892, -70.787603

GPS HACKMATACK PLAYHOUSE: 43.288375, -70.787119

HOURS: Consult website, https://www.hackmatackplayhouse.org, for performances and showtime

FEE: Admission charged

ADDITIONAL INFORMATION: Hackmatack Playhouse, 538 School Street/Route 9, Berwick, ME 03901; (207) 698-1807; www.hackmatack.org

DIRECTIONS: From the center of Ogunquit (junction of U.S. 1/Main Street, Shore Road & Beach Street), drive north on U.S. 1/Main Street for 0.1 mile, turn left onto Berwick Road/Ogunquit Road/Boyds Corner Road/Lower Main Street, and head northwest. After ~9.0 miles, you will reach North Berwick. Turn left onto Route 9/Wells Street and proceed southwest for 0.1 mile.

Then bear left onto Route 4/9/Elm Street and head southwest for <0.5 mile. Turn right onto Route 9/Somersworth Road, go southwest for 2.7 miles, and then left into the parking area for the Hackmatack Farm Playhouse.

DESCRIPTION: The Hackmatack Farm Playhouse is a summer stock theater located on a working farm that showcases the talents of regional professionals and developing thespians.

HISTORY: The Hackmatack Farm Playhouse was founded in 1972 by Samuel Carleton Guptill. It is presently owned and run by Michael Guptill.

The Guptills have been associated with this land since the mid-1600s when Thomas Guptill (then spelled Gubtail) erected a log house on the property.

The present farmhouse was constructed in 1716 and then modified and remodeled several times since. The large barn that houses the theater is not the original, which burned down after being struck by lightning in 1934. The replacement barn already existed and was owned by a neighbor on the opposite side of Somersworth Road. Lewis Guptill (Samuel Guptill's farther) purchased the barn, put it on rollers, and then managed to maneuver the 54-foot-long, 42-foot-wide structure across the road to its present location. It took three days to accomplish the feat.

After the barn was repurposed as a theater in 1972, an addition was added to the back and the packed-earthen floor was replaced by a cement surface. Today, the theater can seat up to 218 guests.

The word Hackmatack is a botanical one, referring to several types of North American conifers, particularly tamaracks.

{6}

SOUTH BERWICK AREA

South Berwick was set off from Berwick in 1814. It was first settled by Europeans ~1631. At that time, the area was known as *Newichawannock*, an Abenaki name for "river with many falls," an apt description of the Salmon Falls River.

Berwick was named for Berwick-upon-Tweed, England.

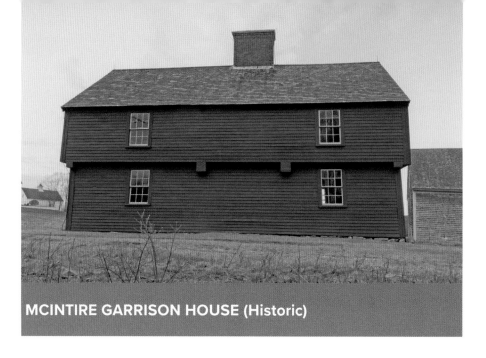

MCINTIRE GARRISON HOUSE (Historic)

LOCATION: Southeast of South Berwick (York County)

MAINE ATLAS & GAZETTEER: Map 1, AB4

GPS MCINTIRE GARRISON HOUSE: 43.167909, -70.712895

ACCESSIBILITY: Privately owned; not accessible to the public; visible from roadside

ADDITIONAL INFORMATION: McIntyre Garrison House, 274 Cider Hill Road, York, ME 03909

DIRECTIONS: From the center of Ogunquit (junction of U.S. 1/Main Street, Shore Road & Beach Street), drive south on U.S. 1 for ~8.5 miles (or 0.7 mile past right turn to Maine Turnpike/I-95 entrance), turn right at a traffic intersection onto Route 91/Cedar Hill Road, and proceed northwest for ~2.6 miles. The McIntyre Garrison House is on your left, opposite Harriets Way.

DESCRIPTION: The McIntire Garrison House dates to c. 1707 and is considered to be one of the oldest houses in Maine.

HISTORY: The McIntire Garrison House, located on the bank of the York River, was built by John McIntire, the son of Micum McIntire, a Scottish highlander who was deported to America by Oliver Cromwell for his role in the 1650 Battle of Dunbar. The garrison was made of 9-inch milled logs, dovetailed at the joints to make them impervious to weathering (a technique introduced by the Scots). It also made the house virtually impregnable in the event of an attack by Native Americans.

In *New England Miniature: A History of York, Maine* (1961), George Ernst writes, "*Farther on, in Scotland, stood the McIntire garrison for seven families and one soldier, or thirty-five souls.*" In such unsettled times, you had to be ready for anything, including protecting your neighbors.

The garrison may also have been known as the Scottish Garrison.

Between 1908 and 1909, the house underwent extensive restoration. The exterior was overlaid with clapboard and shingle sheathing, the windows were double hung, and a new chimney was installed. Still, the basic structure of the house, with its second-story overhang and unadorned façade, remain unchanged.

The second story's conspicuous overhang is a throwback to Medieval Europe, where overhangs were intentionally done to compensate for the crowded, narrow streets below.

The house was designated a National Historic Landmark in 1968. A photograph of the house can be seen in James Phinney Baxter's *Agamenticus, Bristol, Georgiana, York* (1904).

There is some ongoing debate that the garrison may have had an even earlier origin. The American Forts website *northamericanforts.com* contends that the house was constructed sometime between 1660 and 1690 by Alexander Maxwell and that upon his death, John McIntire, a neighbor, acquired the property.

The McIntyre Garrison was by no means the only garrison in York. In the *History of York Maine. Vol. 2* (1935), Charles Edward Banks lists several other garrisons: Alcock's Garrison (<1609), named for Captain Jacob Alcock; Preble's Garrison (1691), named for Lieutenant Abraham Preble; Harmon's Garrison (1692), named for John Harmon or his father; Norton's Garrison (? date), named for George Norton; and Junkins Garrison (~1700), possibly named for Robert Junkins and which was one of the last overhanging houses of its time.

HAMILTON HOUSE & GARDENS

LOCATION: South Berwick (York County)

MAINE ATLAS & GAZETTEER: Map 1, A3

GPS PARKING: *Hamilton House*—43.213977, -70.815352

GPS DESTINATIONS: *Hamilton House*—43.212956, -70.81553125; *Goodwin Barn*—43.213234, -70.814880; *Visitor Center/ Garden Cottage*—43.212863, -70.814629; *Covered well*—43.213200, -70.815159; *Cemetery on hill*—43.214828, -70.812402; *Dock on river*—43.213654, -70.816642

HOURS: *House*—Open seasonally from June—October; Check website, historicnewengland.org/property/hamilton-house, for details; *Land*—Daily, dawn to dusk

FEE: *Grounds*—free; *Hamilton House*—admission charged to tour house

ADDITIONAL INFORMATION: Hamilton House, 40 Vaughans Lane, South Berwick ME 03908; (207) 384-2454

DIRECTIONS: From the center of Ogunquit (junction of U.S. 1/Main Street, Shore Road & Beach Street), drive south on U.S. 1 for ~8.5 miles (or 0.7 mile past right turn to Maine Turnpike/I-95 entrance), turn right at a traffic intersection onto Route 91, and head northwest for >7.5 miles. When you come to Route 236, cross over the road and continue west on Old South Road for <1.0 mile. Then turn left onto Brattle Street/Vaughans Lane, proceed west for 0.5 mile and park to your left before reaching the estate.

From the parking area, walk south for 0.05 mile to reach the Visitor Center, grounds, and the Hamilton House.

To dock on Salmon Falls River—From the parking area, follow a path southwest from the lower road for 250 feet to reach the long dock, from where watercraft can be launched or received.

To Vaughan Woods State Park from the Hamilton House—From the south side of the gardens (GPS: 43.212792, -70.814960), follow a 0.2-mile-long path that leads southeast from the Hamilton House grounds to the Vaughan Woods State Park, coming out near where the breached dam on Hamilton Brook is located.

DESCRIPTION: Overlooking the Salmon Falls River, this c. 1785 Georgian mansion, was built for merchant Jonathan Hamilton in the eighteenth century, farmed by the Goodwin family in the nineteenth century, and then restored as a summer retreat in the twentieth century.

Today, Hamilton House reflects the occupancy of the Tyson family in the early twentieth century.

HIGHLIGHTS:

- Elegant eighteenth-century house
- Sweeping views of Salmon Falls River
- Historic gardens
- Contiguous with Vaughan Woods State Park

WALK: Enjoy a stroll through the Colonial Revival grounds, including a perennial garden, a sundial and marble fountain, enclosed garden rooms and views of the Salmon Falls River, an iconic elm tree, and more.

If you wish to do an additional walk, you can connect with the adjacent Vaughan Woods State Park Trails see next chapter].

HISTORY: Jonathan Hamilton was born in South Berwick in 1745. Starting off in poverty, he worked his way up as a trader in salt fish and then, applying a keen sense for business, purchased forests in Lebanon (the westernmost town in Maine). This was followed by the purchase of mill rights in Quamphegan and at the Chadbourne mill on the Great Works River. From there, Hamilton hit his full stride when he expanded his business into shipbuilding and amassed a fortune.

Following Jonathan Hamilton's death in 1802, the house was occupied by Hamilton's sons for a short period. Sometime between 1811 and 1815, Hamilton's daughter and son-in-law, Olive and Joshua Haven, purchased the property from the sons.

It was next owned by Nathan Folsom as an investment property during which time the home was likely leased out.

In 1839, the property was purchased by Alpheus and Betsy Goodwin who farmed the land during the nineteenth century and raised sheep. The Goodwin barn (the first building encountered as you approach the estate), was originally located next to the house.

In 1898, Bostonian Emily Davis Tyson and her stepdaughter, Elise Tyson Vaughan, acquired the property after being introduced to it by Sarah Orne Jewett. They restored the house, which had gone into decline, and created the colonial, revival-style perennial gardens, which today are used for weddings and special occasions. The restoration work was done by Herbert C. W. Browne and Arthur Little. The Tysons also had the Goodwin Barn moved away from the house to its present location.

When Emily died in 1922, the estate was inherited by Elise, who bequeathed the land in 1938 to the Society for the preservation of New England Antiquities (today, called Historic New England).

As a point of interest, Sarah Orne Jewett [see chapter on the Sarah Orne Jewett House Museum] made the Hamilton House and the Piscataqua River the setting for her 1901 novel, *The Tory Lover*.

Salmon Falls River—Per Ava Harriet Chadbourne in her 1970 *Maine's Place Names and Peopling of its Towns*, *"Salmon Falls River was named from the abundance of salmon there."*

VAUGHAN WOODS
Vaughan Woods State Park

LOCATION: South Berwick (York County)

MAINE ATLAS & GAZETTEER: Map 1, A3

GPS PARKING: *Lower*—43.212010, -70.812506; *Upper*— 43.212184, -70.809204

GPS DESTINATIONS: *Breached dam*—43.212137, -70.814255; *Site of Warren House*—43.204267, -70.816014

HOURS: *Vaughan Woods*—Daily, 9:00 a.m. to sunset.

FEE: During regular season, a modest entrance fee is charged. For further details, consult https://www.maine.gov/dacf/parks/park_passes_fees_rules/park_day_use_fees.shtml

ADDITIONAL INFORMATION: Vaughan Woods State Park, 28 Oldfields Road, South Berwick ME 03908; (207) 384-5160; off season (207) 490-4079 c/o the Lyman Forestry Office

The Audubon Society Field Guide to the Natural Places of the Northeast: Coastal by Stephen Kulik, Pete Salmansohn, Matthew Schmidt and Heidi Welch provides extensive information about the variety of trees that populate Vaughan Woods.

A seasonal restroom is located by the lower parking area.

Dogs must be kept on leash.

Trail map—https://www.maine.gov/dacf/parks/docs/maps/vaughan-woodstrailmap.pdf Note: first Google *"Old Gatc,, ,' Home Site(Rest Rooms Group Picnic ..."* to reach site

DIRECTIONS: From the center of Ogunquit (junction of U.S. 1/Main Street, Shore Road & Beach Street), drive south on U.S. 1 for ~8.5 miles (or 0.7 mile past right turn to Maine Turnpike/I-95 entrance), turn right at a traffic intersection onto Route 91, and head northwest for ~7.5 miles. When you come to Route 236, cross over the road and continue west on Old South Road for <1.0 mile.

From the junction of Old South Road and Brattle Street, turn left onto Brattle Street/Vaughans Lane, go west for <0.2 mile and then left onto Oldfields Road. Head southeast for 0.2 mile, turn right into Park entrance, and proceed west for 0.1 mile. The parking is sufficient for 40–50 cars.

If you are arriving during off-season, park by the road and walk in.

DESCRIPTION: Vaughan Woods State Park, aka Vaughan Woods Memorial State Park, consists of a number of hiking trails, one which follows next to the Salmon Falls River, in a historic area that is associated with the adjacent Hamilton House.

HIGHLIGHTS:

- Salmon Falls River
- Old stands of pine and hemlock
- Breached dam on Hamilton Brook
- Site of James Warren's home

HIKE: A number of hikes can be taken by combining the two main trails with secondary paths that connect the two longer trails:

River Walk Trail (0.8 mile)—The River Walk Trail follows along the Salmon Falls River, going north/south, with five scenic overlooks—Hamilton House View, Deacon Seat, White Oak Point View, Cow Cove View, and Trail End View. A number of boardwalk footbridges are crossed, several over dry gullies. Benches are strategically placed along the way.

The hike is not difficult, but the trail does consistently take you up and down, and hikers need to be mindful of roots that can easily catch the toe of your boot.

From the first lookout, there is a wonderful view of the Hamilton House fronted by a shallow cove of water.

The trail ends where a sign states "Please respect Park limits. Trail ends." At this point, bears left as the trail becomes the Bridle Path.

Bridle Path Trail (0.7 mile)—This path takes you through majestic old growth pine and hemlock as it goes north/south. It passes by a wooden plaque that marks the spot where James Warren, a Scot, lived after completing his indentured servitude. Look for a cellar hole and crumbling gravestones. A little imagination may be helpful here. The area behind the marker is flat and there are a couple of stones that could be construed as grave markers.

An onsite marker states, "*Site of first dwelling and family burial ground of James Warren. Born in Scotland 1620/1 a covenanter. Came to America in 1655 as a prisoner taken at Battle of Dunbar. Settled here on Kittery grant with wife Margaret 1656. A valued citizen died 1702. Tablet presented to the State of Maine by Warren descendants. 1968.*"

The Bridle Path Trail is more level, wider and less rooted than the River Walk Trail, and therefore easier to hike along. On the downside, there are no views of the river. As the name of the trail suggests, it is also used by equestrians.

Hamilton House Trail—This short trail takes you northwest from the River Walk Trail to the Hamilton House [see chapter on the Hamilton House]. Look for two 6-foot-high stone pillars on each side of the trail to announce the start. The path passes by the bench overlooking the breached dam on Hamilton Brook, and then veers right and heads over towards the Hamilton House.

Connector Trails between the Bridle Path and River Walk Trail:

North end—Porcupine Path and Windy Walk.

Midway—Nubble Knoll

South end—Warren Way and Old Gate Trail.

HISTORY: *Vaughan Woods State Park*—The forest south of the Hamilton House was bequeathed to the state of Maine by Elizabeth (Tyson) Vaughan [see Hamilton House chapter] in 1949, which became the Vaughan Woods State Park. Elizabeth Vaughan, who was an accomplished horsewoman, loved the woods and would frequently ride through the forest.

Back in the 1600s, however, the landscape was much different than during Vaughan's time. Native Americans used fire to clear much of the land in order to grow beans, corn, and squash. When a section of land became infertile, they would move onto another section. The land abandoned would then slowly be reclaimed by brush, berry bushes and, finally, trees. By the early eighteenth century, the land was a patchwork of small hayfields, row crops, and pastures. Only three percent of what would become Vaughan Woods State Park was forested. Much of what you see today is a second growth forest.

According to the State Parks website, *https://www.stateparks.com/vaughan_woods_state_park_in_maine.html*, the Vaughan Woods State Park encompasses 250 acres.

It is said that the first cow in Maine was delivered to this area in 1634 by the ship, Pied Cow, at what is fittingly called Cow's Cove (GPS: 43.204588, -70.817422), 0.5 mile downriver from the Hamilton House. A photograph of the cove can be seen in Everett S. Stackpole's *Old Kittery and her Families* (1903).

Salmon Falls River is a 38-mile-long tributary of the Piscataqua River, which rises from the Great East Lake, Newichawannock Canal, and Horn Pond, in the process forming the boundary between York County, Maine, and Strafford County, New Hampshire.

The river is named for the abundance of salmon it once had. The Abenaki called the river *Newichawannock*, meaning "river with many falls."

James Warren was born in Scotland in 1620 and came to America in 1651 as an indentured servant of Richard Leader. During Warren's time of required service, he helped construct the sawmill at the nearby falls on the Great Works River (43.219381, -70.797269). Upon ending his term of indenture, Warren was given 50 acres of land, now part of the Vaughan Woods State Park. Warren is buried in the James Warren Cemetery.

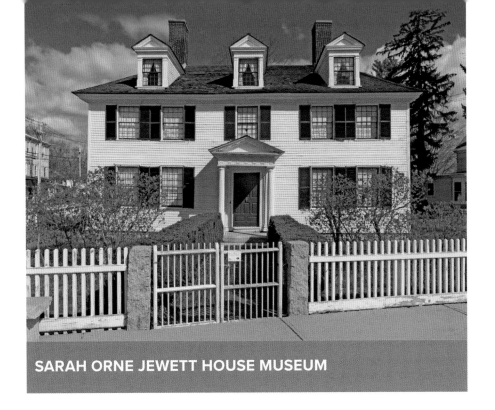

SARAH ORNE JEWETT HOUSE MUSEUM

LOCATION: South Berwick (York County)

MAINE ATLAS & GAZETTEER: Map 1, A3

GPS PARKING: Roadside along Main Street or Portland Street

GPS SARAH ORNE JEWETT HOUSE: 43.234761, -70.808957

HOURS: Open seasonally from June—October; consult website, https://www.historicnewengland.org/property /sarah-orne-jewett-house-museum-and-visitor-center, for details

FEE: Admission charged

ADDITIONAL INFORMATION: Sarah Orne Jewett House, 5 Portland Road, South Berwick, ME 03908; (207) 384-2454

DIRECTIONS: From the center of Ogunquit (junction of U.S. 1/Main Street, Shore Road & Beach Street), drive south on U.S. 1 for ~8.5 miles (or 0.7 mile past right turn to Maine Turnpike/I-95 entrance), turn right at the traffic intersection onto Route 91, and head northwest for ~7.5 miles. When you come to Route 236, bear right and proceed northwest for <1.8 miles. Turn right onto Route 4, still following Route 236, for another 0.2 mile. The Jewett House is at the intersection of Routes 296/Main Street & Route 4/Portland Street, an intersection that historically has been known as "The Corner."

Park on the side of Route 296/Main Street or on Route 4/Portland Street.

DESCRIPTION & HISTORY: The historic site encompasses two homes. The first was Captain Theodore F. Jewett's Georgian-style home, located in the center of South Berwick at the busy crossroads of Main Street and Portland Street. The house was built in 1774 by John Haggens, a successful merchant and veteran of the French and Indian War. The Jewetts initially rented the house from Haggens and then purchased it in 1831. Theodore Jewett, a merchant ship owner, would later become Sarah's grandfather.

The second home was built next door at 5 Portland Street by Theodore Herman Jewett—a country doctor and Captain Jewett's son—as the size of the extended family grew. Dr. Jewett and his family, including Sarah and her older sister, Mary, moved into the Greek Revival house in 1854. Members could move between the two houses, which Sarah and her sibling most certainly did. As for Dr. Jewett, W. Woodford Clayton, in *History of York County* (1880), writes that "*T. H. Jewett, M.D., became a professor in a medical college and an eminent practitioner.*"

In 1887, Sarah and Mary inherited their grandparents' home and moved back into it. It was Mary who lived in the family house most of the time while Sarah, an established writer by then, lived part of the year in Boston with her life-long partner, Annie Fields. Still, Jewett returned for several months each

year to the South Berwick home she loved. Many of Jewett's novels were written in and inspired by the house, and her bedroom study has been left just the way she last arranged it. Upon Mary's death in 1930, she left the house to Historic New England, a regional preservation organization that was founded in 1910. The Sarah Orne Jewett House was designated a National Historic Monument in 1991 for its association with the famous author. A photograph of the house can be seen in *Maine's Historic Places: Properties of the National Register of Historic Places* (1982) by Frank A. Beard and Bette A. Smith.

Theodore Jewett Eastman, Sarah Orne Jewett's nephew, donated both houses to Historic New England. Today, the house is a visitor center, gift shop, meeting place, and a space for programs.

SARAH ORNE JEWETT & MARY RICE JEWETT: *Sarah Orne Jewett* was a Victorian-era writer who published her first short story, "Jenny Garrow's Lovers," in 1868 when she was 19. She began writing under the pseudonym, Alice Eliot, but had discarded that nom de plume for her own by the time she had submitted her first offering to the *Atlantic Monthly* in 1869. Her first novel, *Deephaven*, was published in 1877. During her lifetime, Sarah wrote many novels and short stories, generally set along the southern coast of Maine.

The book considered to be her masterpiece, *The Country of Pointed Firs*, was published in 1896. It brought to life, using much local color, what life was like in a coastal village in Maine.

In *Maine Immortals: including many unique characters in early Maine history* (1932), William D. Spencer writes that "the outstanding characteristics of [Jewett's] inimitable style are simplicity and respondent personality."

Mary Rice Jewett was very involved in the community and church affairs of South Berwick, and it was there that she made her mark.

As a point of interest, she and Sarah were direct descendants of Mary Chilton, the first woman to set foot ashore when the Mayflower landed at Plymouth Rock.

{7}

WELLS AREA

Wells was incorporated in 1653, named for a small cathedral city in the county of Somerset, England. Edmund Littlefield, who built the first gristmill and, later, a woolen mill on the Webhannet River, is considered to be "The Father of Wells." *Webhannet*, is the Abenaki name for "at the clear stream."

Wells is the third oldest town in Maine. Although nicknamed "The friendliest town in Maine" this application truly applies to most of Maine.

The Wells Chamber of Commerce can be reached at 136 Post Road/U.S. 1, Moody, ME 04054; (207) 646-2451 or at https://www.wellschamber.org.

BEACH PLUM FARM
Great Works Regional Land Trust

LOCATION: Ogunquit (York County)

MAINE ATLAS & GAZETTEER: Map 2, E5

GPS PARKING: 43.262376, -70.597711

GPS SALT MARSH: 43.261080, -70.593687

HOURS: Daily, dawn to dusk

FEE: None

RESTRICTIONS: Regular Park rules & regulations apply

ACCESSIBILITY: 0.5-mile walk

DEGREE OF DIFFICULTY: Easy

ADDITIONAL INFORMATION: Beach Plum Farm, 610 Main Street, Ogunquit, ME 03907; (207) 646-3604; https://gwrlt.org

Trail map—https://www.mainetrailfinder.com/trails/trail/beach-plum-farm

Great Works Regional Land Trust, PO Box 151, South Berwick, ME 03908; (207) 646-3604

DIRECTIONS: From the center of Ogunquit (junction of U.S. 1/Main Street, Shore Road & Beach Street), drive north on U.S. 1/Main Street for <1.0 mile. Turn right onto Beach Plum Farm Road and park to your left after 100 feet, next to the Great Works Regional Land Trust headquarters.

DESCRIPTION: The 22-acre Beach Plum Farm is the last remaining saltwater farm in Ogunquit. It presently serves as the headquarters of the Great Works Regional Land Trust.

WALK: The 0.5-mile-long-loop hike takes you past several old barns on your right and a large community garden on your left as you make your way towards the Ogunquit River through a 0.1-mile-wide open corridor. Along the way, depending upon the season, you will see numerous beach plum bushes (for which the Preserve is named), bayberry bushes, and a variety of field grasses and flowers.

Near the end is a small, circular, cleared area. From here, a 20-foot-long path leads to a tiny tributary of the Ogunquit River. There are great views of the Ogunquit River, its barrier dunes, and houses and camps in the near distance on both sides of the Preserve. Littlefield Village, named for David M. Littlefield Sr. who established a campground here in 1925, is on the south side of Plum Beach Farm.

Cross over to the north side of the field and follow the trail west as it leads along the edge of narrow woods that separate the farm from homes along Riverbank Road. Walk south past the community gardens and return to the parking area, making a complete circuit.

Plum Beach Farm is said to be the only place that you can see the dunes and ocean from U.S 1.

HISTORY: Beginning in the 1920s, the land was farmed by Roby Perkins Littlefield, who sold vegetables from his property. Littlefield later helped develop a tradition of community gardening in the area and became a vigorous conservationist when Ogunquit Beach was threatened by developers [see chapter on Ogunquit Beach]. The middle barn on the property houses the Roby Littlefield Museum.

The property was donated to the Great Works Regional Land Trust by Littlefield's nephew, Joe Douglas Littlefield.

Great Works Regional Land Trust—The Land Trust, which formed in 1986, has conserved over 7,000 acres (and counting) of natural, agricultural, and historic lands in southern Maine, which includes the Berwicks, Eliot, Ogunquit, and Wells.

MOODY FALLS

LOCATION: Wells (York County)

MAINE ATLAS & GAZETTEER: Map 2, E5

GPS PARKING: 43.271295, -70.597444

GPS MOODY FALLS: 43.271179, -70.596991

ACCESSIBILITY: 50-foot-walk

DEGREE OF DIFFICULTY: Easy

ADDITIONAL INFORMATION: Ogunquit River Inn (Ascend Hotels Collection), 17 Post Road, Wells, ME 04090; (207) 261-0947

World Within Sea Kayaking, 17 Post Road (at Ogunquit River Inn), Wells, ME 04090; (207) 646-0455

DIRECTIONS: From the center of Ogunquit (junction of U.S. 1/Main Street, Shore Road & Beach Street), drive north on U.S. 1 for ~1.5 miles. Turn right at the Ogunquit River Inn and park to your right.

DESCRIPTION: Moody Falls is a two-tiered, 8-10-foot-high waterfall formed on the Ogunquit River. From the base of the falls, the river is tidal all the way to the Atlantic Ocean in Ogunquit.

A photograph of the waterfall in heavy flow can be seen in Charles Littlefield Seaman's *Ogunquit Maine, 1900–1971 in Pictures and Words.*

VIEW: *Top of falls*—The top of the fall can be viewed from the north bank, 50 feet from the southeast end of the parking lot by the Ogunquit River Inn's dining area, or from an observation deck overlooking the Ogunquit River behind the Ogunquit River Inn. Upstream, just before the U.S. 1 Bridge, can be seen old abutments from a bridge that once spanned the Ogunquit River.

Lateral views of the fall, at best, are partial. An old sluiceway chiseled out of the bedrock on the north side of the waterfall makes access problematic to nearly impossible if an overflow of water is spilling down the sluiceway.

Bottom of fall—The waterfall can also be viewed by kayaks, which can be rented from the "World Within Kayak Rentals" that operates from the inn. The best time to make the water trek is during high tide.

HISTORY: According to Esselyn Gilman Perkins, in her 1951 book *History of Ogunquit Village*, in 1650 Reverend John Wheelwright petitioned to build a sawmill on the "Falles of the Agunquat River." Other petitioners followed. In 1681, John Littlefield received a grant to build a sawmill on the Ogunquit River.

Later, John Marsters and Abraham Marsters were granted rights to build a sawmill on the upper part of the Ogunquit River.

The name Moody Falls appears in Patricia Hughes's 2009 book *Maine's Waterfalls: A Comprehensive Guide*. She describes it as *..a six-foot drop over a ledge."* Historically, the Moodys were early settlers who lived in the area, Samuel and Joseph perhaps being the most famous in the lineage. Moody Beach (43.276820, -70.580644) and Moody Point (43.285535, -70.570524) are further reminders of the Moody family's past.

On the south side of the Ogunquit River next to Moody Falls is Provision ME (756 Main Street), a catering business. The land is private.

CRESCENT BEACH

LOCATION: South of Wells (York County)

MAINE ATLAS & GAZETTEER: Map 3, E1

GPS PARKING: 43.293718, -70.568409

GPS BEACH ACCESS: 43.294641, -70.568110

GPS CRESCENT BEACH: 43.295175, -70.567938

HOURS: Dawn to dusk

FEE: *Parking*—fee charged; *Beach*—free

RESTRICTIONS: Regular Park rules & regulations apply

ACCESSIBILITY: 200-foot walk

ADDITIONAL INFORMATION: Crescent Beach, 210 Webhannet Drive, Wells, ME 04090 (general address)

Lifeguards are on duty during the summer daily from 9:00 a.m. to 5:00 p.m.

Dogs on leashes are allowed on the beach from 6:00 p.m. to 8:00 a.m. from June 16th through September 15th. During the off-season, dogs are allowed on the beach all day.

Porta potties are located behind bushes at the north end of the parking area.

DIRECTIONS: From the center of Ogunquit (junction of U.S. 1/Main Street, Shore Road & Beach Street), drive north on U.S. 1 for ~3.0 miles. Turn right onto Eldridge Road by the Beach Acre Campground and head east for 1.0 mile. When you come to Webhannet Drive, turn left and head northeast for 0.2 mile. There are limited "pay for parking" spaces available on your right just past Gold Ribbon Drive.

From the north end of the parking area, walk north along the side of Webhannet Drive for <200 feet and then down a cement stairway that leads immediately to the beach.

Slightly southeast of Crescent Beach, 0.2 mile away, is Bucklin Rock, aka Buckman Rocks, a rocky bar some 0.2 mile in length.

DESCRIPTION: Crescent Beach is named for its crescent shape. The beach is rocky in places and at high tide becomes completely covered when the ocean advances to the sea wall. Swimmers should take note of the rocky section of the beach farther out and be especially attentive if tidal currents are strong.

South of Crescent Beach is Fishermans Cove, which is essentially a rocky shoreline without a beach.

WEBHANNET FALLS
Webhannet Falls Park

LOCATION: Wells (York County)
MAINE ATLAS & GAZETTEER: Map 2, E5
GPS PARKING: 43.298333, -70.587633
GPS WEBHANNET FALLS: 43.298625, -70.587769
HOURS: Dawn to dusk
FEE: None
RESTRICTIONS: Regular Park rules & regulations apply
ACCESSIBILITY: 100-foot walk
DEGREE OF DIFFICULTY: Easy
ADDITIONAL INFORMATION: Falls Park, Wells, ME 04090

A photograph of Webhannet Falls near flood stage conditions can be seen in Hope M. Shelley's 1996 book, *Images of America: Wells*.

DIRECTIONS: From the center of Ogunquit (junction of U.S. 1/Main Street, Shore Road & Beach Street), drive north on U.S. 1 for >3.4 miles. Turn left onto Buffum

Hill Road and then immediately right (north) onto Falls Park Road. After <0.1-mile, park at the end of the road in a small parking area.

Due to a proliferation of foliage, viewing the falls from the bridge is not as easy as it once was. The best time to view the fall is in early spring or late fall when the trees are leafless. A photograph of the waterfall at full force can be seen in Hope M. Shelley's *Images of America: Wells* (2003).

DESCRIPTION: Webhannet Falls is a 15-foot-high waterfall formed on the Webhannet River—a fairly robust, 8-mile-long river with an 8,963-acre watershed contained entirely within the town of Wells, energized by five main tributaries, including Pope's Creek, Depot Brook, and Blacksmith Brook. The cascade falls into a shallow pool.

HISTORY: In 1640/1641, Edmund Littlefield erected a sawmill and gristmill at the falls. Not coincidentally, the first permanent settlement of Wells developed near this site as attested to by a plaque affixed to a boulder near the bridge.

In *The Kings Highway from Portland to Kittery: Stagecoach & Tavern Days on the old Coach Road* (1953), Herbert G. Jones writes that from below the falls, Littlefield *"...could raft his lumber down to other settlers on or about Drakes Island."*

According to Sandy Nestor in *Indian Placenames in America. Volume 2: Mountains, Canyons, Rivers, Lakes, Creeks, Forests and other Natural Features* (2005), the word "Webhannet" may be Abnaki for "at the clear stream." During part of the nineteenth century, the Webhannet River was simply known as the Town River.

The remnants of a large, cement dam is still visible by the waterfall.

Bridge of Flowers—The display of colorful flowers and bushes adorning the abandoned bridge that spans the Webhannet River just west of U.S. 1 was developed collaboratively by the Webhannet Garden Club and the Historical Society of Wells and Ogunquit. When we last visited, we noticed more shrubbery and bushes.

A raised rock by the parking area contains two plaques. One provides the history of the waterfall's industrial past; the other recites the names of individuals who made the Park possible.

WELLS BEACH

LOCATION: Wells (York County)

MAINE ATLAS & GAZETTEER: Map 3, E1

GPS PARKING: *Eastern Shore Lot at end of Atlantic Avenue*—43.319934, -70.560433 (lot closes at 11:00 p.m.); *End of Mile Road*—43.302484, -70.566483

GPS WELLS BEACH: 43.310635, -70.561524

HOURS: *Parking*—8:00 a.m. to 8:00 p.m.; *Beach*—Mainly, dawn to dusk; for more specific information, consult https://www.wellstown.org/DocumentCenter/View/4354/Wells-Beaches-Brochure

FEE: Parking fee; metered.

Beach parking passes— For further information, consul website, https://www.wellstown.org/835/Beach-Parking-Passes

RESTRICTIONS: Regular beach rules & regulations apply

ACCESSIBILITY: 0.2-mile walk to beach

DEGREE OF DIFFICULTY: Easy

ADDITIONAL INFORMATION: Wells Beach, 110 Atlantic Avenue, Wells, ME 04090

Restrooms are located at the parking area at the north end of Atlantic Avenue.

Pet owners should consult http://www.wellsmaine.org/notices/animals for current regulations regarding dogs.

Photographs of the Wells beach area can be viewed in Hope M. Shelley's 1997 book, *Images of America: Beaches of Wells.*

DIRECTIONS: From the center of Ogunquit (junction of U.S. 1/Main Street, Shore Road & Beach Street), drive north on U.S. 1 for ~4.0 miles. Turn right onto Mile Road and head east for >0.9 mile:

Atlantic Avenue—Turn left onto Atlantic Avenue and proceed north for 1.2 miles, passing by sixteen public beach rights-of-way (mainly for local homeowner) until you reach a large public parking area at the north tip of the peninsula.

From the southeast end of the parking area, follow a path along Wells Harbor for <0.2 mile that leads to the start of Wells Beach at its north end.

There is also direct access to the Wells Beach Jetty, as well as a 0.2-mile-long pier in Wells Harbor (GPS: 43.319752, -70.561736).

Mile Road—Cross over Atlantic Avenue and proceed to the very end of Mile Road where limited parking is available.

DESCRIPTION: Wells Beach extends for >1.5 miles from the Wells Beach Jetty (north) to Crescent Beach (south).

The jetty at the north end of Wells Beach (GPS: 43.317479, -70.554854) was built in 1961–62 by the U.S. Army Corps of Engineers. They used 20,000 tons of granite to make the breakwater. Jetties in general are a mixed blessing. On the up-drift side, they tend to accumulate sand, which promotes beach formation. On the down-drift side, they tend to increase erosion, and beaches shrink in size.

Virtually on the opposite side of the jetty is Drakes Island Beach.

STORERS GARRISON
Storers Garrison State Historic Site

LOCATION: Wells (York County)

MAINE ATLAS & GAZETTEER: Map 2, E5

GPS PARKING: *Storers Garrison State Historic Site*—43.307039, -70.584390 or 43.307030, -70.585130; *Garrison House*—43.309291, -70.585618

GPS DESTINATIONS: *Storers Garrison State Historic Site*—43.307251, -70.584360; *Commemorative monument*—43.30728, -70.58426; *Covered Bridge (adjacent to the Park)*—43.307150, -70.584441; *Garrison House*—43.309338, -70.585794

HOURS: Dawn to dusk

FEE: None

RESTRICTIONS: Regular Park rules & regulations apply

ACCESSIBILITY: Near roadside

DEGREE OF DIFFICULTY: Easy

ADDITIONAL INFORMATION: Storers Garrison State Historic Site, 1099 U.S. 1/Post Road, Wells, ME 04090

Congdon's Doughnut, 1090 U.S. 1/Post Road, Wells, ME 04090

Mike's Clam Shack, 1150 U.S. 1/Post Road, Wells, ME 04090

DIRECTIONS: *Storers Garrison State Historic Site*—From the center of Ogunquit (junction of U.S. 1/Main Street, Shore Road & Beach Street), drive north on U.S. 1 for ~4.2 miles. Opposite the Garrison Motel, Suites & Cottages, turn left into "Congdon's Doughnuts After Dark Food Truck Park," and park.

Walk across U.S. 1 and enter the park between two flat stones. A covered bridge is to your right, spanning a fairly inconsequential stream.

Storers Garrison House—From the Storers Garrison State Historic Site, continue north on U.S. 1/Post Road for <0.2 mile and turn left into the parking area for Mike's Clam Shack opposite Bayview Terrace, on your right. The Storers Garrison House is near the northwest end of the parking area, facing the road.

DESCRIPTION: Storers Garrison, built in 1678, was a large house that served as a refuge for settlers during the French and Indian War.

The plaque on the stone monument reads, "*To commemorate the defense of Lt. Joseph Storer's Garrison on this ground by Capt. James Converse, 29 Massachusetts soldiers, the neighboring yeomanry of Wells and various historic women;*

June 9, 10, 11, 1692, whereby 400 French and Indians were successfully resisted, and Wells remained the easternmost town in the province not destroyed by the enemy."

HISTORY: *Storers Garrison*—In the late 1600s, a house owned by Joseph Storer was selected by the British for its size and trustworthiness as a stronghold in the event that the Well's community should come under attack by hostile Native American and French forces. The house soon became known as Storers Garrison. Like all garrisons, it was well-stocked with food, water, and ammunition.

In the website *Wells Garrisons and Block-Houses* (Wells Garrison and Block-Houses - FortWiki Historic U.S. and Canadian Forts), a detailed account of the Storers House is provided: The "... *Garrison house was two stories high with a turret at each corner that served as a watchtower. The house was protected by a palisade built with upright logs 10 to 15 feet tall spaced about 10 feet from the house. Storer built several small houses outside the palisade to house families in times of danger. The houses were only occupied during the day and everyone went into the garrison at night.*"

The garrison could hold up to several hundred people, if necessary, when under siege.

In 1692, a force of five hundred Frenchmen and Native Americans attacked the settlement. Major James Converse along with fifteen men under his command, as well as armed Wells settlers, defended the garrison and refused to surrender. After forty-eight hours of being repeatedly attacked, the English settlers proved victorious, and the Native Americans and French soldiers were forced to abandon their assault.

Other attacks occurred in 1703 during Queen Anne's War (1702–1713) and in 1712, when a wedding party was raided.

Storers Garrison State Historic Site—The granite state historic marker, made by William E. Barry (an artist who lived in Kennebunk), was erected in 1904 to mark the site of Storers Garrison.

Sometime between 1730 and 1760, a house was constructed on the old foundation of the garrison using timber from the original house. In 2012, Michael McDermott, the owner of Mike's Clam Shack, purchased the house and moved it to the rear of the parking area by Mike's Clam Shack.

A photograph of the house, taken before its relocation, can be seen in Hope M. Shelley's *Images of America: Wells* (2003).

Covered bridge—This bridge, partially concealed by bushes, was built several decades ago by a prior owner of The Garrison Motel, Suites & Cottages. It is presently maintained by the Town. Even though it is not listed as one of the nine covered bridges in Maine (https://www.mainetourism.com/things-to-do/attractions/covered-bridges), it is a unique landmark.

As a point of interest, at one time there were over 120 covered bridges in Maine.

WELLS HABOR BEACH

LOCATION: Wells (York County)

MAINE ATLAS & GAZETTEER: Map 3, E1

GPS PARKING: 43.319013, -70.565302

GPS WELLS HARBOR BEACH: 43.318690, -70.564865

HOURS: Dawn to dusk

FEE: None

RESTRICTIONS: Regular beach rules & regulations apply; For information on beach parking, consult https://www.wellstown.org/835/Beach-Parking-Passes

ACCESSIBILITY: >100-foot walk

DEGREE OF DIFFICULTY: Easy

ADDITIONAL INFORMATION: Wells Harbor, 362 Harbor Road, Wells, ME 04090

DIRECTIONS: From the center of Ogunquit (junction of U.S. 1/Main Street, Shore Road & Beach Street), drive north on U.S. 1 for ~5.5 miles. Turn right onto Harbor Road and proceed east for >0.7 mile. Before you reach Hobbs Harborside at the end of the road, turn right onto a dirt road. Head south for 0.1 mile, going past the Webhannet River Boat Yard, and park in the area at the end of the road.

The beach abuts the Wells Harbor Community Park (located at 331 Harbor Road; GPS: 43.318845, -70.566091)) that contains the Wells Rotary pavilion, Hope Hobbs Gazebo, bocce ball courts, picnic tables, and restrooms.

DESCRIPTION: What makes Wells Harbor Beach unique and different from the other beaches in this area is that it faces a peninsula, making it a protected cove, rather than the Atlantic Ocean. The result is that the harbor's waters are consistently calmer and warmer, although wind can often be a factor if you're out kayaking.

A number of streams merge together in Wells Harbor. To the far north is Blacksmith Brook, aka Gooch Brook, which rises beyond I-95 and enters the harbor west of Drakes Island.

Just slightly north, paralleling Harbor Road, is Depot Brook, which also rises beyond I-95, and flows into the harbor virtually opposite the channel that leads out to the Atlantic Ocean from the harbor.

Around 0.7 mile south of the beach is Pope Creek, which rises west of U.S. 1/Post Road. It is a fairly small stream.

The Webhannet River flows into Wells Harbor south of Pope Creek. In fact, the river is diverted nearly 2.0 miles northeast from where you would expect to see it flow into the ocean (much like the Ogunquit River, which is forced southward for several miles from what would have been its natural exit point).

If you look at a coastal map, the bay that Wells Harbor Beach faces is really the Webhannet River making its way out to the Atlantic Ocean. The other streams coming into the bay are merely tributaries of the Webhannet. In *Pioneers on Maine Rivers, with lists to 1651* (1973), Wilbur D. Spencer writes about the Webhannet River estuary: *"This estuary which ebbs and flows for a long distance in an easterly direction behind Wells Beach, and enters the sea about five miles from the mouth of the Ogunquit River, is supplied with fresh water by a large inland brook* [the Webhannet River]."

The land opposite Wells Harbor Beach is a peninsula filled with seaside homes and cottages. The Wells Public parking area (GPS: 43.319924, -70.560449) is located at the north end of the peninsula.

Hobbs Harborside restaurant (GPS: 43.320520, -70.564721), located at the terminus of Harbor Road, was opened in the mid-2010s by William "Billy" Hobbs, the original owner of the iconic Billy's Chowder House on 216 Mile Road in Wells. Hobbs Harborside was previously known as Lord's Harborside until 2013. For 44 years, it was owned and operated by David Kershaw.

In *A History of Drakes Island: Drakes Island from 1630 to 1950*, compiler Mabel W. Kelley provides a glimpse into how the harbor looked in the 1800s. According to an 1871 report issued by the New England Division of the Army Corps of Engineers: *"This harbor is formed by a small estuary known as Webhannet River, about 1 1/2 miles long, 200 yards wide, having 2 small branches ... A wide sandy beach extends along the coast for several miles on either side of the entrance, causing a bar about five hundred feet in width, with only two and one-half feet of water at mean low tide. The harbor is surrounded by low marshy ground, except at its head, where it is nearly dry at low water."*

The problem early on was that the water at the head of the harbor wasn't deep enough to allow large vessels to make their way in and out safely. The Army Corp of Engineers solved the problem by erecting a 250-yard-long crib-wood jetty ballasted with stone at the harbor's north side entrance, causing the level of the water to rise.

Today, two rubble-mound jetties constructed in 1961–62, and then extended in 1965, protect an 8-foot-deep channel.

A handicapped observation deck built by the Wells Knights of Columbus in 1994 overlooks the beach.

Kayak Paddle—Paddlers can rent kayaks from the Webhannet River Bait & Tackle shop—345 Harbor Road, Wells, ME 04090; (207) 646-9649.

Paddlers should take note that the waters in the harbor can be treacherous at times, a combination of tidal impulses and wind. The safest and easiest trek to undertake is to round the north corner of the harbor by Hobbs Harborside (Restaurant) and follow open water passageways west through marshlands on the north side of Harbor Road (the road you drove in on). Remember to pay attention to the turns you make because this marshy wonderland is a virtual labyrinth.

If you stay close to Harbor Road, you will eventually pass by the Fisherman's Catch (43.321182, -70.574386), a well-known restaurant to your left, where there is a tiny harbor, and then, after 0.1, to where Depot Brook, a small, unnavigable stream, enters. The Fisherman's Catch has been in business for over four decades.

Expect to see great and little blue herons, snowy egrets, and glossy ibises which use the salt marsh, salt pans, and tidal mudflats for feeding and nesting habitats.

FOUNDERS PARK

LOCATION: Wells (York County)

MAINE ATLAS & GAZETTEER: Map 2, E5

GPS PARKING: *In front, off road*—43.321607, -70.591771; *Inside Park*—43.321184, -70.592238

GPS FOUNDERS PARK: 43.321403, -70.592024

HOURS: Dawn to dusk

FEE: None

RESTRICTIONS: Regular Park rules & regulations apply

ACCESSIBILITY: 0.1-mile walk

DEGREE OF DIFFICULTY: Easy

ADDITIONAL INFORMATION: Founders Park, 238 Sanford Road/Route 109, Wells, ME 04090

DIRECTIONS: From the center of Ogunquit (junction of U.S. 1/Main Street, Shore Road & Beach Street), drive north on U.S. 1 for ~5.3 miles. Turn left onto Route 109/Sanford Road (that, if taken further, leads to the Maine Turnpike/I-95 in <1.0 mile), and head west for 0.6 mile. The Park is on your left ~0.1 mile after the Wells Town Office, and just before the Wells Elementary School.

Pull off to the side of the road in front of the John Wells House or drive into the Park and park in a small area at the end of the road.

DESCRIPTION: Founders Park contains the first settlement home in Wells, the John Wells House.

A large boulder containing a memorial plaque lists the names of the founding families of Wells.

HIKE: A short walking path takes you through the Park. Just east of the John Wells House is a paved walkway that passes by a dozen large rocks scattered to your right that were placed there intentionally.

HISTORY: The John Wells House (GPS: 43.321532, -70.591654) is a Cape style home that dates to at least 1709 when it was purchased by John Wells. An interior beam, engraved with the date 1696, suggests that the house may have been constructed prior to the eighteenth century. According to a 1969 *National Register of Historic Places Nomination Form*, the Wells House was burned by Native Americans in 1702, and then rebuilt in 1710.

It was listed on the National Register of Historic Places in 1979.

In 2021, a time capsule created by fourth-grade students from the Wells Elementary School was buried in Founders Park, to be reopened in 2121. The capsule includes a student-created book, two pandemic masks, a discovery map of Wells, local restaurant menus, a stone from Wells Beach, photographs in a scrapbook, as well as a variety of other items. A round metal plaque with the inscription "Wells Maine 200 Time Capsule — Buried May 26, 2021, to be opened in 100 years" marks the capsule's spot.

WELLS RESERVE AT LAUDHOLM
Wells National Estuarine Research Reserve at Laudholm

LOCATION: Wells (York County)

MAINE ATLAS & GAZETTEER: Map 3, D1

GPS PARKING: 43.338629, -70.551044

GPS DESTINATIONS: *Little River Viewing area on Farley Trail, #1*—43.341928, -70.546528; *Little River* viewing area on *Farley Trail, #2*—43.339240, -70.544497; *Viewing area off Laird-Norton Trail*—43.335001, -70.545073; *Viewing area of Webhannet Sanctuary at end of Pilger Trail*—43.332096, -70.555202; *Laudholm Beach* at end of *Barrier Beach Trail*—43.329493, -70.545403

HOURS: Daily, 7:00 a.m. to sunset

FEE: Small day-use fee during peak season

RESTRICTIONS: Regular Park rules & regulations apply

No bikes, domestic pets, smoking, or collecting artifacts are permitted

ACCESSIBILITY: Lengths of hikes vary; *Cart Path/Farley Trail to dock*—0.4-mile walk; *Barrier Beach Trail to Laudholm Beach*—0.7-mile walk

DEGREE OF DIFFICULTY: Easy

ADDITIONAL INFORMATION: Wells Reserve, 342 Laudholm Farm Road, Wells, ME 04090 ME; (207) 646-1555; https://www.wellsreserve.org

Trail maps are available at the kiosk by the parking area.

DIRECTIONS: From the center of Ogunquit (junction of U.S. 1/Main Street, Shore Road & Beach Street), drive north on U.S. 1 for <7.0 miles. At a blinking traffic light, turn right onto Laudholm Farm Road and proceed east for >0.4 mile. Bear left onto Skinner Mill Road and go northeast for >0.1 mile. When you come to the entrance to the Wells Reserve, turn right and head southeast for >0.2 mile to the parking area.

Trailhead—From the parking area, follow the paved walkway southeast towards the farm buildings. At the first building (where the restrooms are located), turn left. Follow the building to its end and then bear left, now heading towards the Visitor Center where the trails begin.

DESCRIPTION: The Wells Reserve is managed by the Wells Reserve Management Authority and is one of thirty areas in the National Estuarine Research Reserve System where rivers meet the sea.

Estuaries are special places where tidal waters meet freshwater currents.

HIKE: There are a variety of trails that can be taken, many of them interconnecting: *Saw-whet Owl Trail*—0.2 mile-long; *Laird-Norton Trail*—0.4 mile-long; *Farley Trail*—<0.7 mile-long; *Knight Trail*—0.4 mile-long; *Barrier Beach Trail*—0.6 mile-long; *Pilger Trail*—<0.6 mile-long; *Muskie Trail*—<0.7 mile-long; *Cart Path*—0.25 mile-long.

The Farley Trail provides an interesting destination leading to two viewing areas of the Little River.

The Barrier Beach Trail (an old road) takes you to a 0.6-mile-long beach that lies between private homes on Drakes Island to the southwest, and the Little River to the northeast. The end of the Barrier Beach Trail is marked by two large stone cairns. From here, the walk continues along Old Farm Lane past private residences for 0.1 mile to a set of wooden steps that lead directly onto the beach. You will be in close proximity to private homes, so be respectful of landowners' properties. The Wells Reserve recommends that you walk northeast along the beach past the last three houses and then utilize the section of the beach beyond for swimming or sunning. Take note that it can be fairly rocky near the shoreline, but this seems to be a seasonal phenomenon. In summer, sand comes in and covers many of the rocky areas, leaving only a few cobbles exposed.

The Pilger Trail ends at a viewing area of the Webhannet estuary.

The Laird-Norton Trail takes you to a viewing area looking across the mouth of the Little River. Its entire length is one continuous boardwalk.

HISTORY: The Reserve land was originally inhabited on a seasonal basis by the Webanaki, but there is no evidence that they ever maintained year-round residency.

The land was first settled by Europeans in 1642 by Henry Boade (a founder of the Town of Wells) and turned into a saltwater farm. Over the next two hundred years, the property became known as Farm Hill and went through a series of owners. William Symonds, a land speculator who worked the farm for nearly two decades, was the first. During King Philip's War, Symonds and his family fled to a nearby garrison and the abandoned house was burned to the ground .

In 1717, Nathaniel Clark and his family built a new farmhouse on the site, and several subsequent generations of Clarks occupied the land.

In 1881, George Clement Lord, President of the Boston & Maine Railroad, purchased the property with the intention of transforming it into a summer home and a gentleman's farm. Around this time, the property became known as "The Elms." Lord's son, Robert, took an interest in the farm, and after importing purebred Guernsey cattle in 1892, assumed ownership of the farm.

In 1908, Lord's other son, Charles, took charge of the farm. It was Charles who named the property Laudholm Farms. It's unclear where the name Laudholm comes from. However, if you break it down into two words, "laud" and "holms," with *laud* meaning "to praise or glorify" and *holm* meaning an "islet in a river or near a mainland," then it seems that Laudholm might mean "praise be to the islet."

After George Lord's death in 1893, several generations of the Lord family continued to operate the farm until 1968 when George C. Lord II sold 199 acres, which included Laudholm Beach, to the State of Maine. Serious efforts to save the farm began in 1978, culminating in 1982 with the establishment of the Laudholm Trust, a 501c nonprofit organization.

Joyce Butler's *Laudholm: The History of a celebrated Maine Saltwater Farm* (revised and updated 2020) provides extensive information about the farm's history.

Wells National Estuarine Research Reserve—The Reserve's mission is to understand, protect, and restore coastal ecosystems of the Gulf of Maine through integrated research, stewardship, environmental learning, and community partnerships.

DRAKES ISLAND BEACH

LOCATION: Drakes Island (York County)

MAINE ATLAS & GAZETTEER: Map 3, E1

GPS PARKING: *Municipal Lot*—43.326730, -70.552702; *Jetty Lot*—43.321047, -70.556501

GPS DRAKES ISLAND BEACH: 43.323990, -70.551003

HOURS: Beach parking opens at 8:00 a.m.

FEE: *Parking*—Resident of the Town of Wells must show proof of vehicle registration to obtain s beach pass; Non-residents must purchase a ticket via the Pay and Display meters located at all five municipal beach parking lots; *Beach*—free

RESTRICTIONS: Regular beach rules & regulations apply

ADDITIONAL INFORMATION: Drakes Island Beach, 3 Island Beach Road, Wells, ME 04090

During summer, dogs are only permitted on the beach after 6:00 p.m., with the exception of service animals.

Lifeguards are on duty on weekends from Memorial Day weekend to the last week of June; then, daily from the last week in June through Labor Day; and finally, on weekends from Labor Day through Indigenous Peoples Day (usually ending on Columbus Day).

Restrooms available.

DIRECTIONS: From the center of Ogunquit (junction of U.S. 1/Main Street, Shore Road & Beach Street), drive north on U.S. 1 for <6.5 miles and turn right at a blinking traffic light onto Drakes Island Road:

Municipal Parking Lot—Head southeast for 1.1 miles, and then turn left into the municipal parking area. From here, it is <0.2 mile walk to the beach along Drakes Island Road.

Jetty Lot—Head southeast for 1.2 miles, turn right onto Island Beach Road, and proceed southwest for <0.4 mile to reach the parking area for the beach and the jetty seawall, which includes bathroom facilities.

From here, it is a >0.1-mile walk next to an enormous stone block jetty, on your right, to reach the beach. Likely, children will find it irresistible to scamper about on top of the jetty.

Drakes Island Road—There are a couple of spaces at the end of Drakes Island Road designated for handicapped parking.

Viehmann's Way—Near the northeast end of Island Beach Road is a beach access, but only for locals or for those walking down from the Wells Reserve at Laudholm, for no parking or drop-offs are allowed. It connects with the Laudholm Reserve's Barrier Beach Trail and leads immediately to Laudholm Beach.

DESCRIPTION: Drakes Island Beach is 2,800 feet long with dunes and lots of sand. The Wells Harbor seawall lies directly southwest. To the northeast, 0.2 mile past Goulds Rocks (a rocky bar), is Laudholm Beach.

HISTORY: Drakes Island is named for Thomas Drake, a Casco Bay trader and voyager who in the 1600s established trading posts with Native Americans between Wells and Yarmouth. It is believed that Drake set foot on this island in 1652, but little else is known about the extent of his involvement with the island that came to bear his name.

Today, a substantial sized community of residences and summer homes exists on the island. Most are located near the ocean. The first summer cottage in this area was built by John Lord in 1897.

The island is separated from the mainland by Blacksmith Brook and marshlands.

{8}

Kennebunks: Kennebunk, Kennebunkport & Kennebunk Beach

From the center of Ogunquit (junction of U.S. 1/Main Street, Shore Road & Beach Street), drive north on U.S. 1 for ~7.0 miles to Cozy Corners to reach all the destinations in this section.

Kennebunk is the Native American word for "long cut bank," believed to be a reference to the Great Hill (GPS: 43.344303, -70.513151) at the mouth of the Mousam River. The town was first settled in 1621, became a trading and, later, shipbuilding center, and was part of Wells until 1820.

Kennebunkport, a shipbuilding and fishing village ~1.0 mile up the Kennebunk River from the Atlantic Ocean, followed suit and was incorporated in 1821.

The Kennebunk-Kennebunkport-Arundel Chamber of Commerce can be reached at 16 Water Street, Kennebunk, ME; (207) 967-0857 or at https://gokennebunks.com.

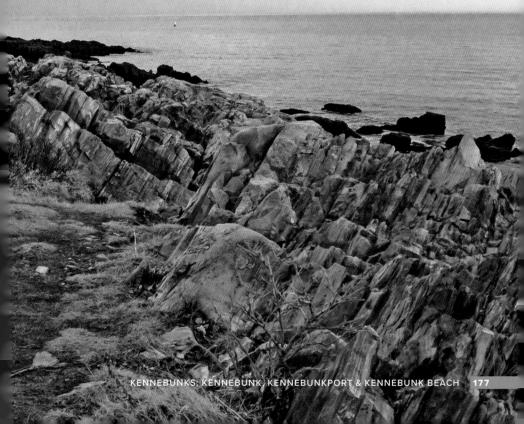

RACHEL CARSON NATIONAL WILDLIFE REFUGE
Rachel Carson National Wildlife Refuge: Headquarters

LOCATION: Northeast of Cozy Corners (York County)

MAINE ATLAS & GAZETTEER: Map 3, D1

GPS PARKING: 43.347197, -70.548416

GPS RACHEL CARSON NATIONAL WILDLIFE REFUGE: 43.347102, -70.548243

HOURS: Daily, 8:00 a.m. to 5:00 p.m.

FEE: None

RESTRICTIONS: Regular Park rules & regulations apply; dogs must be leashed and picked up after

ACCESSIBILITY: ~1.0-mile walk along trail system

DEGREE OF DIFFICULTY: Easy

ADDITIONAL INFORMATION: Rachel Carson National Wildlife Refuge, 321 Port Road/Route 9, Wells, ME 04090; (207) 646-9226

DIRECTIONS: From Cozy Corners (junction of U.S. 1 & Route 9), turn right onto Route 9/Post Road and head northeast for 0.6 mile. Bear right onto Headquarters Access Road at the sign for Rachael Carson National Wildlife Refuge and drive southeast >0.1 mile to the U-shaped parking area.

DESCRIPTION: This portion of the Rachel Carson National Wildlife Refuge protects 1,167 acres of uplands and an estuary salt marsh formed where the Little River makes its way into the Atlantic Ocean.

HIKE: The hike along the Carson Interpretive Trail, heading counterclockwise on a loop trail, first takes you southeast and then northwest through tall while pines and near salt marshes bounded by the Merriland River to the west, and the Branch Brook to the east. There are eight observation spots and decks along the way providing views of the marshlands and rivers. A plaque at observation deck #1 tells you how a landslide in 2005 significantly changed the trail. The observation decks farthest south overlook the Merriland River at GPS 43.343417, -70.545656, and Branch Brook at GPS 43.344284, -70.544707.

At deck #5 is the Rachel Carson memorial boulder (GPS ~43.344143, -70.546314).

The dirt trail is >3 feet wide and well-maintained. This is one walk where you can look around without worrying about being tripped by a root or uneven ground.

Take note that as you follow the loop trail, the banks get lower and lower as you approach the salt marshes, and then higher as you return towards Route 9.

The Trail Guide, which you can pick up at the kiosk, provides information about what you are seeing at the various numbered sites.

Junior Ranger Program—The Rachel Carson National Wildlife Refuge Preserve has just recently started a Junior Ranger Program where youngsters can earn a badge in one day of training. The badges, made out of recycled wood, show either a saltmarsh sparrow, New England cottontail, or piping plover.

HISTORY: The Rachel Carson National Wildlife Refuge encompasses 9,125

acres of National Wildlife Refuge land that are contained in a number of parcels along 50 miles of Maine's southern coast, several which are included in this book.

The Little River estuary is formed by the 13-mile-long Merriland River, rising from swamps east of Oak Hill, and the sinuous Branch Brook, rising from swamps and lowlands north of Wells. In a *History of a Maine 'Little River'* (2015), Joseph W. Hardy writes, *"The Merriland River's third distinctive feature is the collection of marshes in those locations where it flattens out, places where the early settlers could pasture their cattle, and which gave rise to the name 'Merriland' or marshlands."* Branch Brook's gooseneck turns suggest a creek of some antiquity. The two streams come together in the upper mile of the estuary to form the Little River. The Little River, in turn, follows a 1.8-mile-long, serpentine path to reach the ocean.

In total, the Little River watershed encompasses an area of 31.5 square miles.

The refuge was created in 1966, named for Rachel Carson, an environmentalist whose 1962 book *Silent Spring*, documented the adverse environmental effects on songbirds and other creatures resulting from the indiscriminate use of pesticides. Her other famous book was *The Sea Around Us* which assessed the impact of fisheries on the marine ecosystem. She worked as a biologist, and then as a writer-editor, for the U.S. Fish and Wildlife Service from 1936 to 1952

The refuge's headquarters is located on this parcel of land.

MOUSAM RIVER PADDLES

LOCATION: South of Kennebunk (York County)

MAINE ATLAS & GAZETTEER: Map 3, D1

GPS LAUNCH SITE: 43.351699, -70.517795

GPS PARKING: *Route 9—43.351894, -70.516061; Parsons Road—43.345714, -70.518578*

GPS DESTINATIONS: *General site of Fort Larrabee—43.365603, -70.528090; Railroad Bridge—43.374883, -70.535868; Mousam River Wildlife Sanctuary —43.378989, -70.540186*

HOURS: DAILY: Dawn to dusk

FEE: None

ACCESSIBILITY: 25-foot carry to river

DEGREE OF DIFFICULTY: Easy

DIRECTIONS: From Cozy Corners (junction of U.S. 1 & Route 9), drive northeast on Route 9:

Parsons Beach Road (Secondary access)—After 2.0 miles, turn right onto Parsons Beach Road and proceed southeast for <0.5 mile to where Parsons Beach Road (a dead-end road) crosses over a wooden bridge spanning one section of the Mousam River. Park on the opposite side of the road facing west. Be sure to arrive early due to the small number of parking spaces available (presently only six).

Carry your watercraft over the guardrail and put in within 25 feet. Paddle east for <0.2 mile to reach the river proper, <0.2 mile upriver from the Atlantic Ocean. Head upstream.

Route 9 (Primary access)—After ~2.3 miles, turn left into the small launch site (GPS: 43.351573, -70.517837) at the northeast end of the Mousam River Bridge, <0.5 mile upriver from the Atlantic Ocean.

There is not a lot of room to park here. So, after dropping off your watercraft, drive east on Route 9 for several hundred feet and park along the right side of the road where parallel parking spaces are available. A second option is to park at the Madelyn Marx Preserve (named for the founding board member of the Kennebunk Land Trust), on your left, 0.05-mile from the launch site.

PADDLE: Due to the fact that the Mousam River is tidal all the way up to Kennebunk, time your trek so that you arrive at your destination at high tide. By doing so, you will be paddling with the current in both directions.

Route 9 Access—This section is less affected by the tides. Still, it makes good sense to take into account tidal impulses.

Starting at the Route 9 access, paddle upstream. Within 1.2 miles, you will pass by the general area where Fort Larrabee, on your right, was located. A railroad bridge crosses above the river at ~2.5 miles. At ~3.0 miles, you will pass by the 38-acre Mousam River Wildlife Sanctuary, with its 2,400-foot river front, to your right. Rapids are encountered just a short distance further upstream before you get to the Kennebunk dam below York Street. That's as far as you can go under the best of conditions.

Parsons Road Access—Paddlers should consider that this section of the Mousam River is *very* tidal and plan accordingly. Add on another 0.3 mile to the distances given for launching at the Route 9 bridge site as you proceed upriver.

HISTORY: *Mousam River* is a 30-mile-long river that rises from several sources, including Mousam Lake in Shapleigh, and flows into the Atlantic Ocean between Parsons Beach and Kennebunk Beach. Along its route, the river drains an area of 122 square miles. According to Sandy Nestor in Sandy Nestor in *Indian Placenames in America. Volume 2: Mountains, Canyons, Rivers, Lakes, Creeks, Forests and other Natural Features* (2005), Mousam is possibly the Abenaki word for "grandfather." According to Edward Emerson Bourne in *History of Wells and Kennebunk from the earliest settlement to the year 1820, at which time Kennebunk was set off, and incorporated Vol. 2* (1875), "Henry Sayward named it 'Mousam' but neither record nor tradition reveals to us why he did so." It was around 1672 that Sayward built a saw mill at the falls in Kennebunk, followed by a grist mill.

Herbert G. Jones, in *The Kings Highway from Portland to Kittery* (1953), states that *"The Mousam River in ages past was known to the Indians as the Maguncook, meaning 'Ponds at the Head' as it takes it source from three lakes of considerable size—Square Pond (which feeds into Mousam Lake), Middle Pond, and Shaker Pond."* The river was also known as Cape Porpoise River and Cape Porpus River.

Fort Larrabee—Nestor mentions that *"during the 1730s a fortification was built along the river [near Kennebunk] by Sergeant Larrabee and used for protection against the Indians."* It was erected on the site of an earlier garrison built by Larrabee's father, William. The fort, enclosing five single-story, square-shaped houses, lasted until the French & Indian War came to an end in 1762. A line drawing of the garrison can be seen in John Stevens Cabot Abbott's 1892 book, *The History of Maine*. The site of this fort is reputedly marked by an 8-foot-tall monument built in 1908 that contains a bronze-plate designed by historian William Barry. Unfortunately, the monument is located on private property off of Oceanview Road. In *History of Wells and Kennebunk from the earliest settlement to the year 1820, at which time Kennebunk was set off, and incorporated Vol. 2* (1875), Edward Emerson Bourne adds that the *"walls were of large, square timber, about fourteen feet high....on the four corners were four flankers* [guards]."

The Mousam is said to be one of the most heavily dammed rivers in Maine. According to an 1890 report by the Hydrographic Survey of Maine, there were nineteen mills in operation near the end of the nineteenth century. Many of these early dams were created by the Kennebunk Manufacturing Company to power its cotton mills. In *The History of Maine. 1661–1900* (2010), Edwin Emery writes that *"there are nineteen mill privileges within an aggregate fall of 306 feet."* Most of the dams today are used for generating hydroelectric power.

PARSONS BEACH

LOCATION: Kennebunkport (York County)

MAINE ATLAS & GAZETTEER: Map 3, D3

GPS PARKING: 43.345395, -70.518292

GPS PARSONS BEACH: 43.344011, -70.518829

RESTRICTIONS: Consult https://www.kennebunkmaine.us/308/beaches for specific details. Presently, dogs are prohibited on the private portion of the beach from April through October 31; Leashed dogs are allowed on the private portion of the beach from November 1 through March 31.

ADDITIONAL INFORMATION: Parsons Beach, Parsons Beach Road, Kennebunk, ME 04043; (207) 329-8900

DIRECTIONS: From Cozy Corners (junction of U.S. 1 & Route 9), drive northeast on Route 9 for 2.0 miles. Turn right onto Parsons Beach Road and proceed southeast for <0.5 mile to where Parsons Beach Road (a dead-end road) crosses over a wooden bridge spanning a section of the Mousam River. Park on the opposite side of the road facing west. Be sure to arrive early due to the small number of parking spaces available, currently only six.

From the end of the road, walk 250 feet south to reach the beach.

DESCRIPTION: Parsons Beach is a sandy, 0.7-mile-long beach that stretches east to the mouth of the Mousam River and southwest to a small projection of land on which stands The Big House (a grand family home dating back to the late 1800s).

According to one source, the beach is owned by descendants of the Persons family who generously allow public access. This is corroborated by a sign at the end of the road that reads, "Access to this private beach may be terminated by the adjacent landowners at any time."

HISTORY: Parsons Beach is at the entrance to the Mousam River Estuary, an area of saltwater, salt marshes and mudflats that extends upriver for ~3.0 miles to the head of tide. It is not an entirely natural area, for many parts of the marshes have been diked.

The beach itself is a barrier spit that protects the salt marshes along the backwaters of Mousam Creek/Back Creek.

In 2020, piper plovers, an endangered species, returned to Parsons Beach after being absent for three years. Visitors with dogs should first check to find out if piper plovers are presently nesting on the beach. If so, dogs are not permitted back until August. By then, the hatched, infant plovers are able to take flight. Anyone seen violating this prohibition should be immediately reported to the Maine Warden Service at 1-(800) 452-4664.

KENNEBUNK BEACHES: MOTHER'S BEACH, MIDDLE BEACH & GOOCH'S BEACH

LOCATION: Kennebunk (York County)

MAINE ATLAS & GAZETTEER: Map 3, D2

GPS PARKING: Along Beach Avenue

GPS DESTINATIONS: *Mother's Beach—* 43.343855, -70.498935; *Middle Beach—* 43.345214, -70.488392; *Gooch's Beach—* 43.347453, -70.481580

HOURS: Dawn to dusk

FEE: *Parking—*Beach passes are required for parking along the Kennebunk Beaches. Parking passes for residents can be obtained from the 2nd Floor of the Town Hall at 1 Summer Street (GPS 43.360322, -70.475507).

Parking passes for non-residents can be purchased at kiosks along Beach Avenue via credit card or debit card.

Passes are required from June 15th through September 15th for all three beaches. All passes (whether they are a sticker, card, or kiosk print-out) must be displayed in the lower right (passenger side) of the vehicle dashboard/windshield; *Beach—*no fee

RESTRICTIONS: Regular beach rules & regulations apply

ACCESSIBILITY: Near roadside

ADDITIONAL INFORMATION: Consult https://www.kennebunkmaine.us/308/ beaches for updates on beach permit regulations and dogs on the beach. Presently, dogs are permitted on Gooch's, Middle, Mother's and a portion of Parsons beaches from June 15th through Labor Day, from 5:00 p.m. to 9:00 a.m. At all times, dogs must be under voice control or on a leash.

Lifeguards are on duty from mid-June through early September at Gooch's Beach and Mother's Beach.

DIRECTIONS: From Cozy Corners (junction of U.S. 1 & Route 9), drive northeast on Route 9 for <3.0 miles. Turn right onto Sea Road and head south for <0.7 mile. Bear left at a junction and drive east, now on Beach Avenue. You will come to Mother's Beach in 0.2 mile, Middle Beach in 0.4 mile (a narrow beach composed mostly of smooth pebbles and rocks), and Gooch's Beach in 0.9 mile.

*Mother's Beach—*Park facing the ocean where there are a limited number of parking spaces.

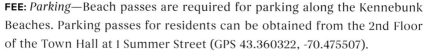

Middle Beach—Park along Beach Avenue to take advantage of parallel parking spaces.

Gooch's Beach—Park along Beach Avenue where parallel parking spaces are available.

DESCRIPTION: Kennebunk Beach consists of three separate beaches: Mother's Beach, Middle Beach, and Gooch's Beach.

Mother's Beach is a 0.1-mile-long stretch of beach between rocky Lords Point (a narrow, 0.3-mile-long projection of land containing private estates) to the southwest, and a rocky area to the east topped by a private residence. Mother's Beach was named for being an ideal beach for families with small children, thanks to its calmer waters and confined area. A children's play area is located next to the beach.

Middle Beach, aka Rocky Beach, is narrow and filled with stones that have been smoothed and polished over millenniums by the erosive action of beach waves.

Most visitors congregate at the southeast end of Middle Beach on the west side of Oaks Neck (a rocky promontory; GPS: 43.342151, -70.487498) where there is mostly sand and few rocks. Oaks Reef, looking like the undulating back of a sea monster, extends southwest from Oaks Neck for ~0.5 mile.

As a point of reference, directly across Beach Avenue is the Narragansett-by-the-sea condo (GPS: 43.345345, -70.486934), which John Curtis opened as a hotel in 1905.

Gooch's Beach, aka Long Beach, is a 0.6-mile-long expanse of beach that lies between the Kennebunk River jetty (GPS: 43.346855, -70.475983) to the east, and Oaks Neck (GPS: 43.344408, -70.485868) to the southwest. It is the longest of the three named beaches. If you look closely south at the ocean, you should be able to glimpse waves breaking at Fishing Rock [GPS: 43.335968, -70.480587) and Little Fishing Rock (GPS: 43.336470, -70.479304), some 0.7 mile distant. A spire was erected on Fishing Rock in 1834.

It seems likely that the beach was named for John Gooch, the area's first settler, who arrived in 1637. He was commissioned by Fernando Gorges, the British proprietary founder of Maine, to set up residence at the of the mouth of the Kennebunk River and to ferry travelers across the river.

HISTORY: Kennebunk is said to be the Abenaki word for "the long cut bank," supposedly referring to the long bank behind Kennebunk Beach. Purportedly, there is no other village in the world named Kennebunk. A photograph of Kennebunk Beach as it looked in 1892 can be seen in Kenneth Joy's *The Kennebunks: "Out of the Past"* (1967).

It was first settled in 1621 as a trading center thanks to its location on the Mousam River.

PICNIC ROCK
BUTLER PRESERVE: KENNEBUNK LAND TRUST

LOCATION: Kennebunk (York County)

MAINE ATLAS & GAZETTEER: Map 3, D2

GPS PARKING & TRAILHEAD: 43.370589, -70.493239

GPS PICNIC ROCK: 43.373335, -70.491222

HOURS: Dawn to dusk

FEE: None

RESTRICTIONS: Regular Park rules & regulations apply

ACCESSIBILITY: >0.3-mile hike

DEGREE OF DIFFICULTY: Moderately easy

ADDITIONAL INFORMATION: Kennebunk Land Trust (office), 6 Brown Street, Suite 2, Kennebunk, ME 04043; (207) 985-8734. *Trail map*—https://www.mainetrailfinder.com/ trails/trail/ butler-preserve

DIRECTIONS: From Cozy Corners (junction of U.S. 1 & Route 9), drive northeast on Route 9 for ~4.0 miles. When you come to Route 35/Port Road just before crossing over the Kennebunk River, turn left and head northwest on Route 35/Port Road for 0.6 mile. Then bear right onto Old Post Road and drive north for 0.4 mile. Park off-road by the trailhead sign that reads "Kennebunk Land Trust: Butler Preserve."

Parking is limited.

DESCRIPTION: Picnic Rock is a large area of exposed bedrock overlooking a deep-water section of the Kennebunk River.

HIGHLIGHTS:

- Historic Picnic Rock
- Views of Kennebunk River

HIKE: Follow the trail, an old woods road, northeast. After 0.2 mile, take the main trail left as a smaller path goes off to your right. The main trail heads downhill and then climbs to the top of Picnic Rock in <0.1 mile.

If you continue east on the trail system, you will end up at the cul-de-sac at Ledgewater Drive.

Note: If you want to experience a "virtual walk" along the trail, log onto the Land Trust's website, https://kennebunklandtrust.org/preserves/butler-preserve.

HISTORY: Picnic Rock, located in the 14-acre, forested Butler Preserve, is an historic rock that has been a destination for picnickers, kayakers, and swimmers for centuries.

The rock may also have been known historically as Sunset Rock. This conclusion is based on antique postcards of Sunset Rock showing what looks like Picnic Rock as seen from the Kennebunk River. A postcard image of Sunset Rock can be seen in Paula H. Koches' 1989 book, *Having a Grand Time!: Postcards of Ogunquit. Wells, the Yorks and the Kennebunks. 1900–1930.*

Picnic Rock consists of two distinct levels: The upper level encompasses a large area of exposed bedrock, 20 feet above the river. It is the perfect spot to sit and enjoy views of the river below.

The lower, plateau-like level, is 10 feet above the river and can be accessed via a short path from the upper rock's north side. From the lower level, it is possible to scamper further down to the edge of the river, or to even jump into the deep waters below (although this is not recommended).

The Preserve is named for G. Robert Butler, co-donor of the land.

The property is overseen by the Kennebunk Land Trust (KLT), which was established in 1972.

ADDITIONAL PROPERTIES MANAGED BY THE KENNEBUNK LAND TRUST:

- **Alewive Woods Preserve** (>625 acres), Cole Rad, Kennebunk, ME; GPS: 43.430567, -70.621664

- **Clark Preserve** (90 acres), End of Emmons Emmons Road, Kennebunk, ME; GPS: ~43.418699, -70.546065

- **Mousam River Wildlife Sanctuary** (38 acres), Water Street, Kennebunk, ME; GPS: ~43.380741, -70.538929

- **Sea Road Preserve** (13 acres), Sea Road (access from the Sea Road School, Kennebunk, ME; GPS: 43.377463, -70.530166

- **Wonder Brook/Murphy Preserve** (80 acres), End of Plummer Lane, Kennebunk, ME; GPS: 43.384846, -70.524897

- **Secret Garden** (40 acres); 1.5-mile loop trail; located between Sea Road and Route 35. Entrance is presently closed.

- **Madelyn Marx Preserve** (24 acres), Western Avenue/Route 9, Kennebunk, ME; GPS: 43.352067, -70.516280

- **Oxbow Preserve** (14 acres), Spiller Drive, Kennebunk, ME; GPS: 43.395513, -70.557224

- **For All Ever Preserve** (111 acres), Webber Hill Road/Route 99, Kennebunk, ME; GPS: 43.399470, -70.603935

- **Hope Woods** (72 acres), Wood Pond Lane cul-de-sac, Kennebunk, ME; GPS: 43.391772, -70.543304

- **Tributary Preserve** (50+ acres), behind the Drala Drive neighborhood off Alfred Road, Kennebunk, ME; GPS: 43.411010, -70.597969 (general area)

WEDDING CAKE HOUSE
(Private)

LOCATION: Kennebunk (York County)

MAINE ATLAS & GAZETTEER: Map 3, D1

GPS WEDDING CAKE HOUSE: 43.381715, -70.516793

ACCESSIBILITY: Roadside. This is a private residence that isn't generally open to the public

ADDITIONAL INFORMATION: Wedding Cake House, 104 Summer Street, Kennebunk, ME 04043

For more information, consult Thomas W. Murphy Jr.'s *The Wedding Cake House: The world of George W. Bourne* (1978).

DIRECTIONS: From Cozy Corner (junction of U.S. 1 & Route 9), drive northeast on Route 9 for ~4.2 miles. Turn left onto Route 35/Port Road/Summer Street and head northwest for ~2.3 miles. The Wedding Cake House will be directly to your right. Park off-road in the front, making sure not to park on the grass.

DESCRIPTION: The Wedding Cake House, aka Cake House, is named for its unusual facade that resembles a wedding cake. It is said to be the most photographed house in Maine.

A beautiful, white, roadside sign announces the presence of the house.

HISTORY: The Wedding Cake House, formally known as the George W. Bourne House, was a wedding gift to George Washington Bourne, a shipbuilder, from his parents in 1825.

In the following years, Bourne added on a frame barn that was connected to the main house by a carriage house. Twenty-seven years later, the barn caught fire. In order to save the house, Bourne destroyed the barn and connecting

carriage house, but later rebuilt both utilizing a gothic design that he had observed in Milan, Italy.

Bourne attached six buttresses with pinnacles to the house, joining them together with intricate woodwork. He spent the rest of his life embellishing his house using mostly hand-held tools. He completed the final work project just four months before his death in 1855.

In *An American Heritage Guide: Historic Houses of America* (1971), editors Beverley Hilowitz and Susan Eikov Green write that the house is "*an excellent relic of the scroll-saw era. The 2-story brick house with central doorway and Palladian window above were built sometime before the elaborate wooden gingerbread trim was added. The slim wooden pinnacles on the roof, Gothic tracery over windows, and crenelated canopy over the doorway give the effect of an old-fashioned lacy valentine.*"

From 1983 to 1998, Mary Ann Burnett and her daughter Anne, who lived in the house, used the barn as an art studio and gallery. The house was subsequently bought by James Hunt Barker, who continued the renovations that the Burnetts had started. After Barker died in 2020, Hunt Edwards (Barker's nephew) and Lela Cason acquired the property and have continued the work on restoring the house to its original condition.

Two hundred feet behind the house is the Kennebunk River. It seems only fitting that Bourne, a builder of ships, would end up living in close proximity to water.

ST. ANTHONY'S FRANCISCAN MONASTERY & FRANCISCAN GUEST HOUSE

LOCATION: Kennebunkport (York County)

MAINE ATLAS & GAZETTEER: Map 3, D1

GPS PARKING: *Franciscan Guest House—43.356187, -70.478582; Franciscan Monastery—43.354989, -70.477321*

GPS ST. ANTHONY'S MONASTERY: *Franciscan Guest House—43.356448, -70.478183; St. Anthony's Franciscan Monastery—43.354522, -70.478075*

GPS DESTINATIONS: *Chapel of the Stations of the Cross—43.355570, -70.476431; Our Lady of Lourdes Grotto—43.355318, 70.477701; Statue of Kateri Tekakwitha—43.356600, -70.475934*

HOURS: Daily, sunrise to sunset

FEE: None

ADDITIONAL INFORMATION: St. Anthony's Franciscan Monastery, 28 Beach Avenue, Kennebunk, ME 04043; (207) 967-2011; Gift shop: Open daily, March 1st to December 31st, 10:00 a.m. to noon, and 1:00 p.m. to 4:00 p.m.

Franciscan Guest House, 26 Beach Avenue, Kennebunk, ME 04043; (207), 967-4865; www.franciscanguesthouse.com

A "Walking tour of the shrines" brochure is available at the Franciscan Guest House's front desk.

DIRECTIONS: From Cozy Corners (junction of U.S. 1 & Route 9), drive northeast on Route 9 for 4.2 miles. Before reaching Kennebunkport, turn right onto Beach Avenue and drive south for <0.3 mile. Bear left into the entrance road.

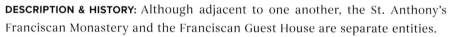

To reach the Franciscan Guest House, turn immediately left into the parking area.

To reach the Franciscan Monastery, follow the road southeast for <0.2 mile, parking in a large area after passing by the monastery. Along the way, you will pass by the Triple Church Monument on your right, just before the monastery.

DESCRIPTION & HISTORY: Although adjacent to one another, the St. Anthony's Franciscan Monastery and the Franciscan Guest House are separate entities.

Monastery—The history of the site dates back to John Mitchell, a professor of Christian religion, who purchased 200 acres of land from Sir William Pepperrell in 1740. In 1744-1745 Mitchell constructed a garrison for protection during the French and Indian War. In 1900, the Michell family sold the property to William A. Rogers, a Buffalo industrialist, who commissioned the Buffalo-based architectural firm of Green & Wicks to construct the large Tudor-style home that you see today. The monastery's beautiful grounds were designed by the Frederick Law Olmstead brothers.

In 1937, the property was sold to entrepreneur William N. Campbell, a wealthy businessman who owned homes in several states.

The St. Anthony's Franciscan Monastery was established when the Lithuanian Friars of St. Casimir acquired the property from Campbell in 1947. In 1952, the friars erected the Shrine of St. Anthony (commemorating a thirteenth-century Portuguese Catholic priest and friar of the Franciscan order) and added to the estate grounds the Grotto of our Lady of Lourdes in 1953, and the Chapel of the Stations of the Cross in 1959. The new St. Anthony's Chapel was built in 1965-1966.

Guest House—The Franciscan Guest House was built in the 1950s by the friars to serve as a High School, primarily for boys of Lithuanian heritage. Stables were converted for school use, and new brick buildings were added on in the early 1960s, including a gymnasium and pool.

When the High School closed in 1969, the property became a year-round guest house and retreat center.

Our Lady of Lourdes Grotto—The shrine was designed by Lithuanian architect Jonas Mulokas and dedicated in 1953. On the southwest side of the shrine is a plaque that reads, *"A piece of the stone on which the blessed Mother appeared in Lourdes, France."*

Chapel of the Stations of the Cross—This chapel was also built by Jonas Mulokas, creator of "Our Lady of Lourdes Grotto." The individual stations contained within the chapel were crafted by Vytautas Kasuba, who won the prestigious Gold Medal for Art in the 1937 World's Fair.

Triple Church Monument—This sculpture, created by Lithuanian artist Vytautas Kazimieras Jonynas, formerly graced the façade of the Vatican Pavilion at the 1964–1965 World's Fair in New York City. It was transported to the monastery in 1967.

HIGHLIGHTS:

- St. Anthony's Franciscan Monastery
- Guest House
- Nature chapels
- Walks near the Kennebunk River

WALK: Short walks take you along the 66-acre estate of rolling lawns and English gardens, down to the Kennebunk River. One of the nicest walks is to follow the paved walkway near the parking area north along the Kennebunk River until you come to the statue of Kateri Tekakwitha, an Algonquin-Mohawk who was a Catholic saint (the first Native American to be sainted). She was informally known as the "Lily of the Mohawks." It's quite possible that the trajectory of Tekakwitha's life changed when she contracted smallpox at age 4 and was left permanently scarred facially and virtually blind. She died in 1680 at age 24.

Along the walk, you will pass by a small pond on your left, and go past Chicks Marina, Kennebunkport Marina, and a Yachtsman Hotel & Marina Club, across the river, to your right.

Another walk leads from the gift shop at the rear of the monastery to a small cove in <0.2 mile where old pier pilons can be seen jutting from the water (GPS: 43.352407, -70.476305)

PERKINS TIDE MILL
Kennebunkport Conservation Trust

LOCATION: Kennebunkport (York County)

MAINE ATLAS & GAZETTEER: Map 3, D1

GPS PARKING: *North Street*—43.363469, -70.477077

GPS DESTINATIONS: *Dam*—43.364336, -70.478170; *Clement Clark Boat House*—43.364947, -70.478407; *Mill Creek*—43.364215, -70.477667; *Launch dock*—43.364464, -70.478405

HOURS: Dawn to dusk

FEE: None

RESTRICTIONS: Regular Park rules & regulations apply

ACCESSIBILITY: Near roadside

ADDITIONAL INFORMATION: Perkins Tide Mill, 8 Mill Lane, Kennebunkport, ME 04046; Kennebunkport Conservation Trust (office), 57 Gravelly Brook Road, Kennebunkport, ME 04046; (207) 967-3465

DIRECTIONS: From Cozy Corners (junction of U.S. 1 & Route 9), drive northeast on Route 9 for ~4.5 mile, entering Kennebunkport and crossing over the Kennebunk River via the Mathew J. Lanigan Bridge at historic Dock Square. When you come to a "T", turn left onto Maine Street (which quickly becomes North Street) and head northeast for >0.1 mile. Turn left onto Mill Lane and drive west for 0.1 mile. This gives you an opportunity to reconnoiter the site, or to drop off your kayak. Take note that the Town and neighbors would rather that you don't park on the site, so turn around and drive back south to park along North Street, a one-way street. Return on foot.

DESCRIPTION: The Perkins Tide Mill, aka the Olde Grist Mill, was constructed by Captain Thomas Perkins, Jr. and two of his sons in 1749 and operated until 1937. The grist mill used tidal forces to turn a waterwheel that powered the mill.

In the *National Register of Historic Places,* William J. Murtagh (1976), etc. describe the mill as a *"frame, shingling; 1 & ½-story main building with additional story above water level, L-shaped, gabled roofs, square cupola, bracketed entrance hood."*

The Grist Mill's last miller was James C. Perkins. When he retired

in 1937, the mill was converted into a tearoom by Louse (Perkin's daughter) and Arthur Lombard who later expanded it into a restaurant. Their son, David, was the last proprietor. He was in the process of selling the mill when it burned down in 1994. The fire is believed to have been set by an arsonist.

The structure that survived the fire that you see today is the Clement Clark Boat House, aka the Boathouse, which was originally part of a boatyard and then was used as an ancillary structure by the restaurant. The boathouse is named for Clement Clark, a twentieth-century, local boat-builder.

The breached dam that you see today was rebuilt in 1963, basically on top of the remains of the old dam. The sluiceway has always been on the side of the river closest to the mill.

Today, visitors can see the sluiceway, the Mill Stream dam, the Clement Clark Boat House, and two commemorative grindstones dedicated to the Reynolds and the Kings.

HIGHLIGHTS:

- Site of Perkins Tide Mill and remnants of mill and dam
- Clement Clark Boat House

PADDLING: The Kennebunk River is navigable for a total of ~5.0 miles. This was not always the case. In Charles Bradley's *History of Kennebunk Port from its first discovery by Bartholomew Gosnold, May 14, 1602, to A. D. 1837,* Bartholomew Gosnold writes that the Kennebunk River was once *"...navigable only about half* *a mile from its mouth. It is a barred harbor, there being only about two feet of water at its entrance at low water."*

The 4.0-mile upriver paddle takes you past Picnic Rock [see chapter on Picnic Rock] at 1.0 mile; the Durrells Bridge (GPS: 43.378787, -70.505035) at ~2.2 miles; near the back of the Wedding Cake House [see chapter on the Wedding Cake House] at ~3.2 miles; and the railroad bridge (GPS: 43.390978, -70.521856) at ~4.0 miles.

While the 1.0-mile downriver stretch of the river from the Route 9/Dock Square Bridge to the ocean can be paddled, typically there is a fair amount of boat traffic. For this reason, it is probably best avoided by paddlers unless you are hugging the shoreline.

HISTORY: In 1973, the mill was listed on the National Register of Historic Places. Unfortunately, one of the last surviving eighteenth-century tide mills in the United States burned to the ground in 1994. Recently, the mill was removed from the National Register of Historic Places since little of it remains, except for a few pieces hidden in the weeds.

In 2006, the property was acquired by the Kennebunkport Conservation Trust—an organization that has protected over 2,800 acres of land from development.

ADDITIONAL PROPERTIES OF THE KENNEBUNKPORT CONSERVATION TRUST:

- Smith Preserve (1,100 acres), Guinea Road, Kennebunkport, ME; GPS: 43.418647, -70.463328

- Tyler Brook Preserve, Tyler Brook Road, Kennebunkport, ME; GPS: 43.389864, -70.444959

- Meadow Woods Preserve (371 acres), 406 Mills Road, Kennebunkport, ME; GPS: 43.416585, -70.411320

- Vaughn Island Preserve [camping] (96 acres), GPS Launch site at terminus of Turbots Creek Road: 43.357759, -70.446664; GPS Vaughn Island: 43.357195, -70.439796

- James Woods ((15 acres), 25 North Street, Kennebunkport, ME; GPS Parking: 43.365997, -70.475518; GPS Trailhead: 43.365525, -70.475549

- Granny's Garden, Ocean Avenue, Kennebunkport, ME; GPS: 43.358532, -70.475104

SEASHORE TROLLEY MUSEUM

LOCATION: Kennebunkport (York County)
MAINE ATLAS & GAZETTEER: Map 3, D2
GPS PARKING: 43.409059, -70.488982
GPS SEASHORE TROLLEY MUSEUM: 43.409222, -70.489280
HOURS: Consult website, https://trolleymuseum.org, for specific details
FEE: Admission charged
ADDITIONAL INFORMATION: Seashore Trolley Museum, 195 Log Cabin Road, Kennebunkport, ME 04046; (207) 967-2712

DIRECTIONS: From Cozy Corners (junction of U.S. 1 & Route 9), drive northeast on Route 9 for >4.5 miles, entering Kennebunkport. When you come to a "T" where Route 9 continues right, bear left onto Maine Street and then immediately right onto North Street. Drive north for 1.3 miles. As you pass through a tiny hamlet, the road becomes Log Cabin Road. Continue north on Log Cabin Road for another 1.8 miles.

Bear right at a green sign that reads: "Seashore Trolley Museum: The museum of Mass Transit" and follow the driveway for >0.1 mile to the parking area.

DESCRIPTION: The Seashore Trolley Museum is the world's first and largest electric railway museum. It contains over 320 transit vehicles and affords visitors the opportunity to ride trolleys from the late 1800s to the mid-twentieth century on the 4-mile-long, private heritage railroad. The trip takes you through fields and woods along a stretch of the electric railway system that once connected the many small towns that were previously only accessible by horse and buggy. The railways also made possible the growth of resorts areas such as Old Orchard by opening them up to the many instead of serving as a playground for the wealthy few.

HIKE: The land surrounding the museum contains several short hiking trails.

HIGHLIGHTS:

- Trolley Museum
- 4-mile-long heritage railroad ride

History: Electric railways were once America's fifth largest industry, the creation of Frank Julian Sprague who developed the world's first successful electric street railway system in 1887. It didn't take long before a vast network of trolley lines extended across Maine. Sixty years later, by the time of World War II, the trolleys were gone except for a few urban lines.

Fortunately, the age of the electric railways and trolleys has not been forgotten. The New England Electric Railway Historical Society was founded in 1939 and incorporated in 1941 to ensure that memory of the glorious age of the electric railway remains intact.

The Seashore Trolley Museum contains three car-houses teeming with restored trolleys and vehicles from major cities in the United States and across the world that made use of streetcar systems. Included are electric streetcars, trolley buses, motor buses, rapid transit cars, light rail vehicles, and omnibuses. An overhead gallery in the restoration shop offers a unique perspective of the complex work underway here.

The museum also offers a souvenir shop and snack bar.

COLONY BEACH

LOCATION: Kennebunkport (York County)

MAINE ATLAS & GAZETTEER: Map 3, D2

GPS PARKING: 43.347169, -70.474467

GPS COLONY BEACH: 43.346858, -70.473752

HOURS: Daily, 6:00 a.m. to 10:00 p.m.

FEE: None

RESTRICTIONS: Regular beach rules & regulations apply

ACCESSIBILITY: Colony Beach lies next to the parking area

DEGREE OF DIFFICULTY: Easy

ADDITIONAL INFORMATION: Colony Hotel, 140 Ocean Avenue, Kennebunkport, ME 04046; (207) 967-3331

DIRECTIONS: From Cozy Corners (junction of U.S. 1 & Route 9), drive northeast on Route 9 for ~4.5 miles into Kennebunkport. Immediately after crossing over the Kennebunk River, turn right onto Ocean Avenue and head south for ~1.1 miles. Finally, turn right onto an unmarked road and proceed west for <0.05 mile to the parking area, passing by condos on your right.

DESCRIPTION: Colony Beach is a 0.1-mile-long, pebbly stretch of sand with a rocky section in its middle. It has sometimes been described as a "pocket" beach due to the way it is hemmed in by rocky cliffs to the west and the diked outflow of the Kennebunk River to the east.

People often go to the beach just to watch yachts and lobstermen make their way back and forth through the breakwater protecting the Kennebunk River.

HISTORY: Colony Beach, aka Arundel Beach, derives its name from the Colony Hotel that is located across Ocean Avenue. In *The Kennebunks* (1967), Kenneth Joy mentions that the hotel was built around 1914 on the site of the Ocean Bluff Hotel (which was erected in 1873 by the Kennebunk Seashore Company and subsequently burned down in 1902). The replacement hotel, originally called Breakwater Court, was commissioned by hotelier Ruel Norton and built by architect Henry Patson Clark using the architectural aesthetics of Colonial Revivalism. It featured white, clapboard siding, a 300-foot-long porch, and a cupola atop the hotel's pitched roof. The hotel was run by the Norton family until 1947, when it was purchased by George Boughton, who renamed it the Colony Hotel and expanded the size of the hotel significantly. For many years, John Banta acted as manager for the Boughtons.

Today, the hotel is still run by Boughton's descendants.

The name Arundel comes from a town in England in West Sussex. The area was previously known as North Kennebunkport until 1957.

A photograph of Ocean Avenue as it looked in the late 1800s from the Colony Hotel is shown in *The Kennebunks: "Out of the Past"* (1967) by Kenneth Joy.

PARSONS WAY

LOCATION: Kennebunkport (York County)

MAINE ATLAS & GAZETTEER: Map 3, D2

GPS PARKING: 43.347169, -70.474467

GPS PARSON'S WAY: *Starting Point—* 43.347297, -70.473209; *End point—*43.344554, -70.462629

GPS DESTINATIONS: *St. Ann's Episcopal Church*—43.342985, -70.471787; *Spouting Rock*—43.3414712, -70.468509; *Blowing Cave*—43.343979, -70.462918

HOURS: Dawn to dusk

FEE: None

ACCESSIBILITY: 1.0-mile walk

DEGREE OF DIFFICULTY: Moderately easy

ADDITIONAL INFORMATION: Parsons Way, Ocean Avenue, Kennebunkport, ME 04046

Consult the next three chapters for specifics on St. Ann's Episcopal Church, Spouting Rock, and Blowing Cave.

DIRECTIONS: From Cozy Corners (junction of U.S. 1 & Route 9), drive northeast on Route 9 for ~4.5 miles into Kennebunkport. Immediately after crossing over the Kennebunk River, turn right onto Ocean Avenue and head south for >1.0 mile. Just past the turn to the Colony Beach, look for off-road parking to your right, and pick up the Parsons Way Trail from there.

DESCRIPTION: Parsons Way is a 1.0-mile trek, partly on paths and partly on paved walkways, which takes you along the rugged Maine coastline around Cape Arundel.

The walk is named for Henry Parsons, the eldest son of George and Sarah Parsons, who donated the land now called Parsons Way to the Town of Kennebunkport. Parsons, who became wealthy through business ventures with his dad, was very involved with Kennebunkport's civic and charitable organizations.

HIGHLIGHTS:

- Walk along Cape Arundel
- St. Ann's Episcopal Church
- Spouting Rock
- Blowing Cave

HIKE: The trailhead starts from near the road leading to Colony Beach and ends just past Endcliff Road (although the sidewalk continues beyond this point). Along the way, there are benches on rocky outcrops overlooking the ocean. The walk takes you along sidewalks and walking paths past St. Ann's Episcopal Church, Spouting Rock (which is diagonally opposite Spouting Rock Road), and Blowing Cave.

If you decide to continue walking northeast along Ocean Avenue/Shore Road from Blowing Cave, you will pass by a restricted road on your right in 0.2 mile that leads to Walkers Point (ex-president Bush's compound) and, at 0.3 mile, a pull-off on your right overlooking the ocean. Heaven Swamp Park is directly across the road from the parking area (GPS: 43.346088, -70.458803) but is trailless and inaccessible as far as we know.

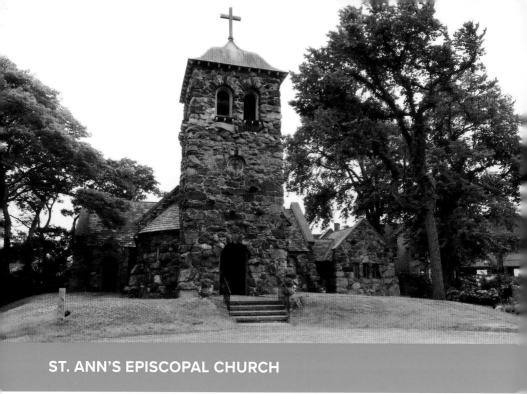

ST. ANN'S EPISCOPAL CHURCH

LOCATION: Kennebunkport (York County)

MAINE ATLAS & GAZETTEER: Map 3, D2

GPS PARKING: 43.344151, -70.4727597

GPS ST. ANN'S EPISCOPAL CHURCH: *Church*—43.342985, -70.471787; *Outdoor chapel*—43.342924, -70.472883

HOURS: *Grounds*—Monday to Saturday, 9:00 a.m. to sunset, and Sunday after church services have ended, to sunset

FEE: None

RESTRICTIONS: No RVs or buses are allowed; consult website, https://stann-skennebunkport.org, for further details

ACCESSIBILITY: 0.1-mile walk

DEGREE OF DIFFICULTY: Easy

ADDITIONAL INFORMATION: St. Ann's Episcopal Church, 167 Ocean Ave, Kennebunkport, ME 04046; (207) 967-8043

DIRECTIONS: From Cozy Corners (junction of U.S. 1 & Route 9), drive northeast on Route 9 for ~4.5 miles into Kennebunkport. Immediately after crossing over the Kennebunk River, turn right onto Ocean Avenue and head southeast for <1.4 miles. Bear right into the driveway for St. Ann's Episcopal Church and park near the church.

You can also park to your right in a small parking area facing the ocean just before the church entrance. From here, walk south for 0.1 mile to the church.

Be sure to visit the outdoor, seaside chapel next to the parking area. Facing the ocean, it is quite extraordinary.

DESCRIPTION & HISTORY: St. Ann's Episcopal Church, located on Old Fort Point, was designed by architect Henry Paston Clark and constructed in 1887–1892 using sea-washed stones from the surrounding area. Since then, the church has served without interruption as a summer chapel. In 1920, the south transept and baptistry were added through a gift made by Nathaniel Wilson in memory of his wife, Annie Edwards Wilson. In 1925, the north transept was added through the generosity of Erickson Perkins and several others, increasing the chapel's seating capacity to 220.

Due to its seacoast location, the church has been under constant assault from the elements and has gone through repeated maintenance and restoration projects. The bell tower was restored in 2007 by monies donated by the family of Dorothy Walker Bush, in her memory.

The seaside chapel was also created through the generosity of the Bush family.

A brochure provided by the church gives more detailed information about the interior and exterior of the chapel and restorations that have taken place.

HIGHLIGHTS:

- St. Ann's Episcopal Church, exterior & interior
- Seaside Chapel

SPOUTING ROCK

LOCATION: Kennebunkport (York County)

MAINE ATLAS & GAZETTEER: Map 3, D2

GPS OFF-ROAD PARKING: 43.342815, -70.469673

GPS SPOUTING ROCK: 43.3414712, -70.468509; 43.3414753, -70.467829 (per Lat-Long.com)

HOURS: Dawn to dusk

FEE: None

ACCESSIBILITY: Near roadside

DEGREE OF DIFFICULTY: Easy

DIRECTIONS: From Cozy Corners (junction of U.S. 1 & Route 9), drive northeast on Route 9 for ~4.5 miles into Kennebunkport. Immediately after crossing over the Kennebunk River, turn right onto Ocean Avenue and head southeast for <1.4 miles. Turn into one of several pull-offs on the left side of the road, opposite a stone wall, and near where Spouting Rock Road is located.

DESCRIPTION: Spouting Rock is one of those rare spots on the Maine coast where, under certain conditions related to the tide and ocean turbulence, incoming waves are ejected high into the air. In Charles Bradley's *History of Kennebunk Port from its first discovery by Bartholomew Gosnold, May 14, 1602, to A. D. 1837,* Bartholomew Gosnold writes, *"In the spouting rock is a small aperture, at the extremity of which is an opening, through which when the sea is rough, the spray is thrown to a great height."*

HISTORY: Spouting Rock Road, named for the rock phenomenon, is nearby, on your left. The road's name is a clear indication that you are in the right area.

A similar rock phenomenon, called Blowing Cave [see next chapter], is nearby.

The most famous spouting rock in Maine is Thunder Hole (GPS: 44.320566, -68.188537), located at Acadia National Park.

Take note that Spouting Rock's spectacle of ejecting water into the air is likely to be seen only during certain times when conditions are right, generally during mid-tide when waves are breaking. Don't be disappointed if there is nothing to see during your visit. There is still the Parsons Way walk to enjoy.

BLOWING CAVE
Blowing Cave Park

LOCATION: Kennebunkport (York County)

MAINE ATLAS & GAZETTEER: Map 3, D2

GPS PARKING: 43.344335, -70.462816

GPS BLOWING CAVE: 43.343979, -70.462918

HOURS: Dawn to dusk

FEE: None

RESTRICTIONS: Regular Park rules & regulations apply; parking is restricted to 15 minutes

ACCESSIBILITY: Near roadside

DEGREE OF DIFFICULTY: Moderately easy

DIRECTIONS: From Cozy Corners (junction of U.S. 1 & Route 9), drive northeast on Route 9 for ~4.5 miles into Kennebunkport. Immediately after crossing over the Kennebunk River, turn right onto Ocean Avenue and head southeast, following the shoreline (as the name Ocean Avenue implies) for ~2.0 miles.

After rounding the tip of Cape Arundel and heading northeast, look for the first pull-off on your right, immediately after Endcliff Road on your left. It will be for Blowing Cave Park overlooking Sandy Cove.

DESCRIPTION: Blowing Cave, aka Roaring Rock, Bouncing Rock, and Thunder Hole, is a waterspout created by incoming waves at high tide that roll into a rocky opening and shoot a jet of water into the air.

WALK: There are two paths that head down from the parking area towards Blowing Cave. One leads to a rocky area in the vicinity of Blowing Cave; the other, past the memorial anchor and down to a viewing area above the rocks where the spouting phenomenon can best be seen.

HISTORY*: Blowing Cave Park*—In Charles Bradbury's 1837 book, *History of Kennebunk Port from its first discovery by Bartholomew Gosnold, May 14, 1602, to A. D. 1837*, Bartholomew Gosnold writes, *"There are two curious rocks on the sea shore, between Kennebunk point and Cleaves's cove* [farther northeast], *called the bouncing and sprouting rocks. The bouncing rock is a small cavern, into which the water rushes at half tide with a tremendous noise."*

Blowing Cave, Kennebunkport, Maine.

Joseph A. Citro and Diane E. Foulds, in *Curious New England: The Unconventional Traveler's Guide to Eccentric Destinations* (2004), describe the cave as 6 feet by 16 feet in size, and capable of sending into the air a plume of water and mist thirty feet high. The authors go on to mention that if you visit the area during low tide, you can walk right into the cave entrance. If you do, just make sure that you're out of the cave by the time the tide begins to roll back in.

D. W. Caldwell, in *Roadside Geology of Maine* (1998), recounts the geology of Blowing Cave: *"The sedimentary layers in the Kittery formation trend almost directly north, and a wide basalt dike cuts across them almost at a right angle. The waves eroded the dike to make a cave with a small hole in its roof. When the tide is rising, waves that break to the back of the cave shoot as much as 30 feet into the air."*

In *Rope's End: Traditions, Legends and Sketches of Old Kennebunkport and Vicinity* (1901), Annie Peabody Brooks writes about what sounds like the traditional legend ascribed to many vertical waterfalls or high cliffs—the story of two Native Americans from opposing tribes that fall in love and, rather than being forcibly separated, jump to their deaths at Blowing Cave.

Other rocks mentioned in Charles Bradley's *History of Kennebunk Port from its first discovery by Bartholomew Gosnold, May 14, 1602, to A. D. 1837* are either lost to history or no longer exist. At the mouth of the Kennebunk River, for instance, stood a perch rock and a riding rock, both which were covered by piers two centuries ago, the first pier being built in 1798. One of the purposes for building the piers was to keep ships from striking the rocks.

Also reported was a large rock called Old Prince near the entrance to Cape Porpoise and a Dinah's Rock near the former house of George Bickford where, legend states, Dinah, while fleeing on snowshoes from pursuers, caught one of her snowshoes in a crevice in the rock/ledge that bears her name and was immediately captured and killed. According to Annie Peabody Brooks, "*the upper part [of the ledge] was removed a few years ago [today, over 120 years ago], and now serves as foundation of two dwelling houses situated at Cape Porpoise near the scene of the murder.*"

Anchor to Windward—Contained in Blowing Cave Park, near roadside, is a 6,000-pound memorial anchor dedicated in 2009 to the 41st President of the United States, George H. W. Bush. The memorial incorporates George H. W. Bush's catchphrase "anchor to windward" which he used to describe where his summer home was located in relation to Kennebunkport.

Walkers Point—Walkers Point, an 11-acre peninsula, is best known today as the location of the President Bush compound/summer home. The estate was jointly purchased in the late 1800s by David Davis Walker—great-grandfather of President George H. W. Bush—and his son, George Herbert Walker. Both men erected mansions on the point in 1902. George Herbert Walker's estate has survived into the present, but David Davis Walker's mansion was torn down some time ago.

CAPE PORPOISE ISLANDS
Porpoise Bay

LOCATION: Northeast of Kennebunkport (York County)

MAINE ATLAS & GAZETTEER: Map 3, D2

GPS PARKING: 43.367748, -70.432448 & 43.367334, -70.431665

GPS DESTINATIONS: *Redin's Island*—43.368588, -70.426648; *Stage Island*—43.371526, -70.420349; *Little Stage Island, aka Fort Island*—43.367610, -70.418100; *Trott's Island*—43.363265, -70.423301; *Cape Island (Preserve)* —43.362449, -70.416818; *Goat Island & Lighthouse*—43.358286, -70.425071

HOURS: Daily, dawn to dusk

FEE: None

DISTANCES FROM LAUNCH SITE: *Redin's Island*—0.2-mile paddle; *Stage Island*—0.5-mile paddle; *Trott's Island*—0.6-mile paddle; *Cape Island*—1.0-mile paddle; *Goat Island & Lighthouse*—0.8-mile paddle.

DEGREE OF DIFFICULTY: Moderately easy in calm waters

ADDITIONAL INFORMATION: The Town plans to raise the causeway four and a half feet higher, possibly in 2023 or 2024, due to rising tides. The impact on the launch site is unknown at this point.

Paddlers should consult the Maine's Weather website, https://www.maineharbors.com/cgi-bin/weather/mhwx.cgi?state=us&forecast=mar-gyx&case=0, for updated weather forecasts. Unlike the other paddles described in the book, this one exposes you to the open ocean where conditions can change dramatically.

DIRECTIONS: From Cozy Corners (junction of U.S. 1 & Route 9), proceed northeast on Route 9 for ~6.7 miles. Turn right onto Pier Road and head southeast for ~0.6 mile to the causeway. Park in a small pull-off on the left where a sign states "Pier Road Kayak Launch. Public and Private Partnership." Limited parking is also available on the right side of the road as soon as you cross over the causeway.

DESCRIPTION: The launch site provides an opportunity for paddlers to explore Porpoise Bay and its archipelago of more than a dozen uninhabited islands that protect the deepwater bay. The paddle described focuses on the islands to the west and southwest of the launch site, deliberately avoiding Cape Porpoise Harbor, just to the east, where boat traffic can be very heavy.

HIGHLIGHTS:

- A variety of islands, some historical
- Goat Island and its lighthouse

PADDLE: From the launch site, explore the islands in the order that you encounter them. The first island reached, on your right, is Redin's Island, aka Redkin Island or Redding Island, named after John Redding, who possibly owned it in 1684. Next is 0.4-mile-long Stage Island, named for the stages that early fishermen constructed during colonial times on which to dry their fish. Granite was also quarried on the island. It is now called Cape Porpoise Stage Island State Park.

In the *History of Cape Porpoise* (1955), Melville C. Freeman mentions that around 1900 a corporation erected a small building on Stage Island to house water tanks. The plan was to make a profit by extracting gold from the ocean's salt water. The enterprise proved to be a scam and money pit that ended up costing $5.00 for every $1.00 worth of gold extracted from the sea.

In *Rope's End: Traditions, Legends and Sketches of Old Kennebunkport and Vicinity* (1901), Annie

Peabody Brooks mentions a fort (most likely a stockade) that was built on Fort Island, a body of rock and land that is connected to Stage Island except at high tide. The fort was occupied by a few soldiers for a short period of time. A battle took place there in 1689. According to Melville C. Freeman, "*Fort Island was also at one time the scene of considerable quarrying.*"

Proceed south to 26-acre Trott's Island, named for John Trott who may have lived there at one time. The island is the largest of the group. Then paddle east to Cape Island, aka East Island, where campsites can be found on its west side. Part of the island is rimmed by tremendous ledges.

Finally, paddle southwest to Goat Island, hidden behind Trott's Island and featuring a lighthouse.

HISTORY: Cape Porpoise is a small fishing village that began as an English settlement. In Charles Bradbury's 1837 book *History of Kennebunk Port from its first discovery by Bartholomew Gosnold, May 14, 1602, to A. D. 1837*, Bartholomew Gosnold writes that Cape Porpoise "*...lies at the extremity of the cape, and is the only safe harbor for coasting vessels between Portsmouth and Portland, being equidistant from them.*" Its center of activity is the Cape Porpoise Pier at the end of Pier Road. One story states that the name Cape Porpoise can be traced back to 1614 when Captain John Smith (of Pocahontas fame) observed a shoal of porpoises frolicking in the cape.

To be sure, Cape Porpoise is not really a cape in the traditional sense of the word. It is more a collection of islands that affect the contour of the coastline.

Goat Island Lighthouse—The Goat Island Lighthouse was established in 1833. Today, the island and lighthouse are owned and maintained by the Kennebunkport Conservation Trust. A small island next to Goat Island, though unnamed on maps, is called Milk Island. It was acquired by Andrew Brown in 1767. The Kennebunkport Conservation Trust has created eight wilderness campsites on three of Cape Porpoise's islands. One of the islands, not included in this trek, is Vaughn's Island, 0.6 mile east of Goat Island, where three of the campsites have been established.

Goat Island was probably named for the livestock that was kept on it at one time.

As a point of interest, when George Bush visited his summer home on Walker Point, accompanying security officials were stationed at the lighthouse.

In 2011, the lighthouse and property were renovated. The walkway that had been washed away during the Blizzard of 1978 was rebuilt, along with the lightkeeper's quarters and the bell tower.

You are allowed to set foot on the island via a small dock (which is most easily accessed around high tide) and explore the grounds.

EMMONS PRESERVE
Kennebunkport Conservation Trust

LOCATION: Kennebunkport (York County)

MAINE ATLAS & GAZETTEER: Map 3, D2

GPS EMMONS PRESERVE: 43.403797, -70.453478

GPS DESTINATION: *Headquarters*— 43.403797, -70.453478; *Emmons Homestead*—43.404051, -70.453765; *Batson River Footbridge*—43.401182, -70.452914; *Community Labyrinth*—43.402057, -70.453581; *Teal Hole Falls*—43.405455, -70.460099 (estimated); *Emmons Cemetery*—43.404232, -70.454655

TRAIL LENGTHS: *Batson River Trail*—1.8 miles; *Jeremy's Trail*—0.4 mile; *Jenne's Loop*—0.5 mile; *Roller Trail*—1.0 mile; *Learning Trail Loop*—0.7 mile

ADDITIONAL INFORMATION: Emmons Preserve, 57 Gravelly Brook Rd, Kennebunkport, ME 04046; (207) 967-3465; kporttrust.org; *Trail map*—https://www.kporttrust.org/emmons-preserve

DIRECTIONS: From Crazy Corners (junction of U.S. 1 & Route 9), drive northeast on Route 9 for >8.0 miles. Turn left onto Beachwood Avenue, head west for 0.4 mile, and then right onto Stone Road. After 0.4 mile, bear left onto Gravelly Road, proceed northwest for <0.2 mile, and then turn left into the Emmons Preserve parking area by the headquarters.

DESCRIPTION: The Emmons Preserve encompasses 146 acres of land, some of which borders the Batson River. There are five trails offering varied treks with a total length of 3.3 miles.

HIGHLIGHTS:

- Teal Hole Falls

- Community Labyrinth

- Variety of trails, some along the Baton River

HIKES: *Teal Hole Falls*—From the land trust's headquarters, follow the yellow-marked Batson River Trail northwest for >0.3 mile. When you come to the red-marked Overlook Trail, bear left and proceed west for 0.1 mile. Then turn left onto the green-marked Jenne's Loop Trail and head northwest for >0.1 mile to reach an overlook, followed by Teal Hole Falls, located at the site of an historic mill. The fall is really a flatly inclined cascade and, from afar, looks like a cascading stream more than an actual waterfall.

Community Labyrinth—From the southwest corner of the parking area, follow the white-marked trail south 0.1-mile to reach the Community Labyrinth.

Circumnavigating the headquarters complex—From the Trust Headquarters, follow the 1.0-mile-long, white-marked Roller Trail, named for longtime volunteers Mark and Gail Roller, as it takes you on a long jaunt around the headquarters complex. Along the way, you will encounter meadows of wildflowers, see beaver dams, follow along a part of the Batson River, and pass by the historic Emmons Cemetery.

Learning Stations—From the southwest corner of the parking area, follow the white-marked Roller Trail southeast for <0.2 mile, bypassing the Community Labyrinth, and crossing over the Batson River Footbridge. After crossing the footbridge, you will come to the blue-marked Learning Trail, which is a 0.7-mile-long lollipop loop. Follow it either clockwise or counterclockwise to pass by thirteen learning stations and the Thompson Cemetery. Each learning station provides information regarding the landscape, flora, fauna, and history of the area.

The learning stations were developed through the collaborative efforts of the "Trust in our Children Program" and the Kennebunk High School.

Batson River Trail—The 1.3-mile long, yellow-marked Batson River Trail goes north towards the Smiths Preserve Trails and southwest to connect with the Tyler Brook Trails. As the name suggests, it follows along a section of the Batson River, crossing the river via a footbridge as you head southwest.

Jeremy's Trail—Both ends of the ~0.3-mile-long, red-marked Jeremy's Trail connect to Gravelly Brook Road, creating a loop. An overlook is reached at the southwest-most part of the loop.

Jenne's Loop—The green-marked Jenne's Loop Trail is accessed from Jeremy's Trail. The long loop takes you past two Batson River overlooks, then Teal Hole Falls, and back out to Jeremy's Trail.

HISTORY: The Emmons Preserve was created on land donated to the Kennebunkport Conservation Trust by Steve and Natalie Emmons. The Emmons' goal was to preserve the land as a place for children and adults to commune with nature.

The Conservation Trust has built a beautiful building near the Emmons Homestead that serves as their headquarters. The original path that Emmons cut through the woods is now Jeremy's Trail, named for 15-year-old Jeremy Walker Georgitis who died on May 10, 1999.

The *Batson River,* aka Gravelly Brook, is a ~6.5-miles long river that flows into Goosefare Bay, north of Cape Porpoise Village. It was originally called Little River according to Charles Bradley's *History of Kennebunk Port from its first discovery by Bartholomew Gosnold, May 14, 1602, to A. D. 1837.*

The river's name likely came from Stephen Batson of Seco, who created a settlement near the west bank of the river in 1642.

The *Community Labyrinth* was constructed using stones donated by members of the community in memory of their loved ones.

The *Kennebunkport Conservation Trust* was founded in 1973 and is recognized nationwide as a model for land trust organizations.

{9}

BIDDEFORD/SACO AREA

From the center of Ogunquit (junction of U.S. 1/Main Street, Shore Road & Beach Street), drive north on U.S. 1 for ~7.0 miles to reach Cozy Corners. Driving directions to the hikes in this chapter begin from here.

Biddeford and Seco are sometimes called the twin cities, being located on opposite sides of the Seco River and its waterfalls. From 1762 to 1805, Seco was earlier called Pepperrellborough for one of its founders, William Pepperrell [see chapter on Lady Pepperrell House]. It was incorporated as a city in 1867, already renamed Seco by 1805.

There are several hypotheses as to how Seco was named, but no definitive answer. One possibility is that it evolved from an old Tuscan personal name,

Saccus (meaning "sack"). A more likely possibility is that it is the Abenaki word for "flowing out" or "the outlet of the river."

Biddeford was named for Bideford, Devon, England. Its first settler, Dr. Richard Vines, spent the winter of 1616-1617 at what he called Winter Harbor, today known as Biddeford Pool. This was four years before the landing of the Mayflower at Plymouth, Massachusetts!

The Biddeford+Saco Chamber of Commerce can be reached at 28 Water Street, Suite 1, Biddeford, ME 04005; (207) 282-1567 or at https://biddefordsaco-chamber.org.

GOOSE ROCKS BEACH

LOCATION: Northeast of Kennebunkport (York County)

MAINE ATLAS & GAZETTEER: Map 3, D3

GPS PARKING: 43.398715, -70.417363

BEACH ENTRANCE: 43.398510, -70.417239

HOURS: 8:00 a.m.—6:00 p.m.

FEE: Parking permit is required

RESTRICTIONS: Regular beach rules & regulations apply

ACCESSIBILITY: <0.1-mile-walk along sandy entrance to beach; for further information, consult the Goose Rocks Beach Visitor Information website, https://www.kennebunkportme.gov/GRB

DEGREE OF DIFFICULTY: Easy

ADDITIONAL INFORMATION: Goose Rocks Beach, Adams Road, Kennebunkport, ME 04046

A parking permit can be purchased at the Goose Rocks General Store (3 Dyke Road), Kennebunkport Police Department (4 Summer Street), or Town Hall (6 Elm Street, Kennebunkport)

For restriction on dogs, which are somewhat complex, consult website, https://www.kennebunkportme.gov/goose-rocks-beach-advisory-committee/pages/dog-rules-goose-rocks-beach

DIRECTIONS: From Cozy Corners (junction of U.S. 1 & Route 9), drive northeast on Route 9 for ~9.5 miles. Turn right onto Dyke Road and proceed southeast for 0.7 mile, parking off-road where allowed with a permit.

From the junction of Dyke Road and Kings Highway, walk south along Adams Road (a road of sand) for 0.1 mile to reach the beach.

DESCRIPTION: Goose Rock Beach overlooks Goose Rock Bay. Nearly 0.4-mile southeast is East Goose Rocks, which is virtually an extension of Goose Rocks Beach, not far from where the Tides Beach Club is located.

West Goose Rocks and Anthony Island lie ~0.7 mile south of the beach entrance, not far from Marshall Point.

HISTORY: Goose Rocks Beach contains a >2.0 mile-stretch of sandy beach. In years past, it was known as Beachwood.

The 7.6-mile-long Little River, which divides Kennebunkport from Biddeford, flows into Goosefare Bay. The beach is bounded by the 6.4-mile-long Batson River (possibly named for Stephen Batson/Badson, an early settler) to the southwest and the Little River to the northeast.

At least 1.5 miles of Goose Rocks Beach is separated from the mainland by Goose Rocks Creek and its marshlands which contact and expand according to the tides.

From 1930 to 1947, the O'Hara Watercolor School, run by Eliot O'Hara, operated by the beach. The school, as well as several other buildings, burned down in the Great Fire of 1947 and were never rebuilt.

LOCATION: Biddeford (York County)

MAINE ATLAS & GAZETTEER: Map 3, D3

GPS PARKING: 43.407351, -70.395473

GPS DESTINATIONS: *Timber Point Peninsula—* 43.401503, -70.395336; *Platform deck on Little River—*43.402838, -70.397974; *Abandoned boat house—*43.402231, -70.397939; *Historic house—*43.398800, -70.397634; *Timber Point* - 43.398728, -70.399470; *Sandbar—*43.397697, -70.400608; *Timber Island—* 43.395076, -70.398579

HOURS: Dawn to dusk

FEE: None

RESTRICTIONS: Regular Park rules & regulations apply; dogs are not allowed on the trail

ACCESSIBILITY: *Timber Point—*0.8-mile trek; *South tip of Timber Island—* 1.4-mile trek

DEGREE OF DIFFICULTY: *Timber Point—*Moderately easy; *South tip of Timber Island—*Moderate (due to sandbar crossing)

ADDITIONAL INFORMATION: Timber Point Trail, 1 Timber Point Road, Biddeford, ME 04005

DIRECTIONS: From Cozy Corners (junction of U.S. 1 & Route 9), drive northeast on Route 9 for >12.0 miles, passing through Kennebunkport along the way.

When you come to Granite Point Road, turn right and head southwest for ~1.5 miles. Park in a small area to your right. There is also space for 2–3 more cars just down the road to your right.

DESCRIPTION: The Timber Point Trail takes you on a hike over varied terrain and flora, ultimately to a sandbar that can be crossed at low tide to access Timber Point Island. The habitat includes salt marshes, freshwater wetlands, saltwater beaches, a deciduous forest, and evergreens.

Over two hundred species of birds make use of the landscape both seasonally and permanently.

HIGHLIGHTS:

- Historic ruins
- Views of Little River
- Opportunity to cross tidal reef to small island

HIKE: From the parking area, follow the Timber Point Road south, with Curtis Cove to your left. In <0.2 mile, you will come to a fork (GPS: 43.405263, -70.396237). Bear right (the road to your left leads in 0.2 mile to private properties held onto by the Ewing heirs) and continue south. Within 50 feet, you will pass around a green-colored, wooden barrier.

In <0.2 mile, an observation deck to your right is reached, from where there are views of the Little River, an oxbow, cattail marshes, mud flats during low tide, fringing salt marshes, and the Sand Point Road neighborhood on the opposite shore.

In another <0.1 mile, you will come to a bench where a spur path on your right leads immediately to an abandoned boat house complex with an old wooden boat that is slowly being reclaimed by the woods. There are also views of the Little River from here.

Continuing south on the old dirt road, you will come to a path in <0.2 mile (GPS: 43.400053, -70.397435). You can either follow the path, which leads to Timber Point, earlier known as Curtis Point, in 0.2 mile, or continue south on the dirt road to reach the historic Ewing estate in 0.1 mile. From the main house, a path can be followed west for 0.1 mile to Timber Point.

To reach Timber Island from Timber Point, be sure to time your hike to coincide with a 1.5-hour window of opportunity on either side of low tide. A land bridge that appears temporarily can then be crossed, taking you over to the northwest corner of Timber Island. Just be sure to pay attention to the tide table and return before high tide approaches.

From Timber Island, looking west, you can see East Goose Rocks (GPS: 43.393491, -70.410377), 0.5 mile away, and further west, West Goose Island (GPS: 43.387656, -70.415645), followed by Anthony Island (GPS: 43.386861, -70.418742). All three of these islands barely rise above the surface of the ocean.

According to *meandermaine.com*, the tip of Timber Island is a great spot to see seals in the spring.

HISTORY: Timber Point is a 98-acre peninsula that lies southwest of Granite Point. At the peninsula's end is Timber Island, which encompasses 13 acres of land with a growth of trees on its midsection.

The trail was opened to the public in 2012.

The area's Youth Conservation Corps built a ramped observation platform that same year to provide closeup views of the Little River.

Historic house & complex at south end of Timber Point—In 1929, Louise Parson Ewing purchased the Timber Point Peninsula, which included a farmhouse, from Charles and Lucie Wicks (who, in turn, had brought the land from the Curtis family). Louise's husband, master architect Charles Ewing, designed the wide, two-story, 14-bedroom, 6,5000-square-foot, Colonial Revival home and protected it from ocean storms by erecting a seawall behind the house. The house and a number of ancillary buildings, including a garage/workshop, boat house, changing shed, laundry, paint shed, truck garage, and greenhouse, were completed in 1931 or during the years following. The Ewings and family used the property to entertain friends, artists, and authors during summers for over 80 years. They called the estate Timber Point.

In 2011, the Ewings' heirs sold the majority of Timber Point land to the Rachael Carson National

Wildlife Refuge, retaining 13 acres for themselves that included the farmhouse (which can be rented out as an Air BnB) and outbuildings on the peninsula's north end.

The Ewing house was listed on the National Register of Historic Places in 2016.

EAST POINT AUDUBON SANCTUARY & BIDDEFORD POOL

LOCATION: Biddeford Pool (York County)

MAINE ATLAS & GAZETTEER: Map 3, C3

GPS PARKING: *East Point Audubon Sanctuary*—43.445926, -70.340083 & 43.445800, -70.339807; *Biddeford Pool Public Beach*—43.442399, -70.351846

GPS DESTINATIONS: *Biddeford Pool* -43.443484, -70.364037; *Site of Fletcher's Neck Lifesaving Station*—43.442592, -70.341624; *East Point Audubon Sanctuary*—43.447421, -70.335228; *Abenakee Golf Club*—43.447312, -70.341931 (*Three surviving concrete platforms on the Abenakee Golf Course*)— 43.447391, -70.339843 & 43.447248, -70.339450 & 43.446986, -70.339133)

HOURS: *East Point Audubon Sanctuary*—Daily, dawn to dusk; *Biddeford Pool*—Daily, dawn to dusk

FEE: None

RESTRICTIONS: *East Point Audubon Sanctuary*—Regular Park rules & regulations apply; Dogs not allowed

ACCESSIBILITY: *East Point Audubon Sanctuary*—0.8-mile hike

DEGREE OF DIFFICULTY: Moderate

ADDITIONAL INFORMATION: East Point Audubon Sanctuary, Lester B. Orcutt Avenue, Biddeford, ME (207) 781-2330

Kayak Excursions—PO Box 2643 Kennebunkport, ME 04046; (207) 495-8036; stefan@Kayak-excursions.com.

Biddeford Pool Land Trust, https://www.mainelandcan.org/ local-resources/Biddeford-Pool-Land-Trust/1139

DIRECTIONS: From Cozy Corners (junction of U.S. 1 & Route 9), drive northeast on Route 9 for >13.5 miles, passing through Kennebunkport mid-way. When you come to Route 208/Bridge Road, turn right:

Biddeford Pool Public Beach—Drive southeast for 0.6 mile. At a "T," turn left onto Mile Stretch Road/Route 208 and head northeast for ~0.9 mile. Opposite the first house on your left, turn right onto Beachhouse Lane (a dirt road just before Elphis Road) and follow it for >0.1 mile to a parking area for the Gilbert R. Boucher Memorial Park—Pool Beach. Beach parking permits are required. For more information, consult https://biddefordmaine.org/2869/Beaches.

East Point Audubon Sanctuary—From the entrance to the Biddeford Pool Public Beach, continue northeast on Mile Stretch Road/Route 208 for another ~0.5 mile. When you come to Lester B. Orcutt Boulevard, turn right and drive east for 0.6 mile. Look for the gated entrance to the East Point Audubon Sanctuary to your left just before the road turns sharply right. There is limited parking in front of the entrance as well as at several pull-offs.

The Gut—Instead of turning right onto Lester B. Orcutt Boulevard, bear left and proceed west for 0.2 mile. Park in a small area for Vines Landing. The Gut (a narrow passage between Biddeford Pool and the ocean) can be seen close-up from the landing ramp.

DESCRIPTION: *East Point Audubon Sanctuary* is a 30-acre sanctuary that abuts the Atlantic Ocean and its rocky shoreline. The sanctuary is favored by bird-lovers.

Biddeford Pool, aka simply "The Pool," is a large tidal pool, located off Saco Bay southeast of the outflowing 136-mile-long Saco River.

Long before the arrival of Europeans and settler colonialism, Native Americans lived here, cultivating crops and fishing to sustain themselves.

HIGHLIGHTS:

■ Audubon Sanctuary

■ Views of Biddeford Pool

■ Views of offshore Islands

HIKE: *East Point Audubon Sanctuary*—From the parking area at the entrance, walk past the gate and follow a dirt road northeast for >0.2 mile through a narrow thicket of woods, with private homes to your right hidden by a wooden fence, and the private golf course to your left, to reach the sanctuary proper. *The Audubon Society Field Guide to the Natural Places of the Northeast: Coastal* by Stephen Kulik, Pete Salmansohn, Matthew Schmidt and Heidi Welch, write that the path leads to where "*...beautiful banded bedrock is exposed. The layers were originally laid down horizontally on a sea floor some 4000 million year ago.*"

When you come out of the woods you will see, to your left, a colorful sign stating, "Monarch Butterfly Habitat." Birds are not the only denizens of this sanctuary.

If you are walking counterclockwise, the road soon becomes a trail paralleling the edge of the cliffs. There are multiple spur paths leading steeply down to the rocky shore, some of them quite eroded. Near the southeast end of the peninsula is a *shingle beach*, formed out of flat-sided rocks that have broken off from the bedrock through weathering and slid down to the seashore.

Eventually, the path reconnects with the road near the northeast end of the peninsula (GPS: 43.448124, -70.335332) where an old, abandoned ramp and a 2016 stone bench dedicated to the memory of Robert R. Melville and Barbara C. Melville can be seen.

From the sanctuary, the 47-foot-high, conical Wood Island Lighthouse on the east end of 35-acre Wood Island (GPS: 43.456791, -70.332888), owned by the Maine Audubon Society, can be seen in the distance, 0.5 mile north. It was built out of granite rubble in 1808 and then reconstructed in 1858. It was finally abandoned in 1986. According to the Maine Audubon Society, the island is occupied by an active heronry (nesting colony). The small island in front of it, some 0.2 mile away, is called Gooseberry Island (GPS: 43.451886, -70.335823). The island 0.7-mile northwest is Stage Island (GPS: 43.456723, -70.352336), with a towering daymark near its northeast end (43.456723, -70.351443).

The island 1.0-mile northwest, just west of Stage Island, is Basket Island (GPS: 43.455821, -70.360422).

The small rock to the east, 0.2 mile from the shore, is Washburn Rock (GPS: 43.445895, -70.328719), which rises 9 feet above water at low tide. An important wreck and rescue occurred here.

Follow the road southwest as it takes you back to your starting point.

DRIVING ALONG BIDDEFORD POOL: *Fletcher's Neck view while driving/walking—*
From the junction of Routes 9 & 208, drive east on Route 208. Within 0.7 mile,
you will start to enjoy views of the Biddeford Pool. After 1.1 miles, you will
be traveling along the Fletcher's Neck stretch of Route 208 (GPS: 43.440464,
-70.359814), where the views of the pool become especially unobstructed. The
eastern tip of Fletcher's Neck is owned by the Maine Audubon Society.

*Days Landing viewing area—*From the junction of Routes 9 & 208, drive
southeast on Route 208 for 250 feet. Turn left onto Old Pool Road and head
north for <0.6 mile. Turn right onto Days Landing (Road) and proceed northeast for >0.2 mile to a cul-de-sac (GPS: 43.449506, -70.374316). Next to the cul-
de-sac is an informational plaque about shorebirds and a short path leading to
a telescope and cement platform. There is no water access from here.

*"Park in the Pines" pocket-park along north shore of lake—*For those who are
able to park along Hills Beach Road, walk down to "Park in the Pines" (GPS:
43.451008, -70.366932), where a tiny lakeside park offers views looking south
across the Biddeford Pool. It's entirely likely that you may observe great blue
herons, green herons, black-crowned night herons, snowy egrets, and glossy
ibises depending upon the time of day and season.

Additional points of interest around Biddeford Pool include the Biddeford
coastal neighborhoods of Hills Beach (a barrier spit beach that separates Saco
Bay from the Pool) on the northwest side of the Biddeford Pool, and Fortune's
Rocks Beach (GPS: 43.432897, -70.371537), south of Biddeford Pool, named for
Francis Fortune who, as a young man, survived a shipwreck in this area.

HISTORY: Biddeford Pool is the site of Maine's first permanent settlement called Winter Harbor, where Captain Richard Vines and his men spent the winter in 1616-1617 on the north side of the pool (not to be confused with today's Winter Harbor, east of Bar Harbor). Biddeford's name came from a market town and seaport in Devonshire, England, named Bideford.

In 1708, Fort Mary was erected near the Pool's entrance at Winter Harbor. Captain John Hill, who commanded the fort, may have named it for his wife, Mary Frost. The fort has also been known as Fort Hill, which is what it was called in John Staples Locke's 1884 book *Historical Sketches of Old Orchard and the Shores of Saco Bay.*

A 7-foot-high monument made of stones cemented in place was erected near the site and a slate plaque affixed to it. The plaque read: *"Fort Mary, 1700-1902. Erected by Rebecca Emery Chapter, Daughters of the American Revolution. Biddeford, Maine."* When the stone monument began to fall apart, the plaque was affixed to a large boulder. The boulder, unfortunately, was later struck by a snowplow and the plaque dislodged. After ending up in a neighbor's garage for several years, the plaque was remounted on the boulder at a new site at the end of Hill Beach Road (GPS: 43.447937, -70.357022) where it can be seen today.

During World War II, from 1941 to 1943, what is now the Abenakee Golf Club was the site of the Biddeford Pool Military Reservation. Four large, circular concrete platforms (Panama Mounts) were set in place for 155 mm guns, three platforms of which can still be seen today [see GPS coordinates listed].

Biddeford Pool has long been a tourist attraction and lobstering ground and is known for its round shape and narrow channel out to the ocean. It is bounded by the mainland to the south and west, by Hills Beach to the north, and by East Point (with its East Point Audubon Sanctuary) to the east. The water level in the pool varies markedly from exposed mudflats during low tide to navigable waters at high tide. The only consistently deep water is found at the mouth of the pool, called "The Gut," where tidal currents flush out accumulated sediment.

Fletcher's Neck Lifesaving Station—This former maritime rescue facility at 18 Ocean Avenue closed in 1971 and was subsequently placed on the National Register of Historic Places. It is now a private residence and has been remodeled. The lifesaving station was built in 1873 to house lifeboats and other storage. The red, seaside double doors of the private residence reveal evidence of the building's past history.

East Point Audubon Sanctuary—The 30-acre plot of land on top of the Biddeford Peninsula for the sanctuary was donated to the Maine Audubon Society in 1976 by a number of Biddeford Pool landowners.

Mile Stretch Road is on a tombolo (an Italian word for a deposition landform) that connects the Biddeford Pool neighborhood to the mainland.

The *Stage Island Daymark* erected on Stage Island in 1825 was designed to serve as a navigational marker for sailors negotiating the waters of Saco Bay. The first 54-foot-high tower collapsed while under construction, killing one worker and seriously injuring another. Following the incident, there were petitions to congress requesting recompense. The second, 60-foot-high tower, built on solid rock instead of loose stone, was successfully completed. It was repaired and repainted in 1913.

Stage Island was named for stages (drying racks) constructed by cod fishermen, who used them for drying their catch. During the War of 1812, the island was bypassed by the British warship HMS Bulwark which went on to attack four local ships and Cutts Store at Biddeford Pool. In the mid-1800s, a two-family house stood on the island, occupied by two brothers, Lyman Frank Verrill and Jacob Verrill, and their families. The island, today, is owned by the Maine Audubon Society.

Basket Island is nearly connected to the mainland by a sandbar, making it possible to walk across it during low tide. A half dozen houses are located on the island.

CLIFFORD PARK HIKES
Clifford Park

LOCATION: Biddeford (York County)

MAINE ATLAS & GAZETTEER: Map 3, C2

GPS PARKING: 43.487970, -70.447891

GPS WATERFALL: 43.483065, -70.442272

HOURS: Daily, dawn to dusk.

FEE: None

RESTRICTIONS: Regular Park rules & regulations apply

ACCESSIBILITY: 2.2-mile hike along Loop Trail

TRAIL LENGTHS: *Yellow-blazed Trail*—0.6 mile long; *Black-blazed Trail*—1.3 mile long; *Blue-blazed Trail*—0.6 mile long; *Green-blazed Trail*—1.2 mile long; *Red-blazed Trail*—0.6 mile long; *Orange-blazed Trail*—0.4 mile long; *White-blazed Trail*—0.2 mile long; *Pink-blazed Trail*—0.1 mile long

DEGREE OF DIFFICULTY: Easy to moderate, the Green-blazed and White-blazed Trails being the most difficult

ADDITIONAL INFORMATION: Clifford Park, 135 Pool Street, Biddeford, ME 04005; *Trail maps* —https://biddefordmaine.org/DocumentCenter/View/4953/Clifford-Park-Trail-Map; https://www.biddefordhistoricalsociety.org/images/Clifford-Park-Biddeford-Trails.pdf

DIRECTIONS: *From Cozy Corners* (junction of U.S. 1 & Route 9), drive northeast on Route 9 for >13.5 miles, passing through Kennebunkport midway.

When you come to the junction of Route 9 with Route 208, continue northwest on Route 9/208, now towards Biddeford, for another ~5.0 miles. Then turn left into the entrance to Clifford Park, opposite the intersection with Parent Avenue.

From the Maine Turnpike (I-95), get off at Exit 32 for Biddeford/Sanford and drive east on the Biddeford Corridor for ~0.2 mile. Turn left onto Route 111/Alfred Street, and head northeast for ~2.3 miles into Biddeford, crossing over U.S. 1 in the process. When you come to Route 9/208/Pool Street, turn right, and proceed southeast for >0.4 mile. Finally, bear right into Clifford Park to park.

DESCRIPTION: Clifford Park contains a network of multi-use forest trails for all levels of abilities.

The hike described passes by interesting rock formations and a scenic waterfall formed on West Brook.

HIGHLIGHTS:

- Waterfall

- Rock formations

- Old quarries

HIKE: *Waterfall Trail*—From the trailhead next to the kiosk and skateboard park, follow a wide path southwest for >0.1 mile. Then bear left, following the black-blazed loop trail clockwise as you head east and then later southwest. Along the way, you will pass by the white-blazed trail and red-blazed trail, all entering on your right. When you come to an intersection with the red-blazed trail, turn left and follow it south as it leads past the informally named West Brook Falls, which lies just outside the boundary of the Park, not far from Parkside Drive. Hikers should bear in mind that the waterfall is on private property.

Other hikes take you past abandoned granite quarries, located on land at a higher elevation near the park's center, where massive stone blocks lay about or in piles. Large quarry holes have filled with water and have been transformed into vernal pools.

HISTORY: Clifford Park opened in 1896 after the Town purchased the initial parcel of land from the Clifford family for a reduced cost, the family's only stipulation being that a sign be placed permanently in the park memorializing their contribution. Donations or low-cost land sales from additional families, including the Boutins and the Freemans, as well as the Maine Coast Heritage Trust increased the size of the park to its present 140 acres.

Historically, the Park was a popular site for mill workers and their families during the late 1800s and early 1900s. One of the attractions was the Park's bandstand, where workers and families could gather together to enjoy music. Some of the Park's old roads were used for transporting granite quarried in the Park. Granite taken from the quarries was used in structures across the country, including the Lincoln Memorial and Brooklyn Bridge.

The Park contains twelve vernal pools (bodies of water that are seasonal), twenty-two miles of wide and narrow trails, and old quarries. Because of the Park's size and extensive trail system, it is best to print out a trail map ahead of time before venturing in too far.

An historic graveyard next to the Park was heavily vandalized in the 1950s.

SACO RIVER WALK & CATARACT FALLS

LOCATION: Saco (York County)

MAINE ATLAS & GAZETTEER: Map 3, C2

GPS PARKING: 43.494121, -70.449504

GPS DESTINATIONS: *Cataract Falls*—43.495138, -70.452391; *Foot-bridge*—43.494054, -70.451038; *View of falls from Saco side of river*—43.495059, -70.453061

HOURS: Daily, dawn to dusk

FEE: None

ACCESSIBILITY: 0.5-mile walk

DEGREE OF DIFFICULTY: Easy

ADDITIONAL INFORMATION: Run of the Mill Pub House & Brewery, 100 Main Street, Saco, ME 04072; *Trail map*—https://mainebyfoot.com/biddeford-riverwalk-biddeford

DIRECTIONS: From Cozy Corners (junction of U.S. 1 & Route 9), continue northeast on U.S. 1 for <11.0 miles to reach Biddeford.

Turn right onto Alfred Street/Route 111 and proceed northeast for ~1.1 miles until you come to Main Street.

Alternate approach—From the Maine Turnpike/I-95, get off at Exit 32 for Biddeford/Sanford and drive east on the Biddeford Corridor for ~0.2 mile. Then turn left onto Route 111/Alfred Street, and head northeast for 2.5 miles, crossing U.S. 1 diagonally in the process, to reach Main Street.

From either approach, bear right onto Main Street/Route 9 and head east for 0.3 mile, crossing over the Saco River in the process. Turn left at the sign for the "Run of the Mill Public House & Brewery" and head into what looks like the side of a parking garage. Follow the ramp down to where you exit into a large parking area by the river.

Accessing view of falls from Saco side of river—From Main Street >0.3 mile before you reach the west end of the Main Street Bridge that spans the Saco River, turn left onto Lincoln Street and head north for 0.1 mile. When you come to Saco Falls Way, turn right and proceed east for 0.1 mile. Then turn right and look for a spot for visitor parking.

Proceeding on foot, walk east between two big apartment complexes—the Lofts at Saco Falls and the Mill at Saco Falls—until you come to a cement ramp that leads down to a spot where you can see the waterfalls.

DESCRIPTION: The River Walk takes you past historic mills and two waterfalls along a section of the Saco River that was heavily industrialized in the past.

HIGHLIGHTS:

- Saco River

- Cataract Falls

- Historic mills

WALK: From the parking area for the "Run of the Mill Brewery" on Factory Island, follow the River Walk Trail northeast as it takes you along the east side of the Saco River. Near the west end of Island Terrace (an enormous apartment complex), walk under the footbridge stairway and continue north to the end of the trail for views of the lower falls through a chain-linked fence. A metal walkway that used to lead to a better viewing area has been closed off.

Return to the stairway.

Climb up the steps to the top of the stairway and then cross over the Saco River via a pedestrian footbridge. From the west end of the footbridge, views of the lower falls can be obtained.

Follow the marked River Walk Trail as it takes you past the North Dam Mill Campus, which consists of a series of former textile mills that have been repurposed for over eighty apartments and ninety businesses. The enormous smokestack belongs to Building #37 which was built in 1916 and served as a steam plant for the mills.

In a moment or two, you will reach the Biddeford-Saco Memorial Bridge that was erected in 1949. Turn left and cross over the bridge. Along the way, take in views of rapids and tiny cascades upriver from the bridge, and moored boats in deeper waters downriver from the bridge.

At the east end of the bridge, follow a flight of stairs to return to the parking area.

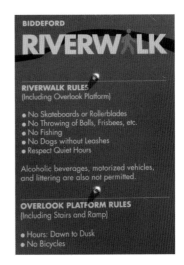

HISTORY: In the early 1800s, Saco became a lumbering center with seventeen sawmills utilizing Cataract Falls for hydropower. The first mill built was Roger Spencer's sawmill in the 1650s.

In 1811, Thomas Cutts and Josiah Calef established the Saco Iron Works on Saco Island, today known as Factory Island. It produced a variety of iron products including nails and iron hoops.

In 1826, the Saco Manufacturing Company erected an enormous, seven-stories-high cotton mill on the island. At the time, it was the largest cotton mill in the United States. After a fire destroyed the mill in 1830 it was replaced in 1831 by a structure built by the York Manufacturing Company.

Within the span of seventy years, the York Manufacturing Company proceeded to construct a total of eight mills on Factory Island. At their peak operation, the mills on Factory Island, Saco, and Biddeford in employed close to nine thousand workers in total.

Times gradually changed over the next half century and by 1958, all the textile mills had closed. Today, the buildings with their amazing architecture have been revitalized and turned into apartment complexes and businesses.

One unique use of Cataract Falls was for ice-harvesting. In *Sands, Spindles, and Steeples: History of Saco, Maine* (2003), Roy P. Fairfield writes about how James Black erected four large icehouses near the Factory Island Wharf for on-loading blocks of ice. *"Then he constructed a trestle-like chute connecting the building and the south lip of Cataract Falls. Taking advantage of another wooden slide around the dam at Spring Island [0.1 mile upstream], he harvested large chucks of ice upriver and skidded them to the falls. Here a fifteen-horsepower engine drove an endless chain conveying the cakes to the long chute which followed the river to the ice houses...Gravity did the rest."*

The Pedestrian Bridge spanning the Saco River between Biddeford and Saco was completed in 2015, funded by the Maine Department of Transportation's Quality Communities Programs.

The Mill at Saco Falls apartment complex, opened in 2010, is a former 170+-year-old, historic textile mill.

The Lofts at Saco Falls is a former nineteenth-century machine shop where machines for weaving textiles were designed and built. The building was converted into an apartment complex and opened in 2016.

Saco River—The 136-mile-long Saco River rises from Saco Lake in the White Mountains of New Hampshire and, after draining a watershed of 1,703-square miles, flows into the Atlantic Ocean at Saco Bay. The river's name means "outlet of the river." Recognizing part of the river's mythology, David W. Caldwell, in *Roadside Geology of Maine* (1998) writes, "*The river was cursed by the Indian Chocorua [a Native American chief or prophet], who jumped to his death from the mountain named for him rather than be captured and killed by settlers. As he leaped, the curse he made stated that one white person would die in the Saco each year.*" Statistically, the Seco is not even one of the top twelve most dangerous rivers in the United States according to *https://usabynumbers.com/most-dangerous-rivers-in-the-us*, so it would seem that Chocorua's curse failed to come true (if you believe in this kind of thing).

CASCADE FALLS
Cascade Falls Park

LOCATION: Northeast of Saco (York County)

MAINE ATLAS & GAZETTEER: Map 3, B3

GPS PARKING: 43.542818, -70.407428

GPS CASCADE FALLS: 43.542632, -70.405722

HOURS: Dawn to dusk

FEE: None

RESTRICTIONS: Regular Park rules & regulations apply

ACCESSIBILITY: >0.1-mile hike to waterfall; 0.5-mile-loop trail hike

DEGREE OF DIFFICULTY: Moderately easy

ADDITIONAL INFORMATION: Cascade Falls, Cascade Road, Old Orchard Beach, ME 04064

Saco Bay Trails, PO Box 720, Saco, ME 04072

DIRECTIONS: *From Cozy Corners* (junction of U.S. 1 & Route 9), drive north on U.S. 1 for ~14 miles to where I-195 crosses over U.S. 1

From the Maine Turnpike (I-95), take Exit 36 for Saco & Old Orchard Beach. Proceed east on I-195 for ~1.5 miles and get off at Exit 2 for U.S 1.

Starting from where U.S. 1 goes under Exit 2 of I-195, head northeast on U.S. 1/Portland Road for >2.5 miles. Turn right onto Cascade Road/Route 98, proceed southeast for >0.3 mile, and turn left into the parking area.

DESCRIPTION: Cascade Falls, aka Bridal Cascade, Bridal Falls, and Cascade Brook Falls, is a 20-foot-high, seasonal waterfall formed on Cascade Brook—a medium-sized stream that rises from two tributaries west of I-95 and flows east into the Scarborough River. The main cascade drops onto an undifferentiated 6-foot ledge of bedrock, and from there into a shallow pool.

HIKE: From the kiosk at the parking area, follow the trail for >50 feet. At a "T", turn right and continue on an old, woods road/trail, heading steadily downhill. At a lower junction, bear left, staying on the main trail as it takes you down to the cascade and head-on views.

Under most conditions, it is possible to rock-hop across the stream to get to the other side of Cascade Brook. A footbridge that was constructed in 2019 by the Maine Construction Corps and City of Saco to enable hikers to effortlessly cross the stream now lies in pieces in the streambed, having been destroyed recently by high waters.

Assuming you have crossed over to the other side of the stream, you are now in position to view the falls laterally. In addition, you can follow a wide path uphill through a ravine that leads in several hundred feet to a metal cage where a bear was kept in the 1950s, apparently for the amusement of visitors.

HISTORY: According to Patricia Hughes, author of *Maine's Waterfalls: A Comprehensive Guide* (2009), the waterfall was used to power a mill during past centuries.

During the Civil War, slate was mined from the bedrock next to the waterfall.

In the 1930s, the site was used by a silent movie company to create the illusion of the action taking place in the Alaskan Yukon.

Cascade Falls is operated by the Saco Bay Trails all-volunteer organization whose goal is to create and maintain trails in the Saco Bay area. The land was donated to the City of Saco in 2005.

ADDITIONAL MUSEUMS & LIBRARIES

1. KITTERY HISTORICAL & NAVAL MUSEUM

ADDRESS: 200 Rogers Road, Kittery, ME 03904; (207) 439-3080
MAINE ATLAS & GAZETTEER: Map 1, B4
GPS KITTERY HISTORICAL & NAVY MUSEUM: 43.101885, -70.742865
MUSEUM WEBSITE: www.kitterymuseum.org

CONTENT: The museum contains a collection of history about Maine's oldest town, Kittery, known as the "Gateway to Maine." Collectables include naval relics from the Portsmouth Naval Yard, old photographs and paintings, ship models, fishing gear, and scrimshaw (carved whale ivory).

DIRECTIONS: From the center of Ogunquit (junction of U.S. 1/Main Street, Shore Road & Beach Street), drive southwest on U.S. 1 for ~13.0 miles.

Get off at the Exit for "U.S. 1, 236 & South Berwick." In 0.2 mile, you will come to Route 236. Tun left and proceed southeast for <0.2 mile. Go partially around the USS Thresher Memorial traffic circle and exit at the sign for "Kittery Mall Road/U.S. 1 North." Head north for 0.1 mile and then turn right onto a short road that connects to Rogers Road. The museum will be directly in front of you.

2. OGUNQUIT FIRE COMPANY MUSEUM

ADDRESS: Corner of Cottage Street & Shore Road, Fireman's Park, Ogunquit, ME; (207) 646-4947
MAINE ATLAS & GAZETTEER: Map 1, A5
GPS FIRE COMPANY MUSEUM: 43.247004, -70.597929
FIRE COMPANY MUSEUM WEBSITE: townofogunquit.org

CONTENT: Steam pumper, memorials, and misc. memorabilia are on display.

DIRECTIONS: From the center of Ogunquit (junction of U.S. 1/Main Street, Shore Road & Beach Street), go southeast on Shore Road for <0.2 mile. The museum is on the corner of Shore Road and Cottage Street.

3. WELLS PUBLIC LIBRARY — FOR PETROGLYPH EXHIBIT

ADDRESS: 1434 Post Road/U.S. 1, Wells, ME 04904; (207) 646-8181
MAINE ATLAS & GAZETTEER: Map 3, E1
GPS WELLS PUBLIC LIBRARY: 43.318372, -70.583273
LIBRARY WEBSITE: www.wellslibrary.org

CONTENT: A Native American Petroglyph is on display.

HISTORY: The Wells Public Library has on exhibit an unusual, 1,800-pound, pink granite rock that contains an ancient petroglyph. The history of the rock goes back to a local quarry where it was taken from, and then used in the construction of the Atlantic House in Fishermen Cove (GPS: 43.290209, -70.570898). When the Atlantic House burned down in the 1870s, the rock ended up as part of a protecting ledge of rocks near the Wells Beach Hose Company (GPS: 43.292581, -70.569572).

The rock was discovered by Captain Austin S. Guest in 1953 while looking for mussels to use as bait. He recognized the rock as something special and, along with his friend, William Abbott, moved the rock up to his front lawn, where it remained until Guest's death in 1973. A family member, not recognizing the rock's significance, carted it off to the breakwaters in front of the fire house. When Guest's grandson, Reginald Guest, discovered that the rock was missing, he was able to locate it and moved it up to his front yard. In 1988, realizing the significance of the rock to Native American heritage, he presented it to the Wells Public Library, where it has remained ever since.

DIRECTIONS: From the center of Ogunquit (junction of U.S. 1/Main Street, Shore Road & Beach Street), drive northeast on U.S. 1/Post Road for ~5.0 miles. The library is on your left, 0.1 mile past Stewart Street.

4. THE MEETING HOUSE MUSEUM/HISTORICAL SOCIETY OF WELLS & OGUNQUIT

ADDRESS: 938 Post Road/U. S. 1, Wells, ME 04090; (207) 646-4775
MAINE ATLAS & GAZETTEER: Map 2, E5
GPS MEETING HOUSE: 43.301557, -70.586425
MEETING HOUSE WEBSITE: www.wellsogunquithistory.org

CONTENT: The museum houses a collection of artifacts from Native Americans, fishermen, local families, farms and businesses. Included is the Esselyn Perkins Memorial Library.

HISTORY: The Meeting House was built in 1862 and serves as the headquarters of the Historical Society of Wells & Ogunquit.

DIRECTIONS: From the center of Ogunquit (junction of U.S. 1/Main Street, Shore Road & Beach Street), drive northeast on U.S. 1 for ~3.8 miles and turn left at the sign for the Historical Society of Wells & Ogunquit, just before Buzzell Road.

5. BRICK STORE MUSEUM

ADDRESS: 117 Main Street/U.S. 1, Kennebunk, ME 04043; (207) 985-4802
MAINE ATLAS & GAZETTEER: Map 3, D1
GPS BRICK STORE MUSEUM: 43.387554, -70.537216
MUSEUM WEBSITE: https://brickstoremuseum.org

CONTENT: The museum contains a collection of Kennebunk's local history, art & culture, including a two-century history of volunteer firefighting and a century of wedding dresses. It houses over 70,000 artifacts related to the culture of the Kennebunks. Historic walking tours of the immediate area are conducted as well.

HISTORY: William Lord's Brick Store, built in 1825, operated as a dry goods store. Constructed of brick, it was somewhat unique in that most buildings at that time were made of wood. The brick store is interconnected with three other buildings on the same block that together constitute the Brick Store Museum. The brick store was opened in 1936 as a museum by Lord's great-granddaughter, Edith Cleaves Barry.

DIRECTIONS: From the center of Ogunquit (junction of U.S. 1/Main Street, Shore Road & Beach Street), drive north on U.S. 1 for ~10.5 miles to Kennebunk. The museum is on your right, just before the right-turn for Route 9A/Route 35/ Summer Street.

6. WHITE COLUMNS

ADDRESS: 8 Maine Street, Kennebunkport, ME 04046; (207) 967-2751
MAINE ATLAS & GAZETTEER: Map 3, D2
GPS WHITE COLUMNS: 43.362737, -70.475667
MUSEUM WEBSITE: kporths.com
CONTENT: The museum contains exhibits on George H. W. Bush, 41st President of the United States, and Bush family memorabilia. Also included are original and rare Victorian furnishings and artifacts of the Perkins and Nott families covering a span of two centuries. A walking tour of the 1853 White Column Home is also an option.

The museum is owned and maintained by the Kennebunkport Historical Society.

DIRECTIONS: From the center of Ogunquit (junction of U.S. 1/Main Street, Shore Road & Beach Street), drive north on U.S. 1 for ~7.0 miles. At Cozy Corners (junction of U.S. 1 & Route 9), turn right onto Route 9 and proceed northeast for ~4.5 mile to Kennebunkport. When you come to a "T," turn right onto Maine Street/Route 9 and parallel park immediately to your right. The museum is directly across the street from the junction.

7. BIDDEFORD MILLS MUSEUM

ADDRESS: 2 Main Street/Suites 18–108, Biddeford, ME 04005; (207) 229-8976
MAINE ATLAS & GAZETTEER: Map 3, BC2
GPS BIDDEFORD MILLS MUSEUM: 43.493093, -70.450250
MUSEUM WEBSITE: https://biddefordmillsmuseum.org

CONTENT: The museum contains exhibits that tell the story of Biddeford's biggest industry, textile mills, and the people who supported it, including its underground canals.

DIRECTIONS: From the center of Biddeford (junction of U.S. 1/Main Street & 111/Alfred Road), drive east on U.S. 1/Main Street for 0.2 mile and turn left into the parking area just before crossing over the Biddeford/Saco Bridge.

8. DYER LIBRARY/SACO MUSEUM

ADDRESS: 371 Main Street/U.S. 1, Saco, ME 04072; (207) 283-3861
MAINE ATLAS & GAZETTEER: Map 3, BC2
GPS SACO MUSEUM: 43.501586, -70.441592
MUSEUM WEBSITE: http://dyerlibrarysacomuseum.org

CONTENT: The museum contains a collection of fine and decorative arts and historic artifacts, including an assortment of eighteenth and nineteenth century paintings, furniture, and other memorabilia. It is the third oldest museum in Maine.

DIRECTIONS: From the center of Ogunquit (junction of U.S. 1/Main Street, Shore Road & Beach Street), drive northeast on U.S. 1 for ~19.5 mile, crossing over the Saco River. Once in Saco on the north side of the Saco River, continue northeast on U.S. 1/Elm Street for another <0.5 mile. The museum is on your right, just after the intersection of U.S. 1 and Main Street at Eastman Park.

GOLF COURSES

lthough it would seem that most visitors to south coastal Maine are irresistibly drawn to its beaches, a surprising number arrive with golf clubs in hand ready to play a round or two—and South Coastal Maine is more than ready to accommodate them!

1. CAPE NEDDICK COUNTRY CLUB (Cape Neddick)

ADDRESS: 650 Shore Road, Cape Neddick, ME 03902;
(207) 361-2011; https://www.capeneddickgolf.net
MAINE ATLAS & GAZETTEER: Map 1, A5
GPS PARKING: 43.224788, -70.586996

DIRECTIONS: From the center of Ogunquit (junction of U.S. 1/Main Street, Shore Road & Beach Street), drive southeast on Shore Road for ~2.1 miles and turn right onto Country Club Lane. Head west for 0.1 mile to reach the parking area.

2. LINKS AT OUTLOOK GOLF COURSE (South Berwick)

ADDRESS: 299 Portland Street/Route 4, South Berwick, ME 03908;
(207) 384 4653; https://www.outlookgolf.com
MAINE ATLAS & GAZETTEER: Map 1, A3
GPS PARKING: 43.244355, -70.799064

DIRECTIONS: From the center of Ogunquit (junction of U.S. 1/Main Street, Shore Road & Beach Street), drive north on U.S. 1/Main Street for 0.1 mile. Turn left onto Berwick Road/Ogunquit Road and proceed northwest for ~5.5 miles. When you come to Emerys Bridge Road, turn left and head southwest for ~6.0 miles. Then bear left onto Agamenticus Road and drive west for ~1.6 miles into South Berwick. When you reach Route 4/Portland Street, turn right, head north for >0.5 mile, and turn right into the entrance to the golf course.

3. LEDGES GOLF CLUB (York)

ADDRESS: 1 Ledges Drive, York ME 03909; (207) 351-3000;
https://ledgesgolf.com
MAINE ATLAS & GAZETTEER: Map 1, A4
GPS PARKING: 43.190435, -70.746641

DIRECTIONS: From the center of Ogunquit (junction of U.S. 1/Main Street, Shore Road & Beach Street), drive south on U.S. 1 for ~8.5 miles. Bear right onto Route 91/Cider Hill Road and proceed northwest for ~5.0 miles, turning right into the entrance to the golf course.

4. OLD MARSH COUNTRY CLUB (Wells)

ADDRESS: 445 Clubhouse Road, Wells, ME 04090; (207) 251-4653;
https://oldmarshcountryclub.com
MAINE ATLAS & GAZETTEER: Map 2, E5
GPS PARKING: 43.305767, -70.625691

DIRECTIONS: From the center of Ogunquit (junction of U.S. 1/Main Street, Shore Road & Beach Street), drive north on Route 1 for ~3.3 miles. Turn left onto Route 9B/Littlefield Road and proceed west for ~1.5 miles. Then, 0.1 mile after crossing over the Maine Turnpike/I-95, turn right onto Clubhouse Road and head northwest for 0.8 mile to the parking area.

5. MERRILAND FARM GOLF COURSE (Wells)

ADDRESS: 533 Coles Hill Road, Wells, ME 04090; (207) 646-0508;
https://www.merrilandfarm.com
MAINE ATLAS & GAZETTEER: Map 3, D1
GPS PARKING: 43.352780, -70.584508

DIRECTIONS: From the center of Ogunquit (junction of U.S. 1/Main Street, Shore Road & Beach Street), drive north on U.S. 1 for ~6.7 miles. Turn left onto Cole Hill Road, head northwest for ~1.4 miles, and then right into the entrance to the golf course.

6. WEBHANNET GOLF CLUB (Kennebunk)

ADDRESS: 26 Golf Club Drive, Kennebunk, ME 04043; (207) 967-2061;
https://webhannetgolfclub.com
MAINE ATLAS & GAZETTEER: Map 3, D2
PS PARKING: 43.346589, -70.497856

DIRECTIONS: From the center of Ogunquit (junction of U.S. 1/Main Street, Shore Road & Beach Street), drive north on U.S. 1 for ~7.0 miles. When you come to Cozy Corners, turn right onto Route 9 and proceed northeast for <3.0 miles. Turn right onto Sea Road/Beach Avenue and proceed south for >0.8 mile. Then turn left onto Ridge Avenue and head north for 0.1 mile. Continue straight ahead across Woodland Avenue, now on Central Ave, and drive north for another 0.1 mile, turning right into the golf club.

7. CAPE ARUNDEL GOLF CLUB (Kennebunkport)

ADDRESS: 19 River Road, Kennebunkport, ME 04046; (207) 967-3494;
https://www.capearundelgolfclub.com
MAINE ATLAS & GAZETTEER: Map 3, D2
GPS PARKING: 43.371712, -70.480431

DIRECTIONS: From the center of Ogunquit (junction of U.S. 1/Main Street, Shore Road & Beach Street), drive north on U.S. 1 for ~7.0 miles. When you come to Cozy Corners, turn right onto Route 9 and proceed northeast for ~4.5 mile to Kennebunkport. Turn left onto Maine Street (which quickly becomes North Street) and head north for 0.8 mile. When you come to River Road, bear left and drive northwest for <0.2 mile. Turn left into the entrance to the golf course and proceed northwest for 0.2 mile to the parking area.

8. SANFORD COUNTRY CLUB (Sanford)

ADDRESS: 588 Country Club Road/Route 4, Sanford, ME 04073; (207) 324-5462; https://sanfordcountryclub.com
MAINE ATLAS & GAZETTEER: Map 2, D4
GPS PARKING: 43.372308, -70.733611

DIRECTIONS: From North Berwick (junction of Routes 4 & 9), drive north on Route 4 for ~5.0 miles. Turn right onto County Club Road and park to your right in the main parking area after 0.05 mile.

9. DUTCH ELM GOLF CLUB (Arundel)

ADDRESS: 5 Brimstone Road, Arundel, ME 04046; (207) 282-9850; https://dutchelmgolf.com
MAINE ATLAS & GAZETTEER: Map 3, C1
GPS PARKING: 43.462310, -70.543324

DIRECTIONS: From the center of Ogunquit (junction of U.S. 1/Main Street, Shore Road & Beach Street), drive north on U.S. 1 for ~7.0 miles. When you come to Cozy Corners, continue northeast on U.S. 1 for another ~5.0 miles, driving through Kennebunk and heading towards Arundel.

Turn left onto Limerick Road (0.3 mile past U.S. 1A Extension, on your right), and drive north for ~4.0 miles, turning into the parking area for the golf club just before reaching Brimstone Road.

10. HILLCREST GOLF (Kennebunk)

ADDRESS: 77 Western Avenue/Lower Village, Kennebunk, ME 04043; (207) 967-4661; https://hillcrestgolf.net
MAINE ATLAS & GAZETTEER: Map 3, D2
GPS PARKING: 43.357953, -70.490568

DIRECTIONS: From the center of Ogunquit (junction of U.S. 1/Main Street, Shore Road & Beach Street), drive north on U.S. 1 for ~7.0 miles. When you come to Cozy Corners, turn right onto Route 9, proceed northeast for ~3.7 miles, and then left into the parking area for Hillcrest Golf (Driving range and mini par 3 pitch and put).

11. SALMON FALLS GOLF COURSE (Hollis Center)

ADDRESS: 52 Golf Course Lane, Hollis Center, ME 04042; (207) 929-5233;
www.salmonfallscountryclub.com
MAINE ATLAS & GAZETTEER: Map 3, A1
GPS PARKING: 43.605550, -70.556966

DIRECTIONS: From Salmon Falls (junction of U.S. 202 & Route 117/Salmon Falls
Road), drive west on US 202 for 0.1 mile, crossing over the Saco River in the
process. Turn right onto Salmon Falls Road and proceed northwest for ~0.6
mile. When you see the sign for the Salmon Falls Country Club, turn right onto
Golf Course Lane and head northeast for >0.2 mile to reach the parking area.

12. BIDDEFORD-SACO COUNTY CLUB (Saco)

ADDRESS: 101 Old Orchard Road, Saco, ME 04072; (207) 282-9892;
https://biddefordsacocountryclub.com
MAINE ATLAS & GAZETTEER: Map 3, BC2-3
GPS PARKING: 43.501576, -70.417093

DIRECTIONS: From Saco (junction of Route 9/Beach Street & U.S. 1/Main Street),
drive southeast on Route 9/Beach Street for <0.9 mile. Turn left onto Old
Orchard Road and head northeast for 0.7 mile. Bear right into the entrance and
parking area for the country club.

13. DEEP BROOK GOLF COURSE (Saco)

ADDRESS: 36 New County Road, Saco, Me 04072; (207) 283-3500
MAINE ATLAS & GAZETTEER: Map 3, B2
GPS PARKING: 43.501576, -70.417093

DIRECTIONS: From Cozy Corners (junction of U.S. 1 & Route 9), drive north on
U.S. 1 for <13.0 miles (or 0.2 mile after crossing over the Saco River). Turn left
onto Temple Street at a traffic intersection and proceed northwest for 0.2 mile.
When you come to Spring Street, turn right and go northeast 0.1 mile. Then
turn left onto Route 5/Bradley Street/New County Road and proceed northwest
for ~1.7 miles, crossing over the Maine Turnpike/I-95 after ~1.3 miles). Turn left
at the entrance to the Deep Brook Golf Course.

14. DUNEGRASS GOLF CLUB (Old Orchard Beach)

ADDRESS: 65 Wild Dunes Way, Old Orchard Beach, ME 04064; (207) 934-4513; https://www.dunegrass.com
MAINE ATLAS & GAZETTEER: Map 3, B3
GPS PARKING: 43.524968, -70.394608

DIRECTIONS: From northeast of Saco (junction of Route 98/Cascade Road), drive southeast on Route 98/Cascade Road for ~1.5 miles.

Turn right onto Ross Road and proceed west for <0.2 mile. When you come to Wild Dunes Way, turn left and head south for ~0.7 mile, turning right into the entrance to the golf club.

15. RAPTOR FALLS: 18-hole miniature golf course (Arundel)

ADDRESS: 1912 Portland Road, Arundel, ME 04046; (207) 477-3131; https://www.raptorfalls.com
MAINE ATLAS & GAZETTEER: Map 3, C1
GPS PARKING: 43.430971, -70.508941

DIRECTIONS: From Cozy Corners (junction of U.S. 1 & Route 9), drive northeast on U.S. 1 for ~6.8 miles and turn left into the parking area for Raptor Falls and its miniature golf course.

16. SCHOONER MINI GOLF (Seco)

ADDRESS: 58 Ocean Park Road, Seco, ME 04072; (207) 590-3429; https://www.schoonerminigolf.com
MAINE ATLAS & GAZETTEER: Map 3, B2–3
GPS PARKING: 43.508521, -70.423660

DIRECTIONS: From I-195, take exit 2. If coming off heading east, drive immediately across U.S. 1 to Route 5. If coming west, drive south on U.S. 1 for 0.1 mile and turn left onto Route 5.

Coming from either direction, proceed southeast on Route 5 for 0.5 mile and turn left into the parking area for Schooner Mini Golf.

FOR CHILDREN AND THE YOUNG-AT-HEART

1. YORKS WILD KINGDOM

See chapter 20 for specific details.

2. FUN-O-RAMA, LLC

ADDRESS: 7 Beach Street, York Beach, ME 03910
MAINE ATLAS & GAZETTEER: Map 1, A5
GPS: 43.175751, -70.609507

DIRECTIONS: From the junction of U.S. 1A/Cape Neddick Road and U.S. 1, drive southeast on U.S. 1A for 0.8 mile. Continue south on U.S. 1A as it now becomes Main Street and drive for 0.6 mile. Park where you can along the village streets or in the parking area for Short Sands Beach. Fun-o-Rama is at the north end of Short Sands Beach.

3. WONDER MOUNTAIN FUN PARK

ADDRESS: 270 Post Road/U.S. 1, Wells, ME 04090; (207) 646-9655; https://www.wondermountainfunpark.com
MAINE ATLAS & GAZETTEER: Map 3, E1
GPS WONDER MOUNTAIN FUN PARK: 43.280078, -70.595519
GPS PARKING: 43.280270, -70.596919

CONTENT: The fun park offers two 18-hole mini golf courses, a go-kart snake pit, New England's largest man-made Human Maze, and Franky's Game Room.

DIRECTIONS: From the center of Ogunquit (junction of U.S. 1/Main Street, Shore Road & Beach Street), drive north on U.S. 1 for ~2.2 miles and turn left onto a road that leads to the parking area behind Wonder Mountain Fun Park.

4. FUNTOWN SPLASHTOWN USA

ADDRESS: 774 Portland Road/U.S. 1, Seco, ME 04072; (207) 284-5139; https://funtownsplashtownusa.com
MAINE ATLAS & GAZETTEER: Map 3, B2
GPS FUNTOWN SPLASHTOWN USA: 43.527580, -70.427868
GPS PARKING: 43.528763, -70.429586

CONTENT: Funtown Splashtown USA consists of two parks—an amusement park with kiddie, family, and thrill rides, and a variety of games; and a water park with slides, pools, and splash pads. Included are Excalibur, Maine's only wooden roller coaster, and Thunder Falls, New England's longest and tallest log flume.

DIRECTIONS: From northeast of Seco (junction of U.S. 1 & Exit 2B of I-195), drive north on U.S. 1/Portland Road for ~1.2 miles. At the traffic intersection, turn left onto Funtown Parkway, proceed northwest for <0.2 mile, and turn left into the entrance for Funtown Splashtown USA.

5. PALACE PLAYLAND

ADDRESS: 1 Old Orchard Street, Old Orchard Beach, ME 04064; (207) 932-2001; https://www.palaceplayland.com
MAINE ATLAS & GAZETTEER: Map 3, B3
GPS PALACE PLAYLAND: 43.515161, -70.374294
GPS PARKING: Park in areas along or off of Grand Avenue or First Street

CONTENT: New England's only beachfront amusement park offers arcades games, the Cascade Falls waterslide, a carousel, an electric wheel, a roller-coaster, and a variety of other rides—all next to Old Orchard Beach and the Atlantic Ocean.

DIRECTIONS: From northeast of Seco (junction of Exit 2B of I-195 & U.S. 1), drive east on I-195 for ~1.0 mile. When I-195 ends and turns into Route 5, continue northeast on Route 5 for >2.0 miles and then bear right onto Old Orchard Street, proceeding southeast. From Old Orchard Street, you can turn right onto First Street or right or left onto Grand Avenue to find places to park.

DOG PARKS

1. BARKS & REC DOG PARK, AKA ELIOT DOG PARK (Eliot)

ADDRESS: Frost Tufts Park Road, Eliot, ME 03903
MAINE ATLAS & GAZETTEER: Map
GPS: 43.123822, -70.804959

DIRECTIONS: From south of Eliot (junction of Old Road & Route 103/State Road), drive west on Old Road for <0.5 mile and turn left onto Frost Tufts Park Road. Head southwest for 0.2 mile to reach the dog park.

2. OGUNQUIT DOG PARK (Ogunquit)

ADDRESS: Spring Hill Road, Ogunquit, ME 03907
MAINE ATLAS & GAZETTEER: Map 1, A5
GPS: 43.249951, -70.617004

DIRECTIONS: From the center of Ogunquit (junction of U.S. 1/Main Street, Shore Road & Beach Street), drive north on U.S. 1 for <0.1 mile. Turn left onto Berwick Road and proceed west for ~1.0 mile. Turn right onto Spring Hill Road and drive north for 0.1 mile. The dog park is next to the Ogunquit Transfer Station.

3. KENNEBUNK DOG PARK (Kennebunk)

ADDRESS: 36 Sea Road, Kennebunk Me 04043
MAINE ATLAS & GAZETTEER: Map 3, D1
GPS: 43.375708, -70.526672

DIRECTIONS: From Cozy Corners (junction of Route 9 & U.S. 1), drive northeast on Route 9 for <3.0 miles. Turn left at a traffic intersection onto Sea Road and proceed northwest for ~2.0 miles. Then bear right at a sign on a snowplow reading" Kennebunk Public Works," go 100 feet on a road that leads to the Kennebunk Recycling Center, and then immediately right into the parking area for the dog park.

4. BIDDEFORD DOG PARK AT ROTARY PARK (Biddeford)

ADDRESS: 550 Main Street, Biddeford, ME 04005
GPS: 43.498682, -70.477208

DIRECTIONS: From Biddeford (junction of U.S. 1/Elm Street & Route 111/Alfred Road), head northeast on U.S. 1/Elm Street for ~1.0 mile. When you come to Main Street, turn left and proceed west for 1.0 mile. Finally, bear right into Parkview Court and head north for >0.1 mile to the parking area for Rotary Park and the dog park.

ACKNOWLEDGEMENTS

Any errors found in the text are the responsibility of the author and not the specialists who have so generously contributed their time and knowledge to making this book as special as it is. I am deeply indebted to:

Tom Bradbury, Executive Director of the Kennebunkport Conservation Trust, for reviewing the chapters on the Emmons Preserve and Perkins Tide Mill.

Christy Butler, author of *Erratic Wandering*, *Berkshire Destinations*, *Connecticut Waterfalls: A Guide*, and *Rockachusetts*, for his photographic contributions.

Karen Casey and Richard Parsons, Biddeford Land Trust, for their review of chapters related to Biddeford.

Ellaine Cooper, Vice-Chair of the Marginal Way Town Committee for reviewing the chapter on the Marginal Way.

Barbara Delaney, coauthor of several history-oriented hiking guidebooks, a novelist, hiking companion, and, most importantly to me, my wife.

Richard Delaney, for proofreading an early version of this book.

Thomas Delaney, author of *Beautiful Place by the Sea*—an amazing novel set in Ogunquit—for sharing his knowledge of Ogunquit and proofreading an early version of this book.

Sandy Gilbreath, Executive Director, and Tony Liguori, Stewardship Committee Chair, Kennebunk Last Trust, for reviewing the chapter on Picnic Rock.

Aram Guptill, Co-Producer, Hackmatack Farm Playhouse.

Claire Julian, Volunteer at Louis T. Graves Memorial Public Library, for consultation on chapters pertaining to the Kennebunks.

Catherine Mayo, regional historian, for reviewing the chapter on Clifford Park and Biddeford Pool.

Melissa Kershaw, Regional Site Administrator, Northern New England Historic New England, for reviewing the chapters on the Hamilton House and the Sarah Orne Jewett House Museum.

Dan Lamontagne, for reviewing the chapter on the East Point Audubon Sanctuary and Biddeford Pool.

Kenneth McAuliffe, Visitor Services Coordinator, Old York Historical Society, for reviewing multiple chapters related to Old York.

Katie Orlando, Executive Director, Seashore Trolley Museum, for coordinating a chapter review of the Seashore Trolley Museum and for sending me three great photographs of the trolley museum to use in the book.

Edward Ramsdell, board member, for reviewing the chapter on the Seashore Trolley Museum.

Allison Ramsey, Executive Director of the Marginal Way Preservation Fund, for reviewing the chapter on the Marginal Way and for the Marginal Way Preservation Fund and their dedicated work in preserving this State treasure.

Scott Richardson, Communications Director, Laudholm Trust, for reviewing the chapter on Wells Reserve at Laudholm.

Karl Sanford, Trustee, St. Peter's-by-the-Sea, for information on the chapel's Memorial Garden.

Samantha Sauls, General Manager at York's Wild Kingdom, for reviewing the chapter on York's Wild Kingdom.

James D. Schantz, president and CEO of the Seashore Trolley Museum for reviewing the chapter on the Seashore Trolley Museum.

Michael Smyser, Communications chairperson, for reviewing the St. Peters-by-the-sea Episcopal Chapel chapter.

Michael Stailey, Marketing Strategist, for reviewing the chapter on the Ogunquit Playhouse.

Bob Taylor, lighthouse photographer and collector, for his photograph of the Nubble Lighthouse.

Charlotte Tragard, Museum curator and Administrator, Ogunquit Heritage Museum, for reviewing the chapter on the Ogunquit Heritage Museum.

Thomas Wall, Ranger/Visitor Services Manager, Rachel Cardon National Wildlife Refuge, for reviewing an early draft on the Rachel Carson National Wildlife Refuge and the Cutter's Island hike.

Devon Zimmerman, PhD, Associate Curator of Modern and Contemporary American Art, for reviewing the chapter on Ogunquit Museum of American Art.

Christy Butler, author of Erratic Wandering, Berkshire Destinations, Connecticut Waterfalls: A Guide, and Rockachusetts, for his photographic contributions, which include Ogunquit Beach, Footbridge Beach, Perkins Cove, Short Sands Beach, Balanced Rock (with Jan Butler in the photograph), and West Brook Falls.

Seashore Trolley Museum for its photographic contributions.

Bob Taylor, lighthouse photographer and collector, for his photographs of the Nubble Lighthouse and the Goose Neck Lighthouse.

York's Wild Kingdom for its colorful photographs of a carousel and peacock.

ABOUT THE AUTHOR

Russell Dunn is the author of ten waterfall guidebooks; five paddling guidebooks; eight guidebooks to amazing boulders and rock formations of New York, Massachusetts, Connecticut, New Jersey, and Pennsylvania; three history-oriented hiking guidebooks of Eastern New York State coauthored with his wife Barbara Delaney; ten photo-books of regional stereographic images; and guidebooks to the Great Sacandaga Lake and Ausable Chasm in New York State.

He lives in Albany, New York, with his wife, Barbara Delaney, and can be reached at rdunnwaterfalls@yahoo.com.